The Octogenarian Yogi:
Finding Wisdom

By Donald R. English

Dedication

To my wife, the sunshine of my life, who encouraged me to write this account of my journey.

Thank you for reading and rereading the various drafts. It never would have come together as it did without your helpful suggestions and support.

Map of India

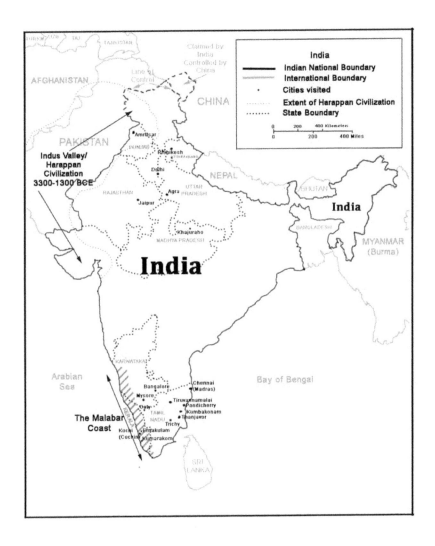

Map of India: Cities visited in 1993 and 2011

Table of Contents

Preface

Carl Jung, that eminent psychiatrist, psychoanalyst, and philosopher, said that until we make the unconscious conscious, it will direct our lives and we will call it fate. That was how I lived my first fifty-five years. Then events conspired to alter the direction of my life and to plant a seed that eventually blossomed into yoga. And now, thirty years later, I continue to teach yoga.

I went through life putting one foot in front of the other, just going with the flow. As a result, I often sabotaged my best efforts in dealing with life's slings and arrows, unaware there was an alternative. I allowed others and life events to shape the course of my life.

In the United States, yoga is marketed as an exercise program that improves strength and flexibility. However, its true goal is not to make us flexible but to teach us, through the poses, to focus and hold that focus, because it is through focus that we begin to assume conscious control of our lives and move the unconscious into our awareness.

Yoga philosophy says our lives are the way they are because we allow our constantly whirling minds to run unchecked. Yoga further tells us that it doesn't have to be that way. We can take control of our minds and, in the process, live more rewarding lives.

Over the years, I tried to sort out my thoughts about yoga and my journey. In the process I created files with names like *The Yoga Sutras Made Simple*, *Yoga: The Full Monty,* and *Yoga: It's Not About the Pose.* As the present work developed, the title *The Octogenarian Yogi* seemed most appropriate. Then I wrestled with various subtitles: *Accidental Discoveries, A Journey of Self-Discovery.* Then *Finding Wisdom* presented itself. And I thought, here I am in my mid-eighties on a path I purposefully ignored for many years. It was not a path of my choosing, but rather one that I was drawn to as if by an invisible hand. It is a path that has brought what I was missing in my earlier years.

For thousands of years, yoga was an oral tradition, and it was finally written down around 500 BCE by a person identified as Patanjali. Today, we know that document as the Yoga Sutras. It contains 196 concise statements evocative of more extensive, more detailed teachings.

Swami Vivekananda brought America's attention to Eastern religions and philosophy when he attended and addressed the World's Parliament of Religions in Chicago in 1893. In his speech, he stressed the unity of all humanity in our spiritual quests. In 1920, the great yogi and philosopher Paramahansa Yogananda lectured around the country on spirituality and the unity of all religions. The messages of both men resonated with many.

Yogananda was the first significant yoga teacher in the United States and the first prominent Indian personality to be hosted in the White House by President Calvin Coolidge in 1927. During the next thirty-two years, he established over a hundred yoga centers in the United States and India.

In 1948, Indra Devi, the first foreign woman to become trained in yoga practices, opened a yoga studio in Hollywood. Gloria Swanson, a famous movie star at the time, was one of her more well-known students. Through Swanson's popularity, yoga gained a measure of status in this country.

I grew up in the Midwest and do not recall hearing the words "yoga" or "yogi" until the Beatles went to India in 1968. This was when Timothy Leary was extolling the virtues of LSD, and the Haight-Ashbury neighborhood of San Francisco had become the de facto center of the counter-culture movement. Yoga was part of that mix and took on some features of modern American yoga we have all come to expect, like music, yoga mats, candles, and incense. This was also the era of the Vietnam War and the anti-war demonstrations it generated. A popular slogan at the time was "Make love, not war," which was taken quite literally in the Haight-Ashbury.

In 1967, I had just gotten out of the Navy after a nine-month deployment to Vietnam and had taken up residence with my wife and two children in the San Francisco Bay Area. My focus was on my family and my work to finish the requirements for a teaching certificate in California and New York. I had no time for any of the crazy stuff that was going on around me.

Despite actively avoiding yoga for the next twenty-nine years, I accidentally took my first yoga lesson when I was fifty-eight. They say that when we are ready, the teacher will come. In the best instances, we greet our teacher at the door. I did not. The teacher banged on my door, and I continually ignored the knock. Eventually, however, I heard the knock and answered the door to yoga.

The woman from whom I took my first yoga classes told us to consider everyone we met and every event we faced as a Buddha there to teach us something. Had someone said those words to me in my youth, I would have thought those were clever words and dismissed them. However, as my practice developed, I came to see her wisdom. Simply put, her remark implied there were lessons to be learned from every encounter.

In this telling, I look back on some of the critical Buddha events in my life and some of the serendipitous happenings that brought me to where I am today. I did not recognize their importance at the time. In yoga, we say you must be present to win and, for the past twenty-eight years, that is what I have tried to do. As a result, yoga has taught me many important life lessons.

When I began this project, I tried to avoid using Sanskrit, the original language of yoga. However, I soon realized that for clarity's sake, it was not possible. For the reader's benefit, I have included a glossary and pronunciation guide of the Sanskrit terms at the end of this work.

Joseph Campbell, the late professor of comparative mythology and religion at Sarah Lawrence College, said that if we're on the right path, we notice that an invisible hand is directing us. This story is also how I came to see and acknowledge that helping hand.

I have laid out my journey in four parts. I begin with the Damascene event that opened me to the richness of Indian philosophy. Then, in Part II, I chronicle my life's mess before that epiphany. Part III follows my discovery of yoga and my developing role as a yoga teacher. The final part details the deepening of my practice in a three-week yoga retreat in Rishikesh, India, devoted to the teachings of the Yoga Sutras.

I am grateful to those who have passed through my life and from whom I have learned so much. I thank you. However, I have changed all of your names in this accounting. It is not my intention to harm anyone or to promote anyone. If you choose to identify yourself, that is your choice. Some conversations have been fabricated to advance the story; some have been edited for clarity. All the experiences, lessons, discoveries, and insights I have learned are real and are as accurately described as possible. Finally, no harm is intended toward any person, place, or thing.

Part I: On the Road to Malabar

On the road to Damascus, Saint Paul had an experience that completely reoriented his life. Sometimes, in a moment of clarity, our world is turned upside down, and we see things as if our blindness were cured.

Chapter 1: An Epiphany

We left our hotel in Ernakulam on the Malabar Coast to look for a taxi to a performance of a traditional Indian dance called Kathakali. This dance style originated here in the southeastern Indian state of Kerala.

Our destination was a quiet street in a residential neighborhood in Cochin on the other side of the bay. When we arrived, I could hear the sound of surf from the Arabian Sea. At the front of one of the houses, a man greeted us. We paid our admission and climbed the stairs to the fourth-floor roof, where chairs were set in rows before a stage with a curtained backdrop. To one side was a statue of a four-armed god, maybe three feet tall.

From the rooftop, I could see the sun sliding into the sea. Birds chattered, vying for the best roosting perch. We found places and watched two men sitting on the stage apply their makeup.

On stage, a man dressed in white walked out from behind the curtained backdrop and, in good English, began to explain the makeup process of the two men sitting on stage.

He told us the performance would be from a section of the Indian epic, the Ramayana, the part where Ram and his friends rescue Sita, his dutiful and devoted wife, from the clutches of the evil Ravana. The performers' features, he said, were exaggerated by the makeup as a way of saying that their characters were bigger than life and were supernatural beings in a struggle between good and evil (*Image 1-1*).

Then he said, "I would like to tell you all about Hinduism. It will only take a minute." Then, with a twinkle in his eye, he said, "Maybe I can do it in thirty seconds. Hindus believe in one god who is without form or substance."

Image 1-1: Ravana, the king of the demons and the abductor of Prince Ram's wife Sita, is depicted here in a kathakali performance from a part of the Ramayana in Cochin, Kerala, India

Really? That wasn't what I thought.

He continued, "To help people understand an aspect, or a facet, of a formless and substanceless god, artists use shapes and images with which people are familiar. To help us recognize and appreciate different aspects of the Supreme Deity, artists have given us the numerous Hindu gods and goddesses."

"Everything comes in threes," he said. "Everything has a beginning, a middle, and an end. In Hinduism, things also come in threes. The gods of the Hindu trinity are Brahma, the beginning, the creator; Vishnu, the middle, the sustainer; and Shiva, the end, the destroyer." He pointed toward the statue in the corner of the stage and said, "Shiva is sometimes shown with four arms to show his power. In one hand, he holds a lotus to symbolize the beginning; in another, he has a wheel for continuing life; in his third hand, he wields a club representing the end of life. And in his last hand, he holds a conch shell as a trumpet to tell us to pay attention to his message."

I thought of the Sistine Chapel paintings of God the Father as Creator and Jesus the Redeemer. Michelangelo was doing the same thing that the Hindu artists were doing with their representations of the indescribable.

By then, my mind was reeling. My God, it's all a metaphor. René Magritte's painting The Treachery of Images *came to mind. I saw it once at the Los Angeles County Museum of Art. It shows a painting of a smoking pipe with the inscription "Ceci n'est pas une pipe" (This is not a pipe). When I first saw it, I was confused—of course it was a pipe—but then I realized it wasn't. It was a representation of a pipe, and that was why Magritte called it* The Treachery of Images. *Like that statue up there wasn't Shiva. It was a representation of a formless and eternal power that this culture symbolically called Shiva, like what was on the ceiling of the Sistine Chapel was a representation of God's formless, eternal power. In the three Fates of Greek and Roman mythology, one spun the thread of life, one determined its length, while the other cut it when life was over—the beginning, middle, and end. They were all saying the same thing. Images could be a trap but so could words. And I realized how easy it was to take things literally.*

If someone had told me that going to India would change my life, I would have laughed. If they had said that within three years I would be taking regular yoga classes, I would have scoffed. I understood that my experiences opened me to a range of possibilities regarding my spiritual outlook. But I could not yet understand how events in my past conspired to bring me to the threshold of these changes. Nor how those changes would shape my life going forward. No, serendipity still had some things in store for me before that could happen.

But here I am, thirty years later, teaching yoga and meditation. My story may not be unique, but it is atypical. Atypical because I am male, took my first class in my late fifties, didn't become a certified teacher until I was almost seventy, and didn't teach my first meditation class until my late seventies. Now, in my mid-eighties, I look forward to teaching in my nineties.

Chapter 2: A Reluctant Decision

The experience at the Kathakali performance was profound. It was a pivotal moment in my life, but it didn't happen in a vacuum, and it nearly didn't happen at all.

In 1986, after our children had settled into their independent lives, Diana, my wife and I relocated from Buffalo, New York, to Eastern North Carolina, where she was hired as a diabetes educator at our local hospital. It turned out to be a good fit for her, and in the meantime, I successfully restarted my wallpapering and interior painting business.

Diana's oldest, Kaitlin, lived in Boston with her husband, Sam. We drove up for a few days' visit. One evening, over dinner, we learned that Sam was going to India for a year to complete research for his degree in South Asian religions. Three months into his stay, Kaitlin planned to take six months off her residency program to volunteer at a hospital in Madras, where they planned to live. In her enthusiastic way, Kaitlin said, "And you guys need to come for a few weeks."

I feigned interest, but I didn't want to go. Three weeks off work would mean three weeks without income. I had been to Asia before. If I returned, there were other places I would choose to go. I wasn't a fan of India or its culture.

In the late 1960s and early 1970s, my friends were reading Hermann Hesse's *Siddhartha*, his fictional account of a man's spiritual journey to becoming the Buddha. Neither my friends' enthusiasm nor the book itself resonated with me. I found the whole Indian thing off-putting. If I had stopped to think about it, I might have traced my views back to my Catholic upbringing. Even though I was no longer a participant, its claims of supremacy over other religions, its teachings, and its rules still dominated my life more than I realized.

Some of my friends were into yoga, but yoga was mixed with the whole Indian thing. One friend made regular trips to an ashram in the Catskill Mountains in southeastern New York State to learn and teach yoga. He was a very grounded, modest, and kind man who practiced yoga and meditated daily, but I also knew psychedelic drugs powered some of his trips in the quest to find a shortcut to enlightenment. He was a spiritual Henry Hudson searching for the Northwest Passage to Enlightenment.

There was another friend who loudly proclaimed the wonders of yoga. At a party one night, he demonstrated how difficult it was to get into a particular pose, insisting we all try it. I did, but it didn't seem such a big deal. It only made me wonder why anyone bothered in the first place.

The 1960s counterculture, yoga, India, and gods with wives made my head spin. But there was something else that held me back. India was no stranger to political violence and death. Several hundred thousand people had died during the Partition of British India in 1947. That's when Great Britain, after a three-hundred-year presence on the subcontinent, withdrew, dividing its former colony into Pakistan and India. Since Partition, serious agitation had occurred among the Sikhs in the Punjab region for greater rights and autonomy. In June 1984, prime minister Indira Gandhi had ordered the military to enter the Sikh Golden Temple complex in Amritsar to apprehend the movement's leaders. Many armed resistors and pilgrims died in the attack. In the pogroms that followed, several thousand Sikhs were killed. Five months later, Indira Gandhi was assassinated by her Sikh bodyguard, resulting in more riots and deaths.

Then there were the Tamil Tigers, a separatist group that operated in Sri Lanka and southeastern India. Only a few months before we discussed going to India, a Tamil suicide bomber had assassinated Rajiv Gandhi, a former prime minister. Fourteen were killed and forty injured in the attack. And this happened in a Madras suburb near where Kaitlin and Sam planned to live.

So, in our talk about going to India, I was circumspect. India just didn't appeal to me, and its political violence didn't make me want to go, even though there was a low likelihood it might affect us. I didn't try to quash the idea but didn't commit. Diana and I discussed Kaitlin's invitation and my concerns on the drive home. Diana was ready to go and that was alright, but I remained undecided.

On long trips, we generally switched drivers every hundred miles or so. After paying the Delaware Memorial Bridge toll, Diana pulled over so we could switch. I opened my door and stepped out. At my feet was a folded ten-dollar bill.

Back in the car, I handed it to Diana and said, "Serendipity just paid our toll."

She replied, "Maybe Serendipity's telling you to go to India with us."

Later, over dinner, Diana said, "Kaitlin, Sam, and I are going to India. We'll share a lot of experiences, and you will feel sidelined and excluded. You need to think about this."

I did and realized she was right. I would feel sidelined and likely send subtle negative messages. I didn't want that. So I put my prejudices aside and agreed to be part of the three-week trip to India.

Chapter 3: A Journey of Revelations

It was late evening when we landed in Madras. I stepped out of the plane's cabin into the night air and was hit by a wall of heavy, hot, humid air. I thought, *This is March; what must it be like in August?* Together, Diana and I descended the mobile stairs. The air felt dense enough to swim through as we crossed the tarmac to the terminal. I expected to step into an air-conditioned terminal, but no, the air inside was hotter, more humid, stagnant, and unmoving. We followed the crowd and queued for immigration and customs.

A faint odor, like raw sewage, hung in the air as we exited the terminal. Kaitlin and Sam were waiting for us in a taxi. The ride to their house in Mylapore, a suburb of Madras just south of the city, seemed long. But even the excitement of being with them was not enough to overcome our jet lag, and we were soon ready to turn in.

At breakfast, Kaitlin and Sam outlined plans for our visit. We would spend a few days in Mylapore before flying to Cochin in Kerala on the southwest coast. They planned for us to see some sights around Cochin, and then we would hire a car and driver to go north to visit temples on our way to Bangalore. From there, we would fly back to Madras, see some sights, and then fly home.

Later that morning, we walked to a nearby tailor shop. Kaitlin wanted her mother to have proper Indian clothes for the temples we would visit. The walk through their neighborhood was pleasant; birds sang from the trees lining the streets. The houses had high brick or stone walls with broken bottles embedded along their tops to deter burglars. Bougainvillea blossoms cascaded over their tops, and jasmine scented the air. On one street, we passed the neighborhood iron *wallah*, or vendor, who toured the streets, announcing his presence with his lilting song. For a small charge, he pressed clothes with his coal-fired iron.

Our route took us from our immediate neighborhood to a bridge over a small stream. The mixed stench of rotting garbage and feces grew stronger as we approached. The water, clogged with every possible plastic item imaginable, hardly moved. We hurried on, hoping to distance ourselves from this open sewer as quickly as possible.

At the tailor shop, the smell had lessened but still hung in the air. Diana and Kaitlin searched for fabrics while one of the owners and I sat on stools and chatted.

"Enjoying India?" He asked.

"We only arrived last night." Then I added, "We're going to Cochin in a couple of days."

"Oh, very good," he said, doing the head wobble that meant approval. "The BJP, the Bharatiya Janata Party, is having a rally at the Mylapore beach in two days only. There is always much trouble with their rallies. Many bad people in the BJP. They cause a lot of trouble."

"Yes," I said. "I've read that there's been a lot of violence at their rallies."

"Ah, indeed. Many injured. Many were killed in riots at BJP rallies. Very unhealthy." His fingers worked constantly over his *misbaha* prayer beads.

Across the shop, Sam looked at neatly folded and stacked fabrics; their bright colors dazzled the eye. A clerk hovered hopefully nearby.

I asked, "Why do their rallies provoke so many people and get them angry?"

"Three months ago, the BJP hooligans tore down the holy Babri Masjid, a mosque built over four hundred years ago. More than two thousand of our Muslim defenders died."

"I read about it in the papers."

Overhead, a florescent tube buzzed, in need of a new ballast.

"Oh, yes," he said. "And one of the BJP's rising lights, Narendra Modi, has a Muslim son-in-law. I do not understand this."

I said, "That is interesting. I didn't know that."

"Newspapers don't report it," he said. His brown eyes looked straight into mine.

"Maybe he'll soften his views. I can only hope so," I said.

"Tigers are not changing colors [sic]," he answered.

I said, "Well, I certainly hope things will be calmer at their rally here."

"I'm hoping so," he said, doing the Indian head wobble again. "Allah be praised."

On the walk back, I mentioned my conversation to Sam.

"Yeah," he said, "just last December the BJP, the Hindu nationalist party, held a rally in Ayodhya and tore down the Babri Masjid, a mosque built in 1528 by a Mogul emperor. The Hindus say that originally there was a temple there on the site of Ram's birth and that the Muslims had destroyed that temple in the late sixteenth century to build their mosque."

"Ram and Vishnu are the same. Is that right?" I asked.

"Yes," he said.

I said, "So, the BJP was playing with fire, inflaming both sides."

"Yeah, that's one of the reasons I planned for us to be on the other side of the country when they have their rally here. Every BJP rally has been violent. Over two hundred thousand BJP supporters attacked that mosque and literally tore it down. And in the violence that followed, a couple of thousand people were killed."

"They do things big in India, don't they?"

> *With the clarity of hindsight, the conversation in the tailor shop took on new significance twenty-one years later when the BJP came to power in India and Narendra Modi became prime minister.*

We returned to the shop to pick up the finished clothes a couple of days later. Then, still jet lagged, we boarded our flight to the western seaside city of Ernakulam on the Arabian Sea's Malabar Coast.

We settled into our hotel and took a short ferry ride across the bay to Cochin. As we crossed the bay, an onshore breeze brought the scents of spices this part of India is famous for. We strolled through a crowded spice market filled with a mélange of smells. Outside the shops sat huge burlap bags of cardamom, coriander, cumin, cinnamon, and peppers of all sorts.

The city is famous for its spices and even maintained trade relations with the early Romans. Before that, there was a sizeable Jewish community. In fact, after Jesus's life on earth, Saint Thomas the Apostle came here to preach his gospel and set up several communities of believers. However, most of Kerala's Jewish residents left for Israel when it was founded after World War II. Forty-five years later, their household belongings still filled the antique shops near the only remaining synagogue that served a handful of members.

That evening, after an early dinner at the hotel, the four of us stepped out of the lobby and looked for a taxi to take us to the Kathakali performance.

In a matter of hours, the street in front had been transformed with flags, buntings, and banners, giving it a festive appearance.

We found a taxi around the corner and asked the driver what was happening. He said the nationalist BJP party was having a political rally at sundown. We had left Mylapore hoping to avoid their violence, only to find them here at our front door. By way of mollifying us, the driver said the rally would probably be over by the time we returned. He also told us the rally in Mylapore had been peaceful, which we hoped was a good omen.

At our destination, we found our seats and listened to the *Reader's Digest* version of Hinduism, of how artists used metaphor to explain the inexplicable nature of the divine. It's hard to describe how I was affected and how I felt for the next several days. It was as though I were in a trance, thoughts tumbling around in my head like clothes in a dryer. It was a profound experience. The concept of God made sense if I stopped thinking about God as a concrete being.

> *The idea of God as it is usually expressed hadn't made sense to me for a long time. How could God be a concrete being? How could Jesus ascend bodily to heaven? Even traveling at the speed of light, he would still be within the Milky Way galaxy. I had gone through agnostic and atheist phases, but a part of me thought that rejecting the idea of God was a simplistic solution tantamount to burying one's head in the sand. But thinking of God as a metaphor for a formless and substanceless essence greater than ourselves made sense. It was how each culture in the world found a way to explain the inexplicable. But unfortunately, most of us turn poetic metaphors into something concrete, mistaking the image for the thing. Later, I learned that an ancient Indian text said that truth is one, but the wise call it by many names. Whether God, Allah, Jehovah, or some other name, they are all paths that lead to one source, like the spokes on a wheel lead to the hub.*

When we returned to our hotel that night, only a handful of people lingered in the street. The rally was over. There had been no violence.

We spent a couple of days seeing sights in Kerala, then hired a car and driver for a road trip north to Ooty, one of the old colonial British hill stations in the Western Ghats mountains. Ooty was where the colonials spent their summers to escape the heat and humidity of the coastal lowlands. I was anxious to experience a bit of old colonial India.

Chapter 4: A Towering Presence

Kerala was a center for training work elephants. On the road north out of Cochin, we passed several elephants learning to carry loads without being distracted by car traffic (Image 4-1). By the time we reached Coimbatore, it was lunchtime. We found a tandoori restaurant atop one of the city's taller buildings that offered a panoramic view of the city and the mountains we would soon enter.

Image 4-1: Elephants learn to ignore traffic

Our driver turned onto a less-traveled country road from Coimbatore through an elephant reserve. We spotted several wild elephants through the trees as we drove through the reserve. From there, we followed an even less traveled road into the mountains toward the city of Ooty, where a sign warned, "This road beyond 17 km from here contains several hair pin [sic] bends & steep gradients. You will have to strain your vehicles to reach Ooty."

The sign was correct, except it failed to mention the sheer drops into the valley below and that there were no safety barriers. Our driver pulled off for a stretch at a lay-by, just a wide spot in the road. A car was in the parking lot, empty of its passengers, its doors open. Hearing voices, I ventured toward the sound. I looked down from a high bank and saw an extended family, its members perched on rocks or wading in a stream. A large sign nailed to a nearby tree proclaimed in Tamil and English, "Fishing, bathing, and washing clothes in the crocodile-infested river is prohibited. Survivor [sic] will be prosecuted."

Once back on the road, I spotted several trucks that had failed to negotiate the hairpin bends and were now lodged in trees far down the slopes. Periodically, we passed trucks that had stopped on the road for repairs. Their drivers had placed coconut-sized stones around them as hazard warnings. More than once, the rear tire of our car spun gravel off the shoulder-less road, sending it tumbling down the mountainside.

Image 4-2: Grotto shrine behind the hotel in Ooty, Tamil Nadu, India

Finally, with jangled nerves, we checked into a British colonial-era hotel at Ooty for a much-needed rest. The next morning, I took a walk before breakfast. The morning air was cool and crisp in the upper fifties. Behind the hotel, I found a trail leading up a small hill and into the woods. When I stepped into a clearing, I saw what appeared to be a stone barbecue similar to what we might find at a state park back home (*Image 4-2*). I moved in front for a closer look. I was momentarily stunned.

Nestled in the protection of this brick grotto was a statue of a multi-armed woman plunging a spear into a water buffalo. It seemed to be more than a simple statue commemorating some saint. Draped around her neck was a garland of fresh flowers with small red and yellow blossoms pressed into every nook and cranny where the statue would accept one. About six feet in front of the grotto, a trident spear was stuck in the ground, points upward, a similar garland draped through its tines.

> *My prejudices kicked into overdrive because what I saw was superstition. I imagined people worshipping this statue as though it were a living being. I was shocked.*

> *Then the rational part of me hit the brakes. I thought of my Catholic background and its statues. I thought of the explanation of Hinduism at the Kathakali performance. I told myself to think metaphorically because that was where I would find understanding and meaning. And then I realized how reflexively I reverted to my habitual thinking.*

Sam was interested in visiting a Jain temple not far from Mysore. So, after breakfast, we traveled further north and out of the mountains. The air became hot and dry.

Jainism is an entirely different religion from Hinduism. The two share many elements but have different belief systems. However, to my untutored eye, Hindu or Jain, the temples all seemed the same.

Shravanabela Gola, the Jain temple, was perched atop a small mountain that jutted over four hundred feet above its surroundings. Our driver dropped us at the visitors' booth and joined the congregation of drivers waiting for their fares to complete temple visits. We exchanged our shoes at the visitors' booth for a claim check from the shoe *wallah*. Next, we purchased "temple socks" and temple entry tickets, then set off to climb the stairs to the temple.

To get to the temple, we needed to climb stairs cut into the rock face.

On that scorching day, we had a choice of how to get to the temple. We could walk up the stairs in the blazing heat or hire two men to carry each of us up in a palanquin, one of those little closed boxes supported by two poles carried on the shoulders of two men, one in front and one behind. I was tempted until I saw someone going up in one. It looked scary beyond belief. The palanquin was not level because the man in front was several steps higher than the man in the back, and the man in the back carried all the weight on his shoulders. Yet, even in the heat, they sped past us. We chose to walk up.

When we reached the top, sweat rolling down our faces, Diana told us there were 729 steps. She had counted them.

"That's interesting," Sam said, "because if you add the digits seven, two, and nine, you get eighteen, and then add those digits and you get nine, which is composed of three plus three plus three. Three, three times. The sacred number three."

> *There it was again,* I thought, *that number three representing the beginning, middle, and end—Brahma, Vishnu, and Shiva.*

The temple builders had planned the steps around the sacred number three. The risers for the steps were hand-hewn into the stone at irregular heights to make the number of steps conform to the formula as a reminder of the nature of things for those who climbed to the temple.

When we reached the temple, heat radiated from the stone floors and buildings. It was like being in an oven, so I stuck to the shade as much as possible. I came around a corner and stepped into a courtyard in the center of the complex, and before me stood a colossal statue of a Jain saint (*Image 4-3*). Carved from the mountain itself, Bahubali stood fifty-seven feet tall. He was so tall that he seemed to peer over the tops of adjacent buildings. But what surprised me more than his height was that he was stark naked except for stone vines growing up his legs. Legend says that Bahubali stood naked in meditation for over a thousand years and was the first person to attain liberation from the cycle of life and death.

We chattered away, gawking at the naked statue like awful American tourists, when I noticed a woman, probably in her mid-thirties, well dressed and affluent, likely the person who came up in the palanquin. She sat cross-legged in meditation. I tried to hush the others, but Sam said, "Oh, she's meditating. We won't disturb her." Then I noticed a fly walking across her face. She didn't flinch. Not a muscle moved. For sure, we wouldn't disturb her.

From Shravanabela Gola, it was a short drive to Mysore, where a major attraction was the royal palace. Rather than fight a losing battle against the British, the Maharaja of Mysore surrendered and was allowed to keep his royal status. When we toured his palace, I saw a representation of Lakshmi painted on a wall. Sam explained she was the consort of the god Vishnu, the sustainer. As such she was the goddess of good fortune and serendipity. In most shops we visited, the owners had an image of Lakshmi and the first rupee the business made.

Just outside Mysore stood Chamundi Hill, a temple perched at its peak. Fortunately, this one had a drivable road to the top. When we got to the temple entrance, we joined a long line waiting to enter.

21

*Image 4-3: Bahubali at the Jain
temple Shravanabela Gola,
Karnataka, India*

In front of us was a family group. A twelve-year-old boy turned to me and asked, "Coming from where, sir?"

"Oh." I was taken aback and needed a second to process his question. "America," I said.

"And what is the product of your country, sir?" he asked as though he were my geography teacher back in grade school.

Momentarily lost for words, I said, "Movies are a major product of my country."

"Oh, liking Michael Jackson, sir?" he asked, then proceeded to moonwalk back to his family.

A man approached Sam and said, "Please, coming this way, sirs and madams. We are having a special entrance for visitors from foreign lands."

He guided us out of the line and around to the side of the temple to a much shorter line.

The temple, we learned, was dedicated to the goddess Chamundi, the local name for Shiva's consort, Parvati. Inside the temple, it was dark. Smells from the candles and oil lamps permeated the interior and cast flickering shadows. People filed past the representation of the goddess one at a time, pausing, hands in prayer, bowed, and moved on. Later, I asked Sam about what we had seen in the temple: devotees standing in long lines in front of the statue of the goddess Chamundi for a moment before moving on.

"It's called *darshan*," he said, "and it means seeing. In the Hindu tradition, simply being in the presence of an image of a god or holy person gives grace and spiritual fulfillment."

According to local legend, back in the mists of time, ignorance and evil reigned throughout the land, infecting the entire population. The local people prayed for deliverance, and when it came, it took the form of Chamundi to destroy the Water Buffalo of Ignorance. Afterward, goodness was restored to the lands, which explained the spear thrust into the side of the water buffalo.

I understood then what I had seen back in Ooty. The statue in the grotto honored the goddess Chamundi, the consort of Shiva, the destroyer, as she thrust her spear into the Water Buffalo of Ignorance. I thought about how ignorance and superstition often masquerade as truth. How hard it is to recognize truth. The trick, of course, is to be able to find the kernel of truth. Robert Pirsig said it so well in Zen and the Art of Motorcycle Maintenance*: "The truth knocks on the door, and you say, 'go away, I'm looking for truth,' and so it goes away. [Isn't that] puzzling." But it would be years before I found that book and its wisdom. Now that I understand the metaphor, I wish I had left a blossom offering at the statue of the Goddess Killing Ignorance. And that Jain meditator—she possessed a tranquility and composure that had stirred something deep within me. But again, that seed would need time to germinate.*

Chapter 5: If India Doesn't Change You

Our three weeks went by fast. On our last full night, Kaitlin, Sam, and I went to their neighborhood temple for a midnight celebration of Shiva and Parvati's marriage. It would be a big deal with a festive procession from the main *gopuram*, or temple entrance tower. It was only a twenty-minute walk from their house on a glorious night, which was dark, and star filled. The air was heavy with the scent of blooming jasmine and frangipani that overpowered any faint, noxious odors. The night was magical.

As we walked, I said to Sam, "All these gods and goddesses have vehicles. What does that mean?"

"All the deities have an animal form," he said. "That's how the gods and goddesses travel. But it's also symbolic of the deity's function. Like with Shiva, his vehicle is the bull, Nandi. It's one way Shiva gets around, so it has a sacred significance."

I said, "A neighbor back home was a marine guard at the United States Embassy in India at the end of World War II. A cow tried to get into the embassy grounds, so he shot it. It nearly caused a riot, and he was shipped back home the next day."

"That's awful," Kaitlin said. "It's like killing God."

"And he thought it was funny. That's the tragedy of it," I said.

By then, we'd reached the temple, where a huge crowd had gathered at the *gopuram*. Lights flooded the area like daylight. A cow pushed its way through the mass of people, and I imagined the injuries it would cause if it panicked. Meantime, we elbowed our way through the crowd, away from the animal and toward a better view of the procession that was about to begin.

The crowd's excitement and tension were palpable and increased exponentially as midnight approached. Suddenly, with a blare of trumpets, the huge wooden temple doors swung open, and out came the procession, led by dancers and musicians playing wooden trumpets. But I was nearly speechless because I recognized what this Indian temple marching band was playing. It was a march by the British composer Sir Edward Elgar. I couldn't name the piece, but I recognized it even on wooden trumpets and slightly off-key.

Image 5-1: Display of Shiva and Nandi at the Kapaleeshwara Temple, Mylapore, Tamil Nadu, India

I turned to Sam, "I can't believe they're playing Elgar—and on wooden trumpets, no less."

"Yeah," he said. "You never know what to expect. India's just one surprise after another."

I stood transfixed at what came next (*Image 5-1*). Forty men, twenty on each side with heavy poles on their shoulders, supported a platform with a statue of Shiva in pure gold. Also on the platform was a statue of Shiva's vehicle, Nandi, in pure silver, framed by an enormous sunburst of flowers. Four shirtless temple attendants sat next to Nandi. Each wore a white *dhoti* trimmed in blue edging wrapped around his waist. Then came more trumpeters, more displays of men, flowers, and images. The crowd cheered wildly with delight.

After the procession, we went to where the images were parked for a closer look, but they seemed lifeless without the crowd's energy. We took a shortcut back through the temple, winding our way through several large halls. A concert of classical Indian music was in progress in one; in another, people slept on the stone floor, apparently waiting for the next cycle of events.

Exiting the back of the temple, we headed back to the house. The air was heavy, but our spirits were high. With each step, the sounds from the temple celebration faded. We excitedly talked about what we had just seen: the crowd, the music, the dancers, and displays of the gods and goddesses.

I turned to Kaitlin and Sam and said, "These three weeks have been amazing. I had no idea India would be like this."

"Yeah," Sam said, "if India doesn't change a person, they just weren't paying attention."

The next evening, we took a taxi to a restaurant for a farewell dinner. On the way, we passed a man on the pavement in the middle of a busy street, an obvious victim of a hit-and-run accident. Cars whizzed past in both directions, but no one stopped. I was sure his back was broken because of his position. His pleas for help were ignored.

My impulse was to stop, but Sam insisted we go to the restaurant, where he would call the police anonymously. He explained there were no Good Samaritan laws in India, and if we were to stop, people would presume it was out of guilt for causing the accident. A crowd would gather, and it would become nasty.

On our return, the man was no longer there, so he must have gotten the care he needed.

A few hours later, we all piled into a taxi for a ride to the airport. We cruised through the night's traffic as cars whizzed past on either side of our slow-moving taxi. Suddenly, the taxi's hood flew up, completely blocking the windshield, and I was certain we would all die on the streets of Madras.

But no, our driver calmly stopped in the middle of the street, casually got out, closed the hood as though this was a common occurrence, got back in, and continued to the airport as though nothing unusual had happened.

Safely at the airport, we said our final goodbyes. In the bookstore, I picked up a book about Hinduism, its temples, gods, and goddesses.

> *On the flight home, I read that Vishnu, the maintainer, represented form, while his consort, Lakshmi, was the personification of his energy—matter and energy—an inseparable duo in an eternal dance. I reminded myself that it was all metaphor, that this depiction represented an aspect of the formless and unknowable nature of something beyond our understanding—something we call the divine.*

While Vishnu maintains, Lakshmi dispenses good fortune and grace on those who maintain proper standards and a sense of harmony. But she also has a bad sister called Alakshmi, who follows Lakshmi wherever she goes, waiting for a chance to undo her sister's good work. And I thought about how she gets that chance to subvert my efforts when I am out of harmony and not focused, present, and aware.

My life is on a balance board. As long as I'm in sync, observant, open, and present, things work smoothly and easily. I see and can welcome Lakshmi's serendipitous gifts. I'm in the zone. But when I lose that sense of balance and become out of sync, it's almost like I trip over myself. And that's how my life seemed to have been for several years: distracted and out of sync.

Part II: "Spiritual Ignorance Is the Source of All Pain and Suffering"

The Yoga Sutras attribute the cause of suffering to *avidya*, or spiritual ignorance. In this sense, ignorance is not stupidity or a lack of knowledge; instead, we have turned away from or are ignoring something that we already know at some level. As a result, we go in directions that ultimately cause suffering.

Yoga Sutra 2.4

Chapter 6: The Pearl Necklace

Not everyone at the Kathakali performance reacted as I did. I am sure I was the only one who had an aha moment. Most people don't need a wake-up call to begin a yoga practice.

India jolted me, but it also piqued my curiosity. I wanted to understand more about the symbolism behind the gods and goddesses. I was curious about the philosophy it grew out of. And I was also struck by serendipity's role in bringing those insights to me.

Whether we believe in coincidences or not or that things happen for a reason, one quality of our humanness is our desire to organize facts and look for meaning. When something happens in real time, like finding an unexpected gift of a folded ten-dollar bill at my feet, it's easy to say, "Oh, that was lucky," and dismiss it. But when I look at certain events in my life, it is hard not to think these serendipitous events were more than simple luck. They seemed connected, like pearls on a necklace, with one thing leading inevitably to the next. In the case of the ten-dollar bill, through a series of events in someone else's life, that folded bill was dropped. Unknowingly, our paths crossed, our lives touched. It sparked a conversation that eventually took me to India, where I experienced amazing things and became more reflective about life and myself. I began seeing the world filled with pearl necklaces of people's life events that intersected, connected, and separated. Sometimes these things were obvious, sometimes not. But life did seem like a web of pearls.

I didn't see things this way before the trip. As far as I was concerned, I was an independent agent doing my thing alongside others doing theirs. I never thought of myself as influenced by or influencing others. India forced me to think about the role serendipity played in the trip. There were connections, the obvious ones, but also the not-so-obvious ones. I saw Lakshmi as the giver of good fortune, gifts, or grace, and how often those gifts influenced my life.

Then I learned about Indra's web. As the metaphor goes, when Indra created the world, he fashioned it as a web. At each intersection of the strands of the web is a pearl. Everything that does, did, or will exist is a pearl in the web. And every pearl reflects every other pearl in the web. Indra's web is a metaphor for a universe of connections and interdependences.

Diana had a story about an old woman who came into the emergency room one night when she was a nurse on duty. The doctor asked the woman what her problem was. And she began by saying, "When I was born . . ." And the doctor looked at Diana, and Diana looked at the doctor, and they knew it would be a long night. Every event in our lives has brought us where we are today, but editing our story for brevity and saliency is essential, and I will try to do this.

My first real yoga teacher urged me to consider people and situations as Buddhas placed in my path with the specific purpose of teaching a lesson. As I reflected on my life, I came to recognize numerous Buddhas. They were sometimes difficult people or situations, sometimes not. They could be ordinary things that brought a lesson. Occasionally, the lessons were immediately apparent, but at other times, they became so only through hindsight.

What follows is the story of recognizing some of those Buddhas, learning to listen, allowing, and trusting the guidance of an unseen hand. It is also about serendipity and the role it played in my life.

Recently, someone posted an old Far Side cartoon on Facebook. It depicts a man who looks like a college professor. He's working at an overhead projector, its image on a screen behind him. Nearly out of sight is a curtained window that lets us know this isn't a college lecture room but a home. In the foreground sits a young boy half hidden by the back of an easy chair. The caption reads, "Eventually, Billy came to dread his father's lectures over all other forms of punishment." I know how Billy felt.

Billy could have been me, and his father, mine. My father was one of my Buddhas. Almost anything prompted him to pull out his battered soapbox and commence a monologue. Being a dutiful son, I sat with feigned attention. His lectures often turned into sermons in which he expounded on some religious point. He was a convert to Catholicism, and as such, he often strove to be holier than the Church, a trait my mother warned against. Occasionally, he might trap Jayne, my younger sister, and me in a group-preach. Somehow, she felt no compunction about walking out and leaving me stuck, which left me wanting to strangle her.

Do I remember any of his sermons? No, not a thing. I have tried to dig them out of the depths of my unconscious, but to no avail. They are permanently lost.

After the death of my older sister, my mother kept my younger sister Jayne and me on a pretty tight leash. In spite of that, we managed to have a fun and active childhood.

Somewhere I had heard about using tin cans connected together with string to create a sort of poor man's telephone. One day with two cans and a large spool of string from our dad's store, we decided to see if it would work. I was maybe eight, Jayne six. She stood in front of our house holding an empty can with a string attached to its bottom. I walked out the string about a block and a half down the street. When I thought I was far enough away, I yelled into the can's open end, "Can you hear me?" From the nearby house of Olie Olson, our school's janitor, came a response, "Yes, I can hear you."

35

Olie Olson was like a grandfather to all the kids in school. I thought he was the wisest person I knew. One night at a play in the school auditorium, I found myself seated next to him. Sitting there, I could hear Olie breathe and the thought occurred to me that if I could match my breath with his, we would be connected forever and by some magic I would tap into his wisdom. But after a few minutes I realized that I wasn't getting enough air and had to breathe at my own rate. I would have to find wisdom some other way.

When my father's job required a move from our small town in South Dakota to Kansas City, I went to the neighborhood Catholic grade school where I didn't find wisdom. There were eight kids in my class, and I hated it. But freshman high school was different. There were lots of kids, better teachers, better classes, and cute girls with whom I flirted endlessly. I loved school. Then, over the summer, I decided I would become a priest.

So, in my sophomore year, I transferred to the seminary in the city. But anyone who knew me from the previous year would have questioned my motives. Why would a kid like this suddenly decide to become a priest?

Over the following summer, my father's job moved us to a small town some distance from St. Louis, necessitating another school transfer. So, beginning in my junior year, I became a boarder. Three years, three schools. It was tough.

> *My brother Hugh was ten years older than me. He was a Buddha, but his lessons taught me how I did not want to live my life.*
>
> *While serving in the post–World War II occupation forces in Italy, he wrote home regularly, but upon transfer to San Francisco, all communications with our parents ceased. In desperation, our mother contacted the chaplain of his unit and learned he had married a non-Catholic before a justice*

of the peace (JP). Not only that, they had a son. The news devastated our parents. Their view, which followed the Church's teachings, was that Hugh's marriage before a JP was not valid in the Church's eye, and that was the only place where it counted for them. He and his wife were living in sin and headed for hell. It was a harsh judgment, but in fact, religion was the primary criterion talked about in our family for a marriage partner, never anything about compatibility of world views, life goals, or anything like that. You got a job, married a Catholic, and had kids. And somehow, everything would fall into place.

My decision to become a priest was motivated by an unconscious attempt to heal the hurt Hugh had caused our family. In addition to receiving the mantle of the Good Son by atoning for his actions, I would be out of the house and not subject to my father's sermons. In Jayne's eyes, I was deserting her, leaving her to bear the brunt of the paternal homilies. And although she never quite forgave me, it did seem fair to me given all the times she'd left me alone with our father's lectures.

On school holidays, I worked at my father's retail store, but in the summers, I chose to work for Joe, my brother, who was nine years my senior. He lived eight hundred miles away in South Dakota. When our father came up in conversations, Joe often began by saying, "Our Father, who art in Missouri . . ." to which I answered, ". . . hallowed be his name," adding a slight bow of my head, vowing never to be like him.

But after five years of seminary life—three years of high school and two of college—the idea of living a noncelibate life won out. I transferred to a Catholic university in St. Louis, where I dated only Catholic girls. After graduation, I joined several friends attempting to salvage a wreck from the bottom of Lake Superior. When I calculated that the recovery costs outweighed income from salvaging steel plate, we called a halt, and I went back to work with Joe until I joined the navy that fall.

The navy sent me to Officer Candidate School (OCS) in Newport, Rhode Island. Then, over Thanksgiving break, I married Vikki, my Catholic college girlfriend, about whom I knew very little as it turned out. Our dating history hadn't prepared us for a life together.

Upon commissioning as a navy ensign, I received orders to a ship in Southern California. With two weeks of leave and an additional two weeks of travel time, we chose to drive, visiting family along the way. For ten days, we were confined in a car together, and it produced the first of many arguments. That was when I realized I had made a mistake I could not easily undo.

Divorce was out of the question as far as my family was concerned. It could also end or severely limit a navy officer's career. And then there was the Catholic Church's position, which was that you could divorce but remarriage was forbidden. I might as well have stayed in the seminary and become a priest. And so I found myself stuck in a bad marriage and just needed to suck it up.

Chapter 7: Resignation

Once in Southern California, we found an apartment two blocks from the beach and settled into the life of a young married couple. But our arguing only intensified. One weekend, a senior officer from the ship invited us to his house for dinner, but at the last minute, I had to cancel because of a screaming match from which we hadn't recovered.

> *Because I was so focused on the hurt my oldest brother had caused our family, I missed the fact that I was living my parents' expectations instead of my own. Neither he nor I had found a middle road. And we'd both caused hurt.*

> *Negative lessons are as important as positive ones, and I recognized Vikki as one of my more important Buddhas, especially when choosing a marriage partner. Throughout my years at home, compatibility of outlook and similar life goals were never mentioned as qualities of a prospective partner. The assumption was that all obstacles would melt away if you were of the same religion. I was young and immature and, as it turned out, incapable of dealing with someone who was the product of an emotionally abusive family.*

A few months after reporting to my first ship, preparations began for the ship's six-month deployment to the Far East. Before the ship sailed, I put my pregnant wife on a plane to her parents' home in New Jersey, where she would give birth to our son in my absence. However, it was six months of a calm and orderly life for me. When the ship returned to the States, Vikki and I enjoyed a short-lived honeymoon before settling back into relating in the only way we knew how: screaming arguments.

And then, in the fall of 1962, the Soviets intervened in our marriage by placing missiles in Cuba. This act of aggression prompted an emergency deployment of a convoy of about two dozen ships from the West Coast to the Caribbean in preparation for an invasion where I would lead waves of boats to the beach. Thankfully, it never happened. After nearly two months, we returned to the West Coast but kept the invasion cargo onboard in case the Soviets reneged on their agreement. At that time, I was "fleeted up" to become the head of the Deck Department's four divisions, meaning I was a junior officer in a billet usually held by a more senior person.

Nine months later, the ship again prepared for its next routine deployment to the Far East. And once more, I left a pregnant wife, this time with a two-year-old son, to deliver our daughter without me. Meanwhile, at sea, I learned to bring the ship alongside another for underway transfers and to recover Oscar, the man-overboard dummy, in less than five minutes.

Finally, after three years of sea duty, a shore assignment sent us to a small naval base in Eastern Maryland. We planned to drive there in our new car. We had a month to drive and find a new place to live before I reported for duty, so we made this a vacation trip. I wanted to see Bryce and Zion Canyons. After that, we would drive to South Dakota to visit Joe and his family before stopping in Southern Indiana, where my parents had recently opened a baby shop.

Back then there were no fast-food places, and restaurants were still very formal places to eat. It was not an optimal time to drive across the country with a two-year-old and a three-month-old.

After our first day of driving, we arrived at our destination late. We were all tired and hungry. We dressed for dinner and, with children in tow, found a table among the other diners. In the middle of the meal, the three-month-old made a fuss, and her two-year-old brother pushed his feet against the table and tipped his highchair backward. The patrons were happy to see us retreat to our room.

The next day, at the entrance to Bryce, Vikki complained of severe abdominal pain. Always ready to take every ache and pain as a sure sign of cancer or some other life-threatening illness, she insisted that we find the nearest medical facility. Panguitch, Utah, was thirty minutes away, so we made a detour and headed there. Its hospital was small, and its doctor was out on call, so she was admitted for evaluation. In the meantime, I explored this town of 1,500 with the kids in tow. By the next day, we had a diagnosis: constipation. Vikki improved rapidly; the next day, we were back on the road, Bryce and Zion in the rearview mirror.

In Maryland, we found a house and settled in. For the next two years, our lives were relatively settled. Vikki recognized that she had issues and sought therapy. We still argued, but without the stress of frequent absences and deployment, the tension in our lives reduced.

However, international events once again intruded on our marriage. This time, it was Vietnam. In August 1964, two United States naval destroyers were fired at off the coast of Vietnam by the North Vietnamese Navy. In response, the United States began around-the-clock bombing of North Vietnam from aircraft carriers stationed in the Tonkin Gulf. In support, multiple ammunition ships ferried ordnance from the Philippines to the carriers in the Gulf.

The operations officer aboard one of those deploying ammunition ships resigned unexpectedly and needed to be replaced immediately. On the Friday before Mother's Day, I received emergency orders to leave Maryland immediately as the replacement operations officer. My orders gave me two weeks to move out, drive to the San Francisco Bay Area, find a house, and move my family in before the ship departed for an expected six-month deployment, which stretched into nine.

This separation was tough on Vikki and the kids. After I returned, I tendered my resignation and returned to the university to fulfill the requirements for a teaching certificate in California and New York. Through the naval reserves, I was chosen to teach that summer at OCS in

Newport, Rhode Island. In the fall of 1968, I began teaching United States history at a high school in Upstate New York.

Things between us continued at a low boil. In the fall of 1970, with ten mutually unhappy years under our belts, we joined a "Coping Group" at the local Unitarian Church. It was for couples to explore and deepen their relationships. We went, met some nice people, and decided to become Unitarians. Somehow, we thought that leaving the Catholic Church would allow us to shed its position on birth control and the attendant anxieties it produced. The decision did provide a seamless transition to a spiritual home where we felt more comfortable. But the old issues and tensions clung like Velcro.

In 1971, Vikki was offered an excellent job in Buffalo, and I found work with a local consumer protection agency. We thought the move might fix things between us. But of course, geography can't fix a marriage, and within a year, we were talking about separating. Stress, tension, and arguments were an integral part of our relationship. Recalling my reactions to my parents' occasional shouting matches behind closed doors, I knew it had to be affecting the children negatively.

That fall, we drove to Southern Indiana for Thanksgiving with my parents. The kids were nine and seven. Sitting around the table after dinner chatting, my father said, "Here, I want to show you an idea I'm trying to sell to a religious goods company." He excused himself from the table to go to a filing cabinet in his home office. His files were sorted into three general categories: God, People, and Things.

He returned with three gold letters about six inches tall. He laid them out alphabetically on the table—D, G, O—and asked, "What does this spell?" Sitting beside her grandfather, my six-year-old daughter looked at them and said, "Dog." He rearranged them and said, "They spell God." She thought momentarily and then said, "I just don't think I believe in God or Santa Claus."

Undaunted, he slid the G with the cross in the center, representing God the Son, over the O, God the Father, and then the letter D, which stood for God the Holy Spirit. When he slid the letters together, they formed a circle with a cross inside, which he told us was "God's symbol." It was an awkward moment that we all chose to ignore.

Later that fall, the lease on the house we were renting was about to expire, so the question became: Do we renew and stay together and continue as we are or find a smaller place with plans of separating? We chose the smaller place. And just before Christmas, we made the final decision to separate. I would move out when I found a place. I found somewhere suitable and moved out on January 1.

I involved myself in an affair with a married friend. Admittedly, it wasn't wise. And after some months, I saw it as a dead-end relationship, one that limited my emotional health and growth. So, with reluctance, I ended it. Many times, I was tempted to reach out to her, but I knew that in the long run, it would only deepen my depression. Instead, I avoided facing my issues, this time using the time-honored strategy of distraction therapy by maxing out my credit cards and spending hours on long bike rides in the country.

> *Looking back on the affair, I came to realize just how deeply depressed I was and had been for several years. Its positive side was that I realized I could love and be loved—a new feeling after the past twelve years. But I also learned how important it was to a relationship to be able to talk freely with each other without holding back secret portions of ourselves, an impossibility in an affair. I grew due to the relationship, but I needed to end it for continued growth. My chief regret is the injury I caused this Buddha by simply cutting off contact. She deserved better.*

One Sunday, I returned from a bike ride and found that my apartment had been vandalized. The place was a total mess; my stereo equipment and a shotgun had been stolen. The sense of violation of my personal space was so strong that I couldn't stay in my home that night. Instead, I asked a friend if I could spend the night at his place. Soon after the break-in, I found someone to take over my lease, and I moved to a flat in North Buffalo.

Things seemed pretty bleak, but it was the memory of an old photograph of me as a four-year-old that sustained me during those times. It's summer and I'm standing in our side yard wearing shorts. I'm holding a ball in one hand. In the other I have an American flag on a small staff resting on my left shoulder. My hair is curly and I have a broad smile on my face. On the reverse side is an inscription: "This is the way he looks all the time, a grin on his face." And I thought, I must get that happiness back (Image 7-1).

Image 7-1: The author at about age four

Then friends at the Unitarian Church invited me to join a singles group, which improved my social life, but it was just another variation of distraction therapy. I still wasn't facing the things I needed to deal with.

> *Without the singles group, I'm sure I would have stumbled and made a worse mess of my life. They were all Buddha-friends who influenced my life in positive ways. It was through this group that I would eventually meet someone who would completely alter the direction of my life.*

But later that fall, I reflected on twelve years of a progressively deteriorating marriage filled with a lot of anger, regret at having left a navy career, low self-esteem, an affair, a robbery, and a love life that was pretty much going nowhere. I wasn't in control of my life, and I sought out a therapist, who, after a few sessions, encouraged me to break out of my habitual routines and see what might happen.

My solution was to go for a walk in the woods. At the next session, I brought in a dried-up milkweed stalk, its pods devoid of last summer's seeds. Its raw beauty appealed to me, but I'm not sure he saw it that way. More than likely, he saw it as emblematic of my life, dead and headed for the compost. That would not have been far off. He encouraged me to look for other ways to escape my rut.

I mulled the question: How can I do something spontaneous and unplanned when it's been suggested that I do something spontaneous and unplanned? Faced with this conundrum, a plan began to coalesce. I thought of something that would present many opportunities for spontaneous and unplanned things to happen. Even though Buffalo had already experienced its first snowfall, I decided to hitchhike wherever I could get a ride. There would be no plan. I would see what happened and deal with it.

Over the Christmas holidays, I took a ten-day vacation from work. I planned to stand on the interstate and hitchhike as far as I could in five days, then turn around and head back.

In preparation, I bought bright red ski pants, a high-quality bright blue down jacket with a hood, and down mittens, all very visible if I were lost in a snowdrift. Again, I also got essential survival gear just in case I didn't die in that snowdrift. For safety, I would carry a hunting knife strapped inside my boot along with a pack of American Express Traveler's Cheques. I would carry high-calorie snacks and the remains of a goose I had cooked for Christmas dinner with friends. The night before I left, a friend gave me a talisman in the form of a yarn leprechaun she had made. We named him Murphy, attached him to my backpack, and walked back to my flat in a light snow, pondering what this adventure might bring.

Chapter 8: The No-Plan Plan

A friend dropped me off at the service center on the westbound side of the New York State Thruway just outside Buffalo. The temperature was in the upper twenties, and huge piles of dingy snow ringed the edges of the three-quarters full parking lot. I picked a stool near the cash register in the coffee shop and conspicuously placed my sign. "WEST," it said in black electrical tape stuck on plywood painted white.

"What can I get you, hon?" the waitress asked; her starched uniform was limp so close to the shift's end. "Coffee and a slice of the lemon pie," I said. The meringue looked stale, but I liked lemon meringue no matter its condition.

I had taken a couple of bites of pie when I heard a stern voice behind me. "Hitchhiking's not allowed on the Thruway." I turned to see the tall figure of a New York State trooper; his eyes bored into me. "Take the back service road, and don't be here when I return." He paid his bill and left without a backward glance. This was my first opportunity to deal with the spontaneous, the unexpected.

I saw no need to panic. I knew there was time to catch a ride before he got back. I lit a cigarette. While the waitress refilled my cup, I tried to think it through. Leaving by the service road seemed the worst option. I could always trash the whole idea and call a friend to pick me up. But I guessed the route the trooper patrolled was a loop of several hundred miles of the Thruway. It would be hours before he returned to this service center, which gave me time to get a ride.

When I was ready, I paid my bill, gathered my things, and prepared to take up a position at the end of the parking lot. As I headed toward the door, a man stepped toward me. He was shorter than I and wore a cap and a heavy Mackinaw jacket. He said he saw the trooper order me off the Thruway. Where was I going? I said California. It was vague but specific enough. He

47

was a trucker driving a load to Erie, Pennsylvania. It was only a hundred miles down the road, but I would be off the Thruway and out of New York State.

At Erie, he dropped me at a truck stop where I got something more substantial to eat before heading to the highway. I pulled a Santa hat from my bag to make my beard and long hair seem less threatening. I counted on pity from passing motorists. After all, it was the day after Christmas.

Eventually, a series of rides brought me to the outskirts of Cleveland, where a guy wearing sandals picked me up. I asked why he wore sandals in the winter. He said he just preferred sandals, simple as that. For the most part, he said, the walks and streets were cleared quickly. If they weren't, he wore boots.

He was an interesting fellow, probably in his mid-thirties, and very chatty. He said he had invented a way to retrofit cars with half-vinyl roofs, turning any car into a Landau version of itself. It was popular in the mid-1970s, at least in that part of the country.

He asked what books I had read recently. I said I'd been reading the Carlos Castaneda books about Castaneda's encounter with Don Juan, the Yaqui Indian mystic. He had just finished *Zen and the Art of Motorcycle Maintenance* by Robert Pirsig. It was a good book, he said, but I should skip over the parts where Pirsig went off on long riffs about quality. I made a note, thanked him, and promised to pick up a copy.

He dropped me at another truck stop, where I felt my luck was changing because I was picked up almost immediately by a Vietnam vet. He was one of those who expressed his frustrations and emotions as anger, not something I felt I could deal with at two in the morning.

He had been in the US Marines, up north near North Vietnam, in I Corps near Danang during the war.

48

"I was nineteen when I shot my first human," he said. "I had nightmares. Still have nightmares, but not about that. About being stalked by the gooks. About body parts."

I could only say, "I can't imagine."

"And you survive it," he said, "but you don't because when you close your eyes, you're still there fighting to stay alive, to keep your buddies alive. And you come home, and they treat you like shit. And you don't want parades because you're not a hero; you just survived, and that's all. But, goddamn it, you don't want to be treated like a piece of shit."

"Yeah," I said. "And you don't want to see anybody else have to go through what you did."

"You just want to feel like what you went through wasn't for nothing. That's all."

He had seen a lot of bad stuff. He saw friends blown to pieces; I could not imagine how anyone could deal with that. I spent my Vietnam time in the navy, comfortably aboard an ammunition ship. Our experiences were so different that I felt guilty. I didn't see my friends get killed. I didn't personally know anyone who died over there.

But as fatigue began to overwhelm me, and his voice droned on and on, thoughts of my own experiences flooded my awareness and drowned out his voice. What we dealt with was so different; my experiences were mild compared with his, yet mine produced a sense of ennui and depression that had eventually ground my life to a standstill. I could only imagine how his experiences might have messed up his view of the world and his life.

No one shot at me. My life was never under direct or immediate threat. I slept in a bed every night. Took a shower every morning. Ate three hot meals a day on a cloth-covered table. My war experiences were from the relative comfort of

49

an ammunition ship delivering bombs to aircraft carriers and ammunition to destroyers that shelled the Vietnam coast.

Our primary mission was to support the frontline ships: the aircraft carriers and the destroyers. The carriers launched continuous bombing missions over the north while the destroyers shelled targets along the Vietnam coast in support of our troops. All these ships constantly needed to be resupplied (Image 8-1).

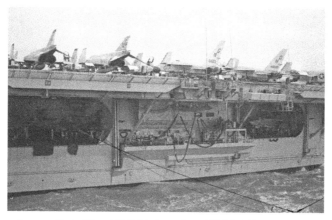

Image 8-1: The USS Enterprise (CVN-65) alongside for an underway re-arming

The routine was simple but grueling. We docked at the Naval Weapons Station at Subic Bay in the Philippines, where it took about three days to fully load. We left port around midnight to be in the Tonkin Gulf at first light two days later, where we rearmed our first aircraft carrier. Then we transited down the coast to resupply the destroyers. Three round trips between the Gulf and the southern tip of Vietnam nearly emptied us. Whatever was left, we transferred to the ammunition ship that relieved us, then we returned to the Philippines to reload.

Halfway through the deployment, the executive officer, second in command, left the ship on emergency leave, which left me the number two. One of my duties as operations officer was to bring the ship into and out of port under the captain's supervision. He generally returned from the officers' club minutes before our departure. One night, after returning from the club, he fell asleep in his cabin, and when it was time to get underway, he could not be roused. With the pilot already onboard, I took a calculated risk and got underway without his presence on the bridge.

Underway rearming could take place day or night, in good weather or stormy, calm or rough seas, even during simultaneous launch and recovery of aircraft. In preparation, the deck crew prepositioned the transfer load on deck, making for a fast, efficient, and safe operation (Image 8-2). This could take hours of hard physical labor. I was our ship's officer of the deck (OOD) for all underway transfers. When we were the receiving ship, I brought us alongside the delivery ship and maintained station within 90 to 120 feet throughout the transfer. .

During all transfers, I was informed of anything that might affect us, whether on our ship, the other ship, or some fishing boat that might present a collision hazard.

On one occasion, we transferred bombs to a carrier alongside to port (our left) and ammunition to a destroyer to starboard. During the transfer, one of our young and inexperienced seamen stepped in the loop of a coiled line on deck. As he did, tension was put on the line, cinching it around his ankle. He was yanked up and outboard, where he

51

dangled between our two ships. When I saw him from the bridge, he was hanging upside down twenty feet above the water. Any slack in the line and he would have dropped into the roiling sea between the ships to an awful death. Fortunately, he was hauled back aboard in a state of shock.

Image 8-2: A transfer load being pre-positioned for an underway re-arming of an aircraft carrier

One transfer took so long that we came within sight of China. With the carrier still alongside and all lines still attached, we made a giant U-turn to the south, away from their territorial waters, and continued the transfer.

After I left the ship, she collided with one of the aircraft carriers she was rearming, damaging the carrier's starboard elevators.

Some weeks later, exhaustion and sleep deprivation led to a serious accident onboard one of the aircraft carriers we had worked with.

Its aircraft had returned from their missions and were in the hangar deck below the flight deck. In the process of removing unexpended ordnance from the aircraft, a large magnesium parachute flare accidentally exploded inside the flare locker room setting off an explosion of some seven hundred additional flares. Forty-four men perished in the ensuing fire that reached temperatures more than twice that required to melt steel. One-hundred-fifty-six others were injured.

I was shaken. Their loss felt personal. These were people we worked with and felt a real connection to. We were all in this thing together. But the truth was that everything you did meant somebody lived and somebody died. It really couldn't get more serious than that.

That incident was another reminder that we lived in constant danger. Six weeks after we first arrived off Vietnam, a coast guard cutter patrolling near Danang was shot up by one of our air force jets. Two onboard the cutter died. One night, we were buzzed and challenged by one of our own. If we had been strafed, only an oil slick would have remained after the smoke had cleared.

The Vietnam vet's chattering seemed to become quieter and quieter as I drifted deeper toward sleep. He dropped me off south of Chicago, but I apologized for not helping him stay awake through the night before he pulled away.

A series of short rides took me across Illinois and Iowa, and I arrived on the outskirts of Omaha in the morning rush. Getting a ride across the city at this hour would be daunting, but I had a map with rudimentary details of Omaha. It was good enough that I could use it to walk to the other side of town, where there was a better chance of getting a ride.

The temperature was just above freezing, with considerable slush on the roads and walkways. But I had only gone a few hundred yards when a car stopped. It was a nurse's aide. She was young; her car was not. She was on her way home from her night shift. "There's no good place around here for you to get a ride," she said. Then, "Let me take you where there's a good truck stop where you can get a ride pretty easily."

She was right. The parking lot was a beehive of activity. I went into the restaurant, found a place at the counter, bags at my feet, sign easily visible. Hash browns, bacon, two eggs over easy, and two cups of coffee later, I headed to the parking lot where it exited onto the highway. I didn't have time to organize myself before a huge Transtar heavy-hauler truck pulled up alongside me.

When I climbed up and opened the cab door, I was greeted with the sound of Bach's second Brandenburg Concerto. "Nice music," I said, stowing my gear on the floor.

"Yeah," he said. "Bach soothes me on these long drives." He reached his hand toward me, "Hi, I'm Hank Christianson. Where are you headed?" We slipped into easy conversation as we exchanged life stories.

Hank had done just about everything. He'd worked trawlers in Alaska, panned for gold in California, and worked for the John Birch Society in Orange County, and had been driving trucks for the past five years. He was a book guy and was interested in the Carlos Castaneda books, even though

54

he hadn't read them. I told him what they were about and the controversy around whether they were fact or fiction. "What difference does it make either way?" he asked. "It's just like with life. The meaning you give it is what's important; otherwise, there isn't any."

We crossed Nebraska together. At Ogallala, we stopped to tank up, him on diesel fuel, me on liver and onions. From the comfort of the truck stop, I looked at what little was left of Nebraska and saw into neighboring Colorado. Then I watched Hank's Transtar disappear down I-80 toward Cheyenne. I planned to take the I-76 split that followed the south fork of the Platte River to Denver. I would visit a friend there, then possibly someone in Fort Collins, before going north to Cheyenne. As I paid my tab, I noticed a book stand prominently displaying a copy of *Zen and the Art of Motorcycle Maintenance*. Wasn't that fortuitous?

It was snowing again, so I went back, sat down, drank more coffee, smoked more cigarettes, and read. I got a lift to Denver, where I crashed with my friend. His recommendation was to go north to Cheyenne and pick up I-90. I took his advice, and in Cheyenne, I got a ride fairly quickly with Stan, who was transporting a car to a dealer in Salt Lake City.

Winter in southern Wyoming can be brutal, which it was that night. A blizzard blew down from the north, sending snow horizontally across the highway. Stan drove on, sometimes at a crawl, at others slightly slower. We passed no other cars and met none either.

By the time we got to Salt Lake City, it was well past midnight and only snowing lightly. Stan insisted that I spend the night at his house. He fixed us salmon steaks from the freezer, and I crashed on the couch.

When I reached Truckee, California, I called my brother Hugh, who was at their family's place on Lake Tahoe, only twenty minutes away. We spent a relaxing day catching up on each other's lives and me on my sleep. Then it was time to turn around and head back.

From Truckee, a series of uneventful rides brought me once again to Cheyenne, where two of Wyoming's not-so-friendly cowboys tried to run over me with their pickups just before a cop pulled up behind me and ordered me into his car.

"Driver's license," he commanded. I considered a smart-ass remark like "I don't have a driver's license; that's why I'm hitchhiking," but thought better of it and handed it over. He called in my information on his radio. And while we waited, we chatted. Where are you going? Why are you hitchhiking? What do you do for a living?

He said the system wasn't usually this slow. He blamed it on the weather. The information had to go to Arizona or somewhere like that and then be relayed to Washington, DC. He apologized for the slowness. Then a call came over his radio about a domestic disturbance.

"I love domestic disturbances," he said. "Get out of the car."

I happily obliged, and almost as fast as I did, a car with three guys pulled over. "We saw that cop harassing you, so we figured we'd get you out of here."

"Thanks," I said as I piled into the back seat.

"Where are you headed?" I said Buffalo; they said Connecticut. I wedged my duffle bag into the back seat between me and the other passenger. As the miles rolled past, I gleaned from their conversation that they were less than savory individuals. There were shared jokes about bar fights, petty larcenies, and firearms stashed in the car, which I suspected didn't mean in the trunk.

When we stopped, I paid for gas, coffee, and snacks. My backseat mate was going to Detroit, so we detoured off of I-90 to drop him off. I suggested we could save time by cutting across Canada's southern peninsula directly to Buffalo. The two in front quietly conferred and opted not to cross into

Canada. I was suspicious that maybe the firearms had factored into their decision. Whatever the reason, it was obvious they intended to keep a low profile when it came to the authorities.

Twenty-one hours after they'd picked me up in Cheyenne, we were at my flat. I invited them in for coffee and cinnamon buns from the bakery on the corner. Honestly, I was a bit nervous that they now knew where I lived, but I had already spent a day with them, and I lived to tell about it.

After they left, and it seemed like they never would, I unpacked, made more coffee, put Murphy, my yard mascot, on the mantle, and thanked him for getting me safely home. Then I pulled out Pirsig's *Zen and the Art of Motorcycle Maintenance*.

> *At one point in the book, Pirsig talks about dogmas and things people fight over. He says people fight over the things they are in doubt about. Everybody knows the sun's coming up in the morning. That's no big deal. Nobody fights over that. The things people get fanatical about are the things they have doubts about, like God. And I thought of my father and his lectures on religion.*

> *When I was fourteen months old, my mother, my five-year-old sister Mary, and I were hospitalized with systemic infections threatening our lives. A few months before we were hospitalized, a medical breakthrough had brought the first wonder drug to market. It saved my mother and me, but unfortunately, Mary had an allergic reaction to the drug, causing sulfur crystals to form around her brainstem. In a matter of days, she was dead. This experience drove both of my parents deep into religion. I'm sure my convert father questioned how an all-merciful God could take his young daughter. I wondered if he was fighting against his doubts when he mounted his soapbox all those years before.*

They blamed themselves. She for not going to a doctor sooner; he for concentrating on his business career. These were crosses they bore for the rest of their lives and that tainted their relationships with the rest of us.

The issues that ran through my head the night the Vietnam vet picked me up hitchhiking resurfaced in my meditation years later. I realized how closely my identity had been connected to my navy career—how much I'd loved ship handling. I saw how its loss, plus the sense that nothing I was doing measured up to what I had done then, contributed to the ennui and depression I was experiencing. Also, layered over that was the fact that although I had resigned to "save" my marriage, I hadn't been able to, which only made matters worse. But, at some deep psychological level, the time spent on the hitchhiking trip did seem to lay the groundwork for putting Humpty Dumpty back together again.

This no-plan plan was filled with Buddhas. There was Stan, who recommended Pirsig's book Zen and the Art of Motorcycle Maintenance. *I would never have read it otherwise. Vietnam vet was the prod that moved me to think back about some important things in my life and reconsider them in light of where I was. He was the key to understanding that I had been seriously depressed for years, which pointed a way forward. Of course, the nurse's aide, my link to Hank, the Transtar driver and Bach lover, taught me that providing meaning to my life was up to me. It seems such an obvious lesson now, but it wasn't then.*

Chapter 9: Finding a Direction

With the hitchhiking adventure behind me, life fell back into a routine. I was back at work and back with my therapist. He, of course, was dumbfounded when I told him about my no-plan plan. In hindsight, it was chancy and probably irresponsible, but afterward, things felt different.

I continued going to the singles parties. Maybe I was less frantic. Still, with each date, I wondered if there would be one of those click moments. But it didn't happen. I thought, *Well, maybe a lifetime of "blessed singleness" wouldn't be so bad. Indeed, it would be better than another bad marriage.*

At one of the parties, I talked with someone who said her parents would be happy if she remarried or got into a long-term relationship. She was surprised when I said mine wouldn't be happy at all. I explained that they would figure I was going straight to hell.

At work, I got pink-slipped and reinvented myself entirely by returning to my college summer job skills. I would be self-employed and post ads in the paper for interior painting and wallpapering. Throughout my working career, I had terrible bosses. Right out of the navy, I sold life insurance, where my boss was just as preachy as my father. That didn't last long. I taught high school, where my department head couldn't look me in the eye when we talked; his focus was somewhere over my head. At the consumer agency, the manager subjected me to long-winded monologues reminiscent of my father's. I'd had it with working for someone else.

In the intervening years since I had worked those summer jobs with my brother Joe, he had relocated his family to Indiana near our parents. So, now, as my business grew, I periodically visited my brother to upgrade my work skills. When I did, I usually stayed at our parents' house, only a short walk away.

One evening at my parents' house, we watched something on public TV about Galileo and his difficulties with the Church over his insistence that the Earth revolved around the sun. Then I suddenly found myself in a fierce argument with my father over these scientific facts.

"The Church was right to condemn him," he said.

"Condemn him for stating an observable, scientific fact?" I asked.

Things got so heated my mother had to intervene, metaphorically pulling us apart before things got out of hand. Despite my new insights about my father, this incident didn't do much to improve our relationship.

Back in Buffalo, things were going well. I decided to have a small dinner party for eight: four men and four women. Just friends from the singles group getting together for a good time. One of the women I invited was Diana. We'd met recently at one of the singles parties. She was chatty, and I thought she would keep the conversation going. It was a Russian-themed dinner because I had a bunch of fresh beets and wanted to make a borscht soup. To round out the menu, I would offer a Russian beef stroganoff, a carrot salad, and *blinchikis*, the Russian version of blintzes, for dessert.

When I brought out the cold borscht, Diana said, "Borscht is always served hot." My mind said, *What the hell are you talking about ALWAYS?*, but my mouth said, "The only way I've had it was cold."

I attended a Flatt & Scruggs concert in Fort Erie, Canada, across the Niagara River from Buffalo a few months later. The music was great, but I came down with the worst cold of my life the next day. It was so bad I couldn't even think about smoking. For a week, I curled up in bed, waiting to die.

By Saturday, I knew I would live and looked for human companionship. I pulled out the proverbial "black book" and looked for someone to go to dinner and a movie with me. One person after another got checked off the list. I called Diana. "Are you available for dinner and a movie tonight?" Her three kids were with their father, and she said yes.

Afterward, we went to her place for coffee and talked till about three in the morning before I left for home. One of the things I learned that night was that she was third-generation Polish, and they always had their borscht hot. After that, we began seeing each other regularly.

As the school year drew to a close, Vikki informed me she was going to Texas to work on an advanced degree in the fall. I knew it would be very stressful if the kids, aged fourteen and twelve, were with her, so I offered to have them live with me till she finished. They planned to go with her to Texas to see where she would live, then return before school to live with me.

When Diana had moved back to Buffalo, she'd promised her kids that she would take them back to Ohio for a couple of weeks to catch up with old friends sometime that summer. She asked if I wanted to accompany her to keep her company on the drive back. So, one Saturday, bright and early, she picked me up in her brown Pinto with her three kids, aged nine to fifteen, wedged into the back seat.

She pulled up to my flat when we returned to Buffalo on Sunday afternoon. I got out but couldn't put my key into the lock. Then I saw plywood over the door and realized the lock was covered. A handwritten sign was taped at eye level that read, "Don: Call me at Sharon's, and I'll explain what happened," signed by my upstairs neighbor. I turned and saw a pile of my belongings in the driveway. I stepped back and looked at the house. Then I realized that all the windows were boarded over.

Neighbors said there had been a violent thunderstorm the night before. Thirteen houses had been struck by lightning, mine included. The neighbors had sprayed garden hoses through the basement windows until the fire department had arrived and put it out.

All I could think about was my kids coming in six weeks.

I mentally reconstructed what I thought had happened and concluded that the lightning had traveled through the electrical wiring to the basement, where most of the fire damage had occurred. In preparation for my kids' arrival, I had moved my bedroom to the basement and covered the ceiling with burlap stapled to the joists overhead. It was this burlap that had caught fire and where the fire damage was concentrated. However, there was smoke damage throughout the entire house.

To contain the fire, the firefighters had smashed every window in the house. So all the windows needed to be replaced before the interior cleanup could begin. I called on some of the contractors I had worked with in my consumer protection days; we could button up the house and start work on the interior.

While the contractors and I worked on cleanup and damage repair, I lived with Diana in the suburbs. Insurance helped cover the minimal repairs to the flat. However, a lot of my personal items were lost to smoke or water damage. By the end of summer, things were ready for the kids' return, just in time for the start of school.

When I looked at the schools the kids would attend in Buffalo, I offered them a choice: the neighborhood schools or the suburban schools where Diana's kids went. I drove them past both schools and asked them to choose which schools they wanted to go to. They could take the city bus to the Buffalo schools, or I could drive them each morning to Diana's, where they would wait for the school bus, and I would pick them up there after work. They chose the suburban schools. And that became our daily routine until I found a rental in the suburban school district.

As our relationship deepened, Diana and I bought a house together and merged our families: my two and her three. A few months later, my mother was diagnosed with advanced cancer, which would soon take her life. In the intervening months, I made several trips to see her. On the final visit, shortly before she died, she asked me to go through the Catholic Church's process of annulling my first marriage so that I could marry Diana. I wondered how my children would feel about becoming illegitimate in the Church's eye. I told her I had never lied to her, but I could not do that. Having to say that saddened me greatly.

When Diana and I married, my father initially said he would not attend the wedding, thinking his presence would indicate his approval. Fortunately, my sister Jayne straightened him out on that point, and he did come, signaling a softening of his attitude.

As my wallpapering and painting business grew, I joined the local chapter of a painting and wallpapering contractors' group. One night, in conversation with a more experienced contractor, I asked how to price jobs effectively. "Keep good records," he said, which I began doing. I kept meticulous records of the time it took to do various aspects of my jobs. In the late 1970s, I got my first computer and created a spreadsheet to calculate the written estimates I presented to potential clients. I also wrote a computer program to estimate wallpaper in stairwells and other complicated areas.

Then, when our youngest went to college, the time seemed right for a significant change. Buffalo's economy wasn't looking exceptionally bright then; Diana had just finished her master's in nursing. For several years, we had vacationed on North Carolina's Outer Banks, so that summer, we decided to see what was on the other side of the dunes, and once again, serendipity entered our lives.

We drove around Eastern North Carolina, visiting several hospitals. At one that served North Carolina's eastern twenty-nine counties, Diana bumped into the director of nursing. In the conversation, Diana learned that the hospital was hiring a diabetes educator, a position she held in Buffalo. With encouragement from the director of nursing, she applied for the job and was hired, so I prepared to move my business to Eastern North Carolina.

I found it interesting that on that Sunday afternoon, when Diana and I pulled into the driveway from Ohio, neither of us saw the fire damage to the house. She parked directly in front of a pile of debris the firefighters had left, and we didn't see that or the boarded over windows and doors.

We saw what we expected to see: the house just as we had left it the previous day. It was fifteen years before I could return to any home without a swell of anxiety. What condition would I find the house in? Had it been broken into? Had there been a fire?

When Diana and I bought the house together, it confirmed my parents' worst nightmare—that the salvation of my eternal soul was at stake. I knew how they felt, but I also knew I needed to find my direction and live my life accordingly. Unlike my older brother Hugh, I kept in touch with them.

Part III: "Now Begins the Study of Yoga"

Atha yoga anushasanam. This first line of the Yoga Sutras is usually translated as "Now begins the study of yoga." It would be easy to skim over this line, but Sanskrit packs a lot of meaning into a single word. *Atha* means now in the sense of after prior preparation. The word "yoga" comes from the Sanskrit root *yuj*, meaning to join or yoke things together, as in yoking a team of oxen together in a disciplined effort. In other words, integrating the life processes toward eventual release. A free translation might read something like this: "Now, after you have tried other ways to deal with life's problems, you are ready to cultivate the wisdom of yoga."

Yoga Sutras 1.1

Chapter 10: Accidents Will Happen

It took three years for the seeds planted in India to germinate. It happened at a workshop, during the morning break. Our presenter said, "This morning, let's do some simple yoga instead of going for coffee and pastries."

A few people couldn't resist the magnetic pull of coffee and pastries, but most were enthusiastic and stayed. I don't know why I stayed; maybe it was peer pressure. In any case, the presenter led us through some simple yoga poses. Then she said, "Let's do some sun salutations. I'll talk you through it if you're unfamiliar."

Because I had avoided yoga all those years, I had no idea what she was talking about, but I followed along. We did a standing backbend, then a forward fold.

She said, "Don't round your backs. Just let your hands rest on your legs wherever they come." Mine were just below my knees. Then she said, "Now go ahead and gently round down. Now drop your hands toward the floor. Go ahead and bend your knees, and then step back into a plank pose. Like this." She did; I followed.

"Okay, now lift your chest and try to pull up from your shoulders. At the same time, let your hips sag toward the floor into a cobra pose." Once again, I followed as best I could.

"Now," she said, "step your feet between your hands into a forward bend. And it's okay to bend your knees." We all followed.

"Come up into another standing backbend, then bring your hands together at your hearts in standing prayer pose."

She turned toward us and said, "And that's one simple sun salutation. We'll do it a couple more times." We all did, and it was great. WOW! *That's amazing*, I thought. *This yoga thing's not so bad after all.* She did it a few more times, increasing the speed with each repetition.

Yes, I was stiff and couldn't reach much below my knees, but I felt energized. It was better than coffee in the morning.

But before we returned to the workshop, I did sneak out for a quick coffee and donut. What we did felt good, but I decided to stick to the morning coffee, at least for the near future.

I was always someone whose body might get out of bed when the alarm went off but whose brain waited until around ten o'clock to come online. After this experience, I incorporated those sun salutations into my morning ritual.

From then on, each morning, as soon as I got out of bed, I did three sun salutations before brushing my teeth. It was a great feeling for my body and brain to be up and functioning together. But sure, I still had my coffee for breakfast.

A few months after the workshop, a notice appeared in the newspaper announcing the beginning of a series of yoga classes. I had no idea there were such things as formal yoga classes. Like so many things, once we've been introduced to something new, we realize it was right before us all along. We see what we are prepared to see.

It was a fall evening, and leaves gently floated through the air as I walked into my first yoga class, just weeks shy of my fifty-eighth birthday. The class was held in a small auditorium. Iris, our teacher, taught from the stage where we could all easily see her. We were fifteen or twenty people, with our yoga mats aligned toward her like iron filings toward a magnet.

She demonstrated and talked us through the poses. The others in the class had been with her for a while. I wasn't sure what I was doing, so I picked a place toward the back. Iris was encouraging. The only way we could do it wrong, she said, was if we didn't try. She encouraged but never pushed. Work at your ability level. She said if your breath gets fast and irregular, back off or come to child's pose and wait.

After that first class, I was hooked. I remember feeling lighter and more relaxed than ever before. It was a great feeling; I knew I had found something of real value and became a committed regular. I promised myself I would not miss a class for six months until going to class was a habit.

In class, as we moved through our poses, Iris referred to what we were doing as meditation in motion. That seemed like a cute, poetic way to describe things. Eventually, the idea of meditating seeped into my consciousness, and I decided to add a couple of minutes just sitting there after my morning sun salutations. I didn't know what I was doing, but when my church later held a fundraiser auctioning members' services, I got the chance to learn more about meditation. Devika, a member of Indian descent and a long-time meditator, offered a thirty-minute introductory meditation lesson. I ran the bid up until I won it.

One evening, while the choir practiced, we met in another room for our lesson.

"We'll start with sitting meditation in a chair," Devika said. We pulled out a couple of folding chairs and faced each other. She placed a small table between us with a candle on it.

"How you are sitting is very important. Sit with a straight spine and balance your head. Maybe drop your chin a bit. When you advance in meditation, this will be very important. Now try to sit with your back away from the chair. Eventually, you may want to sit on the floor, and then it will be important." I did as I was told.

"Before we start," she said, "our minds are like an elephant in a village market in India. It comes in swinging its trunk and picking up whatever it chooses. Maybe bananas, whatever it chooses. But if you give it a stick to carry in its trunk, it will walk through the market, leaving bananas and such behind. That's the way our minds are. They will dart around all over the place. So we need to give them something to hold on to. That is why you will focus on your posture, your breath, or whatever your focus is.

The memory of the elephants plodding along the highway in India came back. They were all carrying something with their trunks. It wasn't to practice carrying something, it was to give them a focus as they walked along the roadway with cars passing in both directions.

"Now sit in a chair, your thighs coming straight from your hips. No angles. Ankles right below the knees, feet straight ahead." Again, I imitated how she sat.

"Now," she said, "rest the back of your hands on your thighs, palms up. That's right. Now index finger and thumb together. We call this *jnana mudra*, which means wisdom. It means you're seeking wisdom."

I followed along.

"Your thumb and finger want to separate. That's natural because you're not used to doing this. Try to keep them together. Let your eyes be half-open only. Maybe a quarter." She lit the candle. "Now look at the flame through half-opened eyes. Try not to focus. Just a soft focus. Concentrate on the flame, and keep your thumb and index fingers together."

"Okay, like this?" I asked.

"Keep gazing at the flame, and concentrate on your thumb and finger. Your mind might wander off. If it does, just come back to the flame and fingers.

No talking aloud or to yourself. Just gazing and holding your fingers together."

We did the exercise for a few minutes. Then she asked me to describe how it had been for me.

"I think I did pretty well. It's like sitting in front of a fireplace in the winter. Just staring and watching the flames dance."

"No thinking," she said.

"Right."

"Now," she said, "do the same exercise but pay attention to your breath this time. Each inhale. Each exhale. No thinking, just doing. Okay? Let's begin by exhaling and then inhaling. Begin with the exhale to get rid of all the toxins, and then the inhale. Okay, now you do it, please."

I took the position again, closing my eyes completely. I felt the exhale empty my chest, and the air came in against the back of my throat. I noticed it in my nostrils and how cool it felt when it came in. I exhaled warm air out. But my mind soon wandered off. *Am I doing this right? Did I miss the last inhale? Oh, am I slouching? Breathe. Pay attention.*

"How was it this time?"

"Well, my mind wandered off a lot more than with the candle."

"That's okay. We're looking for persistence, not perfection. Just keep it up, and you'll improve with practice."

Then she said we would do it again except sitting on the floor. We repeated the candle and breath practices. She said I could sit in a chair or on the floor when I did it alone. Either was okay. Focusing on either the candle or the breath was fine. I should find what worked best for me.

Afterward, I bought a candle, and from then on, after my three sun salutations, I sat and concentrated on the candle flame, which was great until I came home for lunch one day and found the candle still burning. I replaced it immediately with a battery-operated one that flickered like a real flame. Well, not quite, but it was safer. After a while, I stopped using the candle and focused on breathing.

I was a regular in Iris's yoga classes for five years, and then one night, she pulled seven or eight of us aside to say she would teach an intermediate-level class at the Unitarian Church. I was happy to add another class and realized what a gift yoga was—how far those three sun salutations had brought me. I wanted to pass that gift on to others.

Our hospital had just opened its new wellness center with a Saturday morning yoga class. If two classes a week was good for me, maybe three would be better. I went to the class and was appalled. I couldn't help comparing this teacher with Iris, and she didn't come close. Her class was more about demonstrating her flexibility than teaching or working with us. But I stayed with the classes.

One Saturday, I talked with the exercise coordinator and, as diplomatically as possible, gave her my feedback. She told me about a teacher training class and said that if I took it, she would hire me.

The training class was held in a hotel conference room in Raleigh. The course was for people with some exposure to yoga poses who wanted to meet the basic qualifications to teach yoga in a gym setting. The course offered nothing about yoga philosophy. Its main goal was to teach us how to protect our students from injury. A bonus was that they offered a selection of books and yoga music for sale.

During a break on the second day, I struck up a conversation with the woman on the mat next to me. I commented that the previous day was very tiring. It was my first time doing that much yoga for so long.

"I'm so glad to hear it wasn't just me," she said. "I thought my fibromyalgia was coming back."

She had done yoga for about five years, and her fibromyalgia had improved as a result. She took a photo from her wallet. "This was me before I started yoga." The contrast was stark. I would not have recognized her from the photo. The puffiness in her face was gone, and she had lost considerable weight. Sitting on her mat, she looked good, and her eyes were alive.

I knew there was a lot to learn, particularly when it came to knowing how to sequence the poses together. So, wanting to avoid embarrassing myself in front of a class, I haunted the local bookstore for whatever I could find on yoga. I mostly found books on the poses, nothing specific on sequencing, and only occasionally something on yoga philosophy.

Preparing for my first class at the hospital's wellness center, I thought about what made yoga different from a stretching class. Yoga seemed to be most clearly about focus. What yoga tried to teach us was to be consciously aware of each pose as we moved from one pose to the next. So that was how I taught my classes—and I kept them safe, of course.

> *It is interesting how you can cross paths with someone who changes the direction of your life, and they never know it. The workshop presenter was one of those sorts of people for me. She had no idea that what she did on that break would change the direction of my life, so she was one of my Buddhas.*

> *My brother Joe was another Buddha. He was almost a surrogate father. During the summers I spent with him, we built a boat together. I learned to paint a car, to do minor car repairs, to fish for bass, and to hunt ducks. He sought to fill in the gaps in my upbringing without ever saying it.*

During those summers together, he taught me how to be a good painter and wallpaper hanger, telling me it was good to have a trade to fall back on, even with a college degree. When I left for OCS, he advised me not to do like many people he knew in the army, who praised their last duty station and badmouthed their current one. "Enjoy where you are while you're there," he advised, so I credit him as my first mindfulness teacher.

Sam was a very important Buddha for me. His need to go to India and Kaitlin's desire for her mother and me to join them made them important people in my journey. Sam was always someone I could rely on to check out things related to Eastern spirituality.

And Devika, another Buddha. She and her husband joined the Unitarian Church, and for a few short years, our lives ran parallel and then diverged. But in those few years, I had the opportunity to learn basic meditation from her and to acquire a better understanding of Hinduism from her husband.

Iris was an important Buddha, too. She flung open the door to yoga and gave me an idea of what it had to offer. And it was through her that I began to look at people and events in my life more discerningly.

The woman next to me in the training class was one of my Buddhas. From her, I learned the power of yoga to restore the body, mind, and spirit.

Later in my yoga career, I learned that there was a distinction between yoga teachers trained as studio teachers and what was referred to as gym yoga teachers. The studio yoga teachers had completed an exhaustive course of study, including of yoga's history and philosophy. In contrast, the gym yoga teacher might have had a vast repertoire of poses, but they tended to focus on the exercise aspect of the practice rather than the spiritual.

Chapter 11: Hitting the Rocks

I realized that I was learning yoga piecemeal. I wanted to know more about its origins and philosophy. I wanted to know what these ancient geographers of the mind were trying to teach me here at the end of the twentieth century. I needed to pull things together, and the only way that seemed possible was to do a full-scale teacher training program. However, they were generally three to four weeks long, and as a self-employed person with retirement on the horizon, I wondered if it made sense.

Periodically, the thought continued to intrude into my awareness. I reminded myself, *You're sixty-three years old. You're too old to start something like this.*

Both Kaitlin and my daughter, Anne, encouraged my yoga adventure. Anne and I attended a yoga conference in New York, and after a busy day of classes and lectures, we sat talking over our day. Then, completely unbidden, the words popped out of my mouth. "I've been thinking about doing a teacher training."

"That's a good idea," she said.

"But I'm too old."

"If that's what you want, you should do it," she said.

Back home, I began searching for the right program. Most courses were more than three weeks. Travel was involved, which meant three weeks of no income. Add to that the airfare, room and board, and course tuition. It was not cheap. But I eventually found one that was professional and slightly less expensive than the average, so I made a reservation.

At this point I was teaching a few different classes, and one of them involved a weekly visit to a residential program for teens in recovery from substance abuse. They were a fun group to work with, always up for a challenge. We worked a lot on flexibility and balance.

One day, I brought them into a pose called seated wide-angle with a forward fold. First, we spread our feet apart in a "V," then with our backs erect, we hinged at our hips and brought our chests toward the floor.

"Okay, guys. Let's go a little deeper this time," I said.

When I did, I felt a stab in my lower back, like an electric shock. With all the aplomb I could muster, I came out and repeated it on the other side, hoping that whatever had just happened would correct itself.

All seemed well. I finished the class and went on with my day.

The next morning, I hopped out of bed for my three sun salutations but couldn't do a forward fold without bending my knees. *Hmm,* I wondered, *what's going on?* After breakfast, Diana suggested we take a short walk before work.

We hadn't gone fifty feet, and I knew I could go no further. I went back to the house but then went on to work. By noon, however, I was in pain. I left and went to the doctor. In my eagerness to show off to my teens, I had herniated a disc in my lumbar spine.

I asked to postpone teacher training until the following year. Within four months, I was back to work and teaching, without surgery. However, a year after the original injury, and with a new teacher training course only weeks away, the dried-up material that had seeped from the disc was pressing against the nerve. It was as painful as the original injury. This time, I canceled the course and didn't reschedule. The Universe seemed to be sending a message.

As much as I wanted to avoid surgery, it now seemed necessary. All went well, and I got immediate relief. But I still had a twelve-week recovery ahead of me, which meant no work or teaching.

Janet, my younger stepdaughter who lived nearby, invited me to join her in a Mindfulness Based Stress Reduction (MBSR) course in Raleigh. It would be one night a week for eight weeks. I'd heard about the program but didn't know it was taught locally. Doing this during my recovery was perfect.

MBSR is a program that was created by Jon Kabat-Zinn in the 1970s at the University of Massachusetts Medical Center. The program uses mindfulness, which it defines as paying attention to the present moment on purpose and without judgment. It is a tool for reducing stress, anxiety, depression, and pain.

A serious injury is one of life's top ten stress events. Only the loss of a spouse, divorce, separation, imprisonment, or the death of a close family member ranks higher. Not only would learning the MBSR program be good for my teaching, but it would also be personally worthwhile.

We met in a large conference room of a Raleigh hospital. When Janet and I arrived that evening, the lights were slightly dimmed, and chairs were arranged in a large circle to accommodate around thirty people. We found chairs and waited for Ralph, our leader, to welcome us.

We went around the circle, introducing ourselves to the group and saying something about our reasons for wanting to do MBSR.

"Let's do a little mindful exercise," Ralph said. "I'm coming around with a box of toothpicks and some raisins. Please take one raisin on a toothpick and wait until we all have one."

When we were ready, he told us to put them in our mouths. "But don't eat them," he said. "Just roll them around with your tongue and explore them. Feel the creases, the texture."

I caressed my raisin as instructed, noticing its creases and how its hardness began to soften. Then he told us to bring our teeth in contact with our raisins and slowly increase the pressure on them.

It flattened between my teeth, and as the pressure increased, it burst apart, flooding my mouth with its sweetness and flavor. Each slow bite brought more flavor until it was eventually all mashed out, and I swallowed it. Wow! What an experience.

"We usually eat things without paying much attention. What you just experienced is mindfulness," he said. "You have purposefully paid attention to your raisin. You were present throughout the process. And you experienced the raisin without any judgments. You simply observed."

His gaze scanned the room. Then he said, "This is what it's like to be present in the moment. Each moment of life is neither better nor worse than any other moment. Each one is a component of life. Each has value, and each can be witnessed. That way, each can be fully appreciated, dealt with, and acknowledged in whatever way is appropriate. Our goal is to try and apply this to all facets of our lives."

As the course progressed, I learned about the relationship between mindfulness and anxiety, pain, and disease, about paying attention, about not judging, and about being patient. I understood what MBSR called beginner's mind, which was very much like what I called traveler's mind when I hitchhiked and traveled in India.

Another thing stuck with me that evening. Ralph said, "MBSR wants you to learn to trust your inner guide and not to get caught up in the reputation and authority of some teachers who seem to undermine their students' good feelings and intuition, because then you are not paying attention to your present experiences. MBSR is personal. It's a nonstriving practice because to strive takes us out of the present we are experiencing."

I understood that mindfulness wanted me to be accepting but not in passive acquiescence to whatever might come along. Instead, it asked me to show a willingness to see things as they are and then to take appropriate action.

We explored mindfulness through gentle yoga and short sitting meditations throughout the course. By the course's end, I was sitting for twenty minutes of meditation each day and could hold my focus reasonably well.

On the last night of our course, we were scheduled to do a full mindful yoga class. I explained to Ralph that my surgeon had given me the go-ahead to return to teaching yoga. I told him it would mean a lot to me if I could lead our yoga class. He agreed. So, as mindfully as possible, I moved the class from pose to pose. When it was over, I thanked him and briefly told the group what the evening had meant to me.

For the next several years, I honed my teaching skills and searched for the right teacher training program.

> *After the original disc herniation, just months before I turned sixty-five, I fully expected that I would recover and be back hanging wallpaper for another two or three years. However, when it happened again a year later, I knew my working days were over. It was another instance of loss of identity, one that could have dumped me into a depression again, although I did not recognize the fact then. In retrospect, I realized there were parallels to the loss of identity I'd felt when I'd resigned from the navy. However, this time, those feelings didn't last long, and I think one reason was that I was in a much better relationship where I*

felt supported, but also because I saw a way forward as a yoga teacher.

My Buddha teacher was my ego this time, teaching me how easily pride can lead a person into dangerous territory. It was ego that had injured my lumbar spine, but it also led me to cancel the original teacher training I'd planned to take and put me on track with an excellent alternative. The recovery from back surgery allowed me to take the MBSR course and get my mindfulness on track, where I learned, among other things, that it could take fifteen or twenty minutes for a novice's mind to settle down and maintain focus.

A scandal at the Kripalu Center for Yoga and Health still reverberated through the larger yoga community. Its founder was discovered to have been sexually involved with members of the community, forcing him to resign his leadership and move to Florida. Over the years, several other prominent yoga teachers were caught up in similar scandals. In reaction to these scandals, the Yoga Alliance was created to set standards of behavior for its members.

Memories of those incidents circulated in my head during the MBSR course as it emphasized trusting our inner guide. The course warned about getting caught up in the reputation and authority of some teachers who may gaslight students for their ends.

Chapter 12: A Yoga Weekend

In the early 2000s, only a few teacher training courses existed nationwide. They were run by teachers with national exposure and stature and involved travel and several weeks of accommodations. I hoped to find one that would credit my five years of teaching and shorten my time away from work.

I was motivated to do such an extensive training program for several reasons. I had gained so much from yoga already and wanted to be able to pass along the tradition accurately. I have always supported professional organizations, especially when they set training standards and require adherence to an ethical code. For these reasons, I wanted to be certified through a program sanctioned by the Yoga Alliance, yoga's certifying body.

Eventually, I found one that fit my needs. The curriculum was extensive, but I could do much of it online. Its lengthy reading list included books on postures, alignment, and anatomy. There were several chants to learn or be familiar with. The study guide offered a look at the basics of Sanskrit, with a day-long workshop on the language's fundamentals. There were readings on energy, chakras, breathwork, basic nutrition, and Ayurveda, India's traditional medicine. The reading list included yoga philosophy, spiritual development, meditation, the Mahabharata, the Bhagavad Gita, the Ramayana, and some Vedic texts. There was also a requirement to observe and assist various level yoga classes of other teachers and our practice teachings under the watchful eye of Sarah, my mentor teacher.

One of the topics the course covered was the Yoga Sutras. As I delved into them, I searched online for other interpretations than those in the books I already had and found a site with lengthy discussions that were both readable and understandable. It was written by an American-born swami named Swami Shantiananda. Digging deeper, I learned he had a small retreat center in New York's southern Catskills Mountains, not far from where Diana had grown up.

On a visit to his website, a banner announced a retreat over a long weekend at the his center. It would consist of yoga and meditation classes and lectures on yoga philosophy. I immediately signed up.

It turned out to be a great experience in many ways. It was my first exposure to non-Indian vegetarian food. The yoga classes, taught by one of the residents at the center, were not overly demanding but did expose me to some new variations. The meditation classes were interesting. Mostly, they reinforced what I had already learned about meditation.

However, Tanya, the meditation facilitator, did introduce me to something new. It was called the *So-Ham* mantra. Tanya told us that for the proper pronunciation of "ham" the "a" sound was pronounced like the "a" in father. She said that traditionally, the inhale was thought to sound like a softly spoken "so," and the exhale mimicked the sound "ham." Then she said that *"So-Ham"* in Sanskrit, meant "I am That," indicating an identification with the universality of existence.

She said, "As you say the *So-Ham* mantra meditation over and over, the sounds begin to run together. '*So-ham-so-ham-so-ham-so* . . .' and it begins to sound like the Sanskrit word *hamsa* meaning swan." She went on to say that traditionally, the swan was thought to be able to siphon off the milk from a mixture of water and milk. So, symbolically, the swan was thought to be able to glean truth from fiction.

By this point in my yoga career, I had been exposed to many dubious claims about yoga's efficacy—that this pose will cure that disease, and so on. This *So-Ham* thing just seemed like another such claim, so I dismissed it out of hand.

Swami Shantiananda himself was scheduled to give a couple of lecture sessions, and I was excited to meet this man whose writings I greatly

84

admired. He walked into the room wearing a pair of orange slacks and a matching orange shirt. Perched atop his head was a knit cap, again in matching orange.

He introduced himself and told us that his name Shantiananda meant something like Peaceful Bliss, but he said we could address him simply as Swami Shanti. With that introduction over, he forged ahead to explain the symbol OM which, according to the Yoga Sutras, is a fast track to enlightenment or Self-Realization.

"The symbol," he said, "represents consciousness and its various aspects. It represents individual as well as Universal Consciousness. The symbol is the visual representation of the vibrational hum of the Universe. OM is everything."

Then he put a slide (*Slide 12-1*) up on a screen.

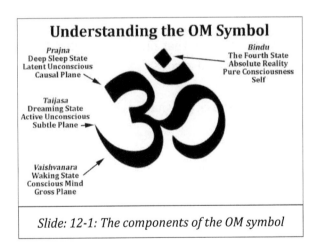

Slide: 12-1: The components of the OM symbol

Swami Shantiananda continued, "We are a collection of conscious and unconscious memories and awarenesses. We know that some things are stored in our memories, but we're not immediately aware of them. When we need them, we can recall them. And there are other things that have been tucked away in the deep, dark cellar of our unconscious that unbeknownst to us drive our behavior.

"The ancient yogis recognized this as three different states of being. Our waking, everyday state of being, where we're out here dealing in the big, wide, wonderful world, they referred to as the Waking State. They referred to the active unconscious state of being as the Dreaming State. And please do not confuse this Dreaming State with your ordinary, everyday, or nightly dreams.

"Not the same." He paused as if to let that sink in.

"Then there's the Deep Sleep State, which is a state of consciousness filled with memories and information that cannot be retrieved—things you may have forgotten or repressed but operate out of sight, so to speak.

"You see the arrows pointing to the various parts of the symbol they represent," he said.

Then a woman in the back asked, "What's that on the far right? In the middle of the diagram that doesn't have an arrow?"

He said, "That's the Dreaming State—the circle-shaped thing—the loop on the right side of the OM symbol."

Several people said they were confused and thought the diagram would be clearer if the label and its arrow were on the other side of the symbol, pointing directly at the loop.

Swami Shantiananda said, "Well, that's not going to change. It's like asking: What's the significance of the M?" I didn't understand what he meant by that.

The woman continued, "To me, it's different. The upper, middle, and lower parts have meaning. And the loop has meaning, and the whole part has meaning, and I was just wondering . . ."

"I know you were wondering, and I'm trying to respond. Maybe it's not a proper response. But how can I respond . . ." A man to my left tried to clarify what the woman had said, but Swami Shantiananda didn't let him.

"I don't have the answer for you," he said, ignoring the man and addressing the woman. "It is what it is."

She persisted, "Every little part seems to have a meaning . . ."

And again, he cut her off, "We've just seen that. And so it's a part of the middle ground."

Then it was her turn to cut off Swami Shantiananda, ". . . the parts all have meaning."

There was a long pause, and then, gesturing toward the OM symbol, Swami Shantiananda said, "See that?"

"Yeah," she said, "that's what I want to know."

He said, very firmly, pointing to each element of the symbol, "A . . . U . . . M and *turiya*, the silence at the end. So that's what it is. And it just is what it is."

It ended there—a sort of standoff between the two, but not before a lot of bad feeling had been generated.

If I had thought before this incident that swamis were perfected beings, that exchange dashed that idea. I realized swamis were just people with a high degree of specialized knowledge. Swami Shantiananda's strong point was his ability to simplify complex concepts in his writings. However, his asmita, *his pride, firmly gripped him, and he couldn't admit his diagram was unclear. I felt bad for him that he did not have the humility to accept an obvious error in his slide. And I felt bad for the retreatants he put down and steamrolled over.*

Despite this incident, I got a lot out of the weekend—extended meditation periods, new insights into the poses, and a realization that swamis had human shortcomings.

But one of the more important things that this weekend did was to spark my thinking about the relationship with my father.

It was the idea of moving memories from the latent unconscious into the active unconscious that prompted reflections on my early childhood. It came in the form of a memory of a very loud shouting match between my parents from behind closed doors.

They had always been friends with our local priest. In fact my mother's older sister Mary was the housekeeper for our parish priest. After an evening church service, the family stopped at the rectory for a social visit.

In the course of the visit, the pastor offered my parents a glass of wine. My mother accepted; my father declined. When we got home, my parents went to their room, and a loud argument ensued about the wine my mother accepted. In hindsight, I think my father considered himself an alcoholic. I never knew him to have any alcohol, and can only assume that they had some kind of agreement that she would not have any either. She finally ended the shouting match by gaging herself and vomiting into the toilet.

At some very deep level, I saw, even at seven or eight, a contradiction between his pious sermons and his actions that evening, and I was never able to reconcile those two aspects of his personality.

Chapter 13: Yoga's Path

Sarah, who ran the teacher training school, required me to be present for certain in-person programs. One was held at the bed-and-breakfast run by her friends in the mountains of Western North Carolina, where the owners had restored an old barn for square dances. It was a huge space for our needs but offered a wonderful view of the mountains and the valley below. For a few moments, I just gazed out over the valley as cloud shadows slid over its forested cover.

When Sarah walked in, we were all on meditation cushions like good yoga students. Sarah was tall and slim, hair pulled back in a bun. She wore a white leotard and tights.

"Good morning," she said. "Today, we're going to do some practice teaching, and then we'll get into a popular part of the Yoga Sutras—the five *yamas* and the five *niyamas*—the prohibitions and the observances. They form yoga's ethical code. Some people call them yoga's Ten Commandments. But that's a misnomer because they are more guides than commandments."

We spent the morning taking turns teaching a twenty-minute class to each other and getting Sarah's feedback. She paid particular attention to how we sequenced our poses and used verbal cues to correct each other. She also wanted to see how we did hands-on corrections. Did we ask permission? Was our touch firm and directive or more like a caress? Afterward, we critiqued each other and got her feedback.

Outside, a large cloud cast a shadow over the restored barn.

Then she said, "I want us to look at and discuss the yamas and the niyamas, but first, let's put them into perspective. They are part of what is called *Ashtanga Yoga*, the eight constituent parts or divisions of the yogic path. In English, it's often called 'the eight-rungs of yoga.' The problem for many of us is that this conveys a linear progression. First, you accomplish this, then you move on to the next one, and so forth.

"B. K. S. Iyengar says in his book *Light on the Yoga Sutras of Patanjali* that these eight parts are more like the petals of a flower that open in unison, not one at a time. I like his idea of petals because we're working on all of them simultaneously. I'm doing my postures but also practicing nonharming and focusing on my breathing. At the same time, I'm working on maintaining focus and controlling my reactions to sensory input. It's all happening at the same time. My emphasis may be shift in my practice to breathing or meditation as I continue work on nonharming and the poses."

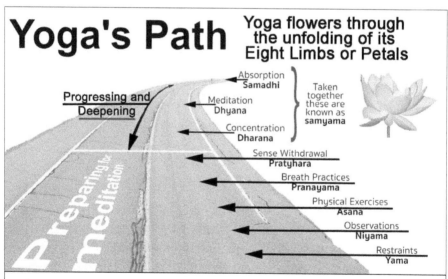

Slide 13-1: The journey of Ashtanga Yoga, as described in Yoga Sutra 2.28, is more often translated as the "Eight Limbs of Yoga." However, B.K.S. Iyengar describes the concept more accurately as eight unfolding petals.

Sarah asked me to set up a movie screen while she unpacked a slide projector. I placed it on a small table, and she dropped a slide into the slot and an image appeared on the screen (*Slide 13-1*).

She asked if there were any questions. The cloud passed down the mountain, and the room was again bathed in bright sunlight.

Sarah moved on. "The graphic is shown in perspective. The road trails off to a tiny point in the upper center. There's a reason I'm showing it this way—because we begin here on the lower left in this big, wide, wonderful world filled with all sorts of people and things. As we travel this path, we move from the general to the particular—from interacting in the public arena to seeking the Essential Self. The yogi has gained independence from all bondage and has achieved absolute true consciousness.

"Now, if you're all with me, we'll look briefly at each of the eight."

Sarah's laser pointer indicated the word "restraints" at the lower right. "The first thing practitioners need to do is to align themselves with their neighbors and community. When the Yoga Sutras were written, people lived in smaller communities and lived out of doors more than we do today in this country. So if a person wanted to sit quietly with their eyes closed, that person needed to have good relations with the neighbors. Otherwise, they would have to be on the lookout for angry folks who wanted to settle some old score.

"The first of the Eight Petals of Yoga, the restraints, or the *yamas*, encourage us to be good citizens. Then the practitioner can begin working on the inner self. This petal is called the observances, or the *niyamas*.

"Next, we begin to work on getting and keeping our bodies in shape, and that is where the postures, or the *asanas*, come in. The next step, or petal, refines things further as we begin to work with the breath practices, *pranayama*, the fourth petal. The next petal is called control of the senses, or *pratyahara*, and refers to becoming nonreactive to external stimuli, like sounds, sights, bodily sensations, that sort of thing."

93

Sarah scanned the room; everyone must have been with her because she smiled and continued. A cloud shadow momentarily dimmed and relit the room with sunlight. "This slide," she said (*Slide 13-2*), "shows yoga's path in a list form. There are some slight differences in the translations between these two slides of the *yamas* and *niyamas* to give a nuanced understanding of the concepts. "

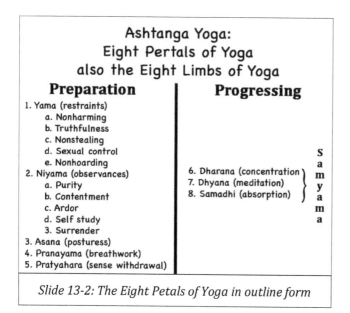

Slide 13-2: The Eight Petals of Yoga in outline form

She paused to give us time to examine it. Then she said, "These five, the *yamas, niyamas, asanas, pranayama,* and *pratyahara,* that is, the restraints, the observances, poses, breathwork, and sensory control, form the preparatory portion of the path. Concentration, meditation, and absorption, or *dharana, dhyana,* and *samadhi,* represent a deepening of the process toward final absorption. When taken together, they are called *samyama.*

"Each of these moves us to deeper and deeper levels of focus and concentration until it is so refined and one-pointed that nothing else exists for us—only is-ness remains. Now, that doesn't mean you go there, and there you are—sort of stuck in that state. No, the yogi moves in and out of it at will. A good example of that might be the Dalai Lama. He's a very public figure who is grounded by his practice to the extent that he can function very well in the day-to-day world."

Sarah let her gaze move across our little circle and said, "Now let's talk about the yamas, the restraints, and the niyamas, the observances. Remember, they are part of the preparations portion of the yoga path. And just so we know we're all on the same page, would someone please tell us what the *yamas* are?"

Someone on the other side of the room offered that the *yamas* were a set of restrictions on our behavior that fostered harmony with our fellow community members. She listed them off: nonharming, truthfulness, nonstealing, sexual control, and nonhoarding.

Then Sarah asked about the *niyamas*. Someone else offered that the *niyamas* were personal observances that aided in ordering our personal and spiritual lives: purity, contentment, ardor, self-study, and surrender.

Sarah said, "Good. We have the restraints and the observances, the *yamas* and the *niyamas*. Then we have the *asanas* and *pranayama*, the poses and the breathwork. These are the first four, and they are preparatory work for what comes next. And what comes next is the real heart of yoga. It deals with the withdrawal of the senses, concentration, meditation, and absorption—*pratyahara, dharana, dhyana*, and *samadhi*. These four are shades or gradations of meditation."

Sarah looked at us and said, "I want to tell you a little fairy tale. It's a story that I call *Prince Uncharming*."

> Once upon a time, a very long time ago, there was a man who was a king and was very mean and cruel to his son, the young crown prince. He taunted him and told him what a completely inadequate person

he was and that he would never grow up to be worth a pfennig. The old king pushed and pushed the young prince, who soon learned that the best way to please his father was to lie about his accomplishments. He learned that he could amass a large fortune simply by not paying the hired workers. And when any of them complained about their treatment, he made some offhand comment to one of his loyal knights that, well, maybe the world would be better off if that malcontent had some sort of accident that might disable him for life.

As the young prince became increasingly shrewd in his dealings, his treasure room brimmed with gold, silver, and precious jewels. He was not beyond trading a cheap trinket from his treasure room for the favors of some comely maiden whose family lived close to the edge of privation. On several occasions, while carousing with his entourage in a local tavern, he might pinch a pretty barmaid or gently caress her firm breasts. And it was not unlike him to slip his hand up a skirt or two. While these intrepid young bar maidens were, for the most part, adept at thwarting his advances without infuriating the prince, one, in particular, seemed not so skilled, and the prince was drawn to her like a hawk to a chicken. "Ah, methinks this one's worth the plucking," he said to one of his henchmen. And so it was that he concentrated his efforts on seducing her with promises of wealth and fortune if she would only do his bidding in her bedding.

Now, the hapless barmaid was utterly convinced that the stories told by the others about him were untrue and that he would look after her and support her and any future offspring, should one spring forth. And so it came to pass that she surrendered herself to the prince's advances one night.

But alas, their time together was short-lived, and promises that he made went unkept. It was not long before the prince's eye found new delights. But unbeknownst to the prince, the maid to whom he had made so many promises had several very strong and rough brothers and some male cousins who were prepared to avenge her dishonoring.

Meanwhile, an itinerant yogi met the prince by happenstance, and in the course of their idle conversations, the yogi convinced the prince that it would be helpful for him to mend his ways.

"You have all read and studied the eight limbs, so this morning, let's imagine that the prince is interested in the yogi guiding him toward absorption, toward enlightenment. How do you suppose the conversation between them might have gone?"

The comments came fast and furiously.

"For starters, the prince's behavior is off the rails."

"Yeah, he's managed to earn the anger of most people in his realm. He's a liar, a cheat, a misogynist."

"Not to mention that he's impoverishing the principality by starving his people half to death. Certainly, to the point that they are willing to endure humiliation to survive."

"No wonder his life is in danger."

"Yeah, from her brothers and cousins."

"And our itinerant yogi is trying to convince him that if he wants to live a peaceful life, he will need to get right with all the people he's offended."

"Assuming that our yogi is going to teach him the Path of Yoga, then our prince will have to make peace with all of those who are getting ready to do him in."

"That yogi's got a lot of work to do."

"The first thing he might consider is to begin to share what he's been hoarding. His precious jewels and stuff. That might help to convince his people of his worthy intentions. It might buy him some time."

"He has to do a range of things all almost at once. He has to convince others of his good intentions. And maybe he'll gain some compassion in the process, which is a good antidote to anger and its associated violence."

"I'd like to say something about the woman he made promises to so he could sleep with her. Promises that he didn't intend to keep. From her point of view, naive as she was, her sense of reality was twisted by his promises to the point that she could not correctly evaluate her situation and circumstances. That's one of the biggest problems when you lie to someone. You mess up their understanding of reality, and that causes them to make decisions that may be in your interests but not theirs. What I mean is that lying twists reality for people. It's gaslighting."

"Good point."

"And violence leads to more violence. The prince's actions have enflamed enough of his people that they are ready to use violence against him. It becomes a never-ending cycle."

"For a person on yoga's path, *ahimsa*, nonharming, is the Hippocratic oath of the yogi. Or at least that's the way I think of it anyway."

"Yeah, I like that."

"Okay," Sarah said. "You all talked about the *yamas*, but nobody named them. What are the Sanskrit and English names for the *yamas*?"

Like a Greek chorus, we answered in unison, "first *ahimsa*, nonharming, second *satya*, truth, third *asteya*, nonstealing, fourth *brahmacharya*, sexual restraint, and fifth *aparigraha*, nongreed."

"Thank you," Sarah said. "That's a look at the yamas, the restrictions to our behavior in the larger world. Let's suppose our itinerant yogi's teachings are successful so far. What might his next teachings be about?"

Someone said, "His next teachings would relate to the *niyamas* of the eight limbs. They are internal observances. They are the things we need to do internally, for ourselves."

"He needs to teach the prince about purity, *saucha*. Purity of his thoughts, words, and deeds. The yogi would encourage the prince to bring order into his life. Get himself organized. Keep his environment tidy to support his practice."

"And *santosha*, contentment—learning to have enough to support his life and his loved ones, and to be content with what he has."

"Live simply, that others may simply live."

"Somebody said about *santosha* that we need to be content but not satisfied. And I think they meant not to be content in a passive way but in an active sort of way. You are content, but you are open to improving. You're not stagnant. Contentment shouldn't mean stagnation."

"Then our yogi would encourage the prince to develop a passion for maintaining his progress on the path. He needs the attitude of keeping his eyes on the prize, so to speak."

"That would be *tapas*, keeping his eyes on the prize."

Sarah interrupted the exchange to say, "*Tapas* is the burning desire, the fire in the belly that pushes us to practice, and yes, to keep our eyes on the prize."

"Which leads naturally into the next part of the progression—to what Patanjali called *svadhyaya*, or self-study."

"Yeah, that's an interesting one, isn't it? You need to constantly mine your own personal thoughts, words, and deeds to better understand yourself and your relationship, not just toward the world at large but toward yourself. And Patanjali and all of the commentators on the Yoga Sutras want us to dip into the wisdom of those who walked the path ahead of us. And apply it to ourselves. That's what he means by self-study."

"This leads us to the last of the niyamas, to *ishvara pranidhana* or the surrendering of the fruits of our labors to something or someone greater than ourselves. Patanjali doesn't say that you surrender to God but rather to a higher power, whatever or whoever that might be is for each of us to decide."

"Yeah, that teaches us humility. It teaches us that we're not in this alone. That we all depend on each other. That we're part of something bigger than ourselves. And maybe that is what we surrender to. You know, the knowledge of our interdependence on each other."

Sarah said, "Okay, we successfully saved the prince and pointed him on a new path. And now that he's learned these, our yogi would help him understand that these are the things he needs to be working on constantly. None of them are ever a 'once and done' thing. The *yamas* and *niyamas* are organic, and we need to keep them in constant focus. Sometimes, one may take priority, but none are ever completely done. These are ongoing practices—these are the *yamas* and the *niyamas*. We're always working on them."

Then she asked, "Any questions?"

Someone asked, "Have you experienced *samadhi*?"

"I have touched it," she said. "As our practice develops, we go through stages, or levels, if you will, as our practice carries us toward full absorption. In the early stages, truth begins to dawn, and then, having experienced truth, insights flow and deepen. I'm sorry, words don't work here." At that point, she seemed focused off in the distance somewhere.

Finally, she said, "If there are no other questions, let's sit for the length of your practice, and we'll call it a day. But first, tomorrow, Asha will join us from the Sanskrit Institute to introduce you to the fundamentals of Sanskrit, the basis for most European languages." And with that said, we each arranged our places for meditation. I closed my eyes and focused on my breath and my bodily sensations.

> *Nonviolence is the center of yogic philosophy. It could almost be considered the yogi's Hippocratic oath. An awful lot flows from restraining the urge to harm. Just controlling the urge to strike back, even verbally, begins to change a person. Life is hard enough without making it more difficult for another. The eye-for-an-eye thing doesn't work. It only provokes the other to feel justified in their first strike and provokes another round of harm. I mean, the Bible even deals with this issue. Turn the other cheek, it says, but people don't take that part very seriously these days.*

Finally, I let it all go and sank into darkness . . . not really darkness, not blackness either . . . maybe a very deep purple . . . then swirling violet light like a murmuring of starlings in fall flight . . . flowing this way and that . . . swirling . . . turning . . . becoming dense in some places, less so in others. It wasn't always like that, this aurora mentalis, *this mental light show. Then it faded to a wisp and was gone. I fell into slow rhythmic breathing. Nothing else. Just meditation.*

Chapter 14: Saying Goodbye

It took about a year to finish all the readings, do all the modules, write a couple of papers, and take my final exam. With all the requirements met, I received my certificate of completion and joined the Yoga Alliance, the accrediting body for yoga teachers. It took eleven years, from my first exposure to yoga, to become a full-fledged and accredited yoga teacher.

Soon after becoming Yoga Alliance certified, an opportunity presented itself to teach a group of people with multiple sclerosis. It was my good fortune that Catherine, one of the preeminent teachers of yoga for this population, offered a training session in nearby Virginia. When I finished the training, I began teaching this group of people yoga. They were a joy to work with and challenged me at every turn. Some could get up and down from the floor. Others could only work from chairs. One man was in a wheelchair, and when class was over, he whipped around the studio, picking up other people's blocks, straps, and chairs. I often wondered, *Who is getting more out of this, them or me?* They all maintained a positive attitude and willingness to work. They were truly inspirational, every one of them. And from them, I learned courage, patience, and acceptance.

A student from one of my regular floor classes approached me after my class one night. She told me she worked in cardio rehab and wanted to do a pilot study on the efficacy of yoga as a recovery program for her population. She asked for my help in designing the yoga portion of the study. I was wading into something I didn't feel comfortable doing, but I found a program that trained yoga teachers to teach cardiac patients.

Our research study group was small. It was too small for the results to be statistically significant. However, finding ways to motivate our participants to do their work was a good challenge.

About this time, Diana woke in the middle of the night and found a lump under her right rib cage about the size and shape of a mango seed. When we saw the doctor, the X-ray of her liver looked like the spots on a Dalmatian. She had cancer that had already spread to her liver. Despite having done everything by the book, including taking regular exercise, eating healthily, and having timely screenings, she had stage 4 colon cancer. We were crushed.

I went with her to chemo. In those first months, she seemed to be declining, but then her condition stabilized, and we planned a trip to Martha's Vineyard with Kaitlin and Diana's son, David. Soon after our return, the blood tests failed to show improvement. Through it all, she remained solid as a rock.

My daughter Anne and her family lived in Los Angeles, and because of the distance, I made an effort to be there every January for my grandson Nick's birthday. On our way to LA that year, we stopped in Dallas to visit one of Diana's oldest and dearest friends. Diana's friend pulled me aside as we left and said, "I know this is the last time I'm going to see her." I assured her Diana was strong and hopefully would pull through. But we both knew it was wishful thinking on my part.

The birthday visit went well, but we could all see the trip was hard on Diana. Our flight home got us into Raleigh after dark. On the hour-and-a-half drive home, she did not complain, but I saw she was not in a good place. I stopped on the roadside to help her into the back seat so she could lie down to rest.

She knew she was dying and, being the pragmatist that she was, said, "Dying is the easiest thing I've ever had to do." Within days of our return, we called the hospice. Then, surrounded by our children, she slipped away.

Through it all, the thought kept coming to me that the Universe had been preparing me to help and support her on her journey all along. All the twists and turns of my life, all the wrong turns, the missteps, the doors that closed, and the new ones that opened led to yoga, to a sense of groundedness, to this moment, to Diana. She was a Buddha who gave me so much, and I could only hope I had given back to her in equal measure.

The next day, I changed into my cycling clothes and went out for a bike ride. I needed it to exhaust my body and clear my head. On the ride home at a stop light, a cycling friend, a clinical psychologist, pulled up alongside me on his bike. I told him that Diana had died the previous night. He said all the right things, and when the light changed, we crossed the street, got out of traffic, and talked. "I'm so sorry," he said. We hugged at the side of the street before going our separate ways.

Several years earlier, Diana and I had decided that when we died, we would donate our bodies to the local medical school. The night she died, I made the phone call, and the undertakers from the medical school arrived to take her remains. Later that summer, our hospice held a social for their clients from the past year. As I circulated, chatting with various people, I noticed one of the undertakers who had come to the house that dark, wintery night.

I introduced myself. He said he remembered me. I asked what he was doing there. He said his wife died of breast cancer shortly after Diana's death. We commiserated, asked each other about our plans, and wished each other well.

What a powerful lesson that meeting was for me. Another Buddha lesson. You never know what burden someone else is carrying. How easily a careless word, tone, or gesture could hurt someone. "If you can't be nice, be quiet." How often did I hear that growing up and casually shrug it off?

Diana was an important Buddha to me. In our relationship, I learned many things I would have learned in my first marriage if Vikki and I hadn't been in a constant emotional tug-of-war. With Diana, I learned to be financially responsible and a good husband and father. More importantly, I learned how to trust another person emotionally. And our life together had let that happy four-year-old come back into my life.

After her death, I understood what people meant about feeling like a part of themselves had been lost. We shared points of view, jokes, and observations, but that sharing abruptly ended with her death. The things to be shared were there but not the person to share them with. I was reaching out to someone but was finding no one there. The mental image I had was of a planet revolving around its sun. Then, suddenly, the sun vanishes, and the planet is flung out into the void with nothing to keep it in its orbit.

Thirteen months before Diana's death, my sister Jayne had died from a blood cancer she dealt with for sixteen years. Three weeks after Diana's death, one of Jayne's sons died of cancer, and three weeks after that, a different cycling buddy died by his own hand. It was a very emotional fifteen months.

To say I was at loose ends would be an understatement, but eventually, I did begin to find my way out of the fog. Or I began to formulate a plan that might eventually allow the fog to lift and me to return to living in the present.

I knew geographical fixes didn't change anything. I knew wherever I went, whatever I did, everything would still be there to be dealt with. What I needed to do was to jolt myself out of the darkness that wanted to take over.

Memories of the winter hitchhiking came back. Something like that might force me to be more present and more focused on living life. Whether you called it traveler's mind or beginner's mind, I knew I needed to push myself to get out of the past and back into the present, into the here and now, to the land of the living.

One of the things I had learned from earlier travels and the MBSR course was the importance of being present and focusing on the here and now rather than spending time in mental ruminations of past events or imagined futures. I hoped an unfamiliar environment would force me to be alert, engage my beginner's mind, stop living in a murky past, and focus on living in the present. Baba Ram Dass, one of the great teachers of the 1960s, reminded me periodically to "be here now," which brought up one of yoga's aphorisms that you must be present to win.

Through the years, I had followed Swami Shantiananda's teachings via his website and an occasional email exchange. The following spring, he was scheduled to conduct a three-week retreat in India centering on the teachings of the Yoga Sutras. I knew him, felt I could deal with his quirks, and thought this might be exactly what I needed to get my life back on track.

Many years ago, Sam said that the power of India has more to do with our inner experience and the changes it puts us through than anything about India itself. Things about India that blow our minds are mundane, everyday realities for Indians. But the shock to our sensibilities, the sensual overload, the cognitive dissonance, and the realization that our world is just another way to dream up a world profoundly undermine our autopilot's grip on reality.

I began formulating a plan to go back to India, where my yoga journey had begun. I would deal with the chaos of

107

India. I would explore the country on my own before the retreat began. Something would happen, and I would deal with it. Sam's words from years ago echoed in my mind: "If India doesn't change you, you weren't paying attention." I needed to change. I would pay attention. But first, there were things I needed to plan.

I returned to teaching my yoga classes almost immediately after Diana's death. I told my students I would be going to India for three months. A woman from India approached me after class and told me, "Remember, whatever they say about India, its opposite is also true." *Yes,* I thought, *I'll keep that in mind.*

My plan developed: I would leave for India at the end of the year. I would go to the South Indian cities of Chennai (formerly Madras) and Kochi (formerly Cochin). Like many Indian cities, they had returned to their former names and spellings before Great Britain colonized the subcontinent.

The only thing that was firm was a three-week course of study of the Yoga Sutras at an ashram in northern India. Until I returned, all major life decisions were on hold.

My departure was only a few weeks away when a friend brought someone new to my noon class. I went over to introduce myself and learned she was new to yoga. She said her name was Louise, and as we made eye contact, I immediately knew this would be an important person in my life. And here I was, nearly packed for India. We only had time for a couple of dates and a Christmas concert at her church. And with promises to email regularly, I boarded a plane for India.

Chapter 15: Transitioning

On December 30, I left Eastern North Carolina. A recent snow covered the ground, and I realized everything would be in full bloom when I returned in April. In Charlotte, I changed planes for Newark, where I had a comfortable wait before my direct flight to Delhi.

I planned to stay awake during the fourteen-hour flight. Every hour or so, I walked the aisles to stay awake and to keep blood from settling in my legs. On one walk, I climbed the stairs to the upper deck to view a sky splattered with stars. On another, I found the cabin crew puttering in the aft galley and chatted with them. One was curious about why I was going to India. I told her I planned to spend a few weeks at an ashram. "Oh, I love yoga," she said, so we did some stretches in her tiny galley.
We landed at India's new Indira Gandhi International Airport around ten o'clock at night. At touchdown, all three hundred passengers leaped to their feet, grabbed carry-ons, and stood waiting to exit the plane.

It was a long walk from our gate, and like lemmings, we followed the person in front down long hallways, around corners, and along more hallways. We came to a balcony overlooking more lines, waiting for the immigration check. Directly over those lines hung large, golden sculptures of hands, each about eight feet high (*Image 15-1*). Each hand formed a *mudra*, or a yoga hand gesture with a specific meaning. I recognized several: the welcome *mudra*, the fear-not *mudra*, and the boon-bestowing *mudra*. *Appropriate messages*, I thought as I descended the escalator and found a place in line.

Once through customs check, I exited into the main terminal. I saw the terminal doors and headed that way just beyond the duty-free section. Indian airports only allow ticketed passengers inside. Outside the terminal doors stood a chaotic mass of humanity peering expectantly into the terminal, hands and noses pressed to the glass doors and windows. Some held signs; others stood stoically.

Image 15-1: Delhi's Indira Gandhi International Airport arrival terminal adorned with yoga hand gestures called mudras

Somewhere in that mass was Jack. We had exchanged photos. He was a short, round fellow with a big smile that lit his face. His beard was closely cropped, compensating for the lack of hair.

Jack spotted me easily because I was a head taller than most of the other passengers. He greeted me warmly like we were old friends. It was a short walk to the taxi and then a quick ride to his colony or subdivision. It was an upper-middle-class neighborhood with tree-lined streets, each home surrounded by a high wall with shards of glass embedded on top. Many houses were four stories. He explained that the owners generally lived on the bottom two floors. In his building, the owner's parents lived on the third floor and rented out the top floor to Jack.

I noticed small guard shacks at each driveway gate as we approached his house. When we pulled up to his flat, Jack greeted the guard with a cheery, "Good evening, sir." The guard replied, "You found your visitor at the airport, sir." Jack introduced us, and then we hauled my luggage across the marble driveway to the vestibule, where Jack punched an elevator button for his fourth-floor flat.

The floors throughout his flat were also marble. We dropped my bags in the second bedroom. He reminded me that it was New Year's Eve and suggested we view the fireworks from the roof.

The roof offered a view of the neighborhood over the tree tops. Some people had turned their rooftops into lounge areas with Astroturf, lawn chairs, potted shrubs, and flowers. While we watched the fireworks, Jack told me his plans for the next couple of days. We would tour the neighborhood whenever I was up, and there was no rush. He had a couple of errands in the city, which would give me an idea of how things were laid out.

After the fireworks, he helped me settle into his extra bedroom. There was a small space heater that didn't put out nearly enough heat to warm a room with a nine-foot ceiling. Delhi was cold at this time of year, and few homes had central heating. Newer homes had air conditioning, including this one, but no heat. I went to bed in my clothes. The next night, I doubled several blankets.

In the morning, Jack had a cereal breakfast ready. Over breakfast, he told me he was a consultant for a large international firm. He was divorced, and his adult kids lived in his house back home. One was in college, the other was working. He had done some yoga but wasn't all that committed. He was a gadget guy: fancy popcorn popper, a reverse osmosis water purifier, beautiful kitchen knives, a food vacuum-sealer, and an inversion table, which he had set up in the dining room.

I had heard about inversion tables but had not seen one before. It was a board, like a fancy teeter-totter. The first thing Jack did was set an adjustment to the length of my body. Next, he set the angle of tilt. With the table in the upright position, I stood against it with my arms at my side.

111

Jack locked my ankles to the board and told me that when I was ready, I should lift my arms to my chest. As I did, the board slowly tilted me into an inverted position. To come out, I simply lowered my arms to my sides. This simple shift in the weight distribution was enough to gently tilt me from inverted to upright. It was a great way to stretch the spine and let blood drain from the legs after a long day of standing. Throughout my stay, I used the table several times.

Foolishly, I had not checked the weather in Delhi for January. The high tomorrow would be in the forties, and I had packed for hot and sticky weather in the south. Thankfully, Jack offered me an extra jacket.

Holiday shopping in Delhi was a participatory sport. The streets and shops were crowded beyond belief. It was bumper-to-bumper traffic on the streets and elbow-to-elbow in the malls and shops. In one strip mall, I nearly tripped over a beggar woman sitting in the middle of the sidewalk. The crowds parted around her like the Red Sea parting for the fleeing Israelites.

In the parking lot of the same mall was a guard tower twenty feet high. In the roofed guard shack, an armed soldier kept surveillance over that entrance to the mall.

On Monday morning, Jack went off to work, and I slept till nine. I did my yoga and meditation, tested the inversion table, and made breakfast. Afterward, I sat in the sun on the balcony, warming my hands on a hot mug of tea. Below me stretched our neighborhood (*Image 15-2*), as birds flitted from tree to tree. Brahminy kites, a cousin to the eagle, circled overhead.

> While I sipped my tea, I thought of the large *mudras at the Delhi airport terminal with their mixed messages of welcome and caution. The beggar woman, perhaps a professional beggar, perhaps a cripple, but who knew for*

sure? The advice to tourists is not to give to beggars directly but through NGOs.

Image 15-2: A upper middle-class home in our Delhi neighborhood

I recalled my first encounter with a beggar. I was about ten or eleven. We lived in Kansas City then, and we went to the train station to meet a visiting relative. At the station entrance, a beggar panhandled the incoming crowd. But as we left the station, I saw him leave in a limousine. Because of this experience, my preference has been to give through NGOs and organizations that directly help where it is needed most.

During our shopping trip, I bought a pair of Ray-Ban Wayfarer sunglasses and paid five times more for them than any sunglasses I had ever bought. I blamed this on being jet-lagged and vowed never to make expensive purchases or important decisions while jet-lagged. I classified this experience as one of my Buddha moments.

Jack was also a Buddha. He even looked like Buddha with a bit of a belly and a jovial laugh. He was courteous, friendly, and inquiring toward everyone he met. He greeted people he met on the street in Hindi. Sometimes, it was a simple namasté; other times, it was a more elaborate greeting. But he addressed everyone he met as sir or madam and always with respect.

I finished my tea and washed the cup. I had come to explore India, so with a guidebook and maps Jack had offered me, I gathered my borrowed jacket and a small backpack and walked to the neighborhood shopping center to find a taxi.

Chapter 16: Discovering Delhi

Getting oriented to the city and the neighborhood took a couple of days. I was anxious to see some of the sights around Delhi. Jack gave me contact information for Mr. Patel's Pronto All-India Tour Company, which would set up sightseeing within the city. I wanted to be over my jet lag before I headed out to explore on my own, so Mr. Patel's Pronto service was a good option.

The next morning, after tea on the balcony, I walked down the marble driveway and greeted the guard in the guard shack, "Good morning, sir," I said. "Having a good day, sir?" he asked.

Image 16-1: The Dancing Girl at the National Museum from the Indus Valley site of Mohenio-Daro 2700-2000 BCE

I took a right into the street since there were no sidewalks. My destination was Basant Lok, about a mile's walk to an upscale shopping center and a taxi. My route took me past an outdoor barber shop where a man was getting a shave. Then past the entrance to the Modern School, a private coed school, and just around the corner, I passed the Happy Feet Play School for preschool and nursery-aged children. At the shopping center, I easily found a taxi.

My first stop was the National Museum, where I was fascinated by an exhibit on the Indus Valley, or Harappan, Civilization, one of the great river civilizations of antiquity located in western India. The collection displayed the Dancing Girl (*Image 16-1*) from the early Indus Valley period.

At the National Gallery of Modern Art I discovered an artist I liked. Upendra Maharathi grew up under British rule and struggled to find his unique style after India became independent in 1947.

I was especially drawn to his painting called *Truth Seeking Man Caught in a Whirlpool of Temptation*. Even the title was exciting, because it spoke to one of the central themes of yoga philosophy, i.e., the role of desire in directing us away from our goals. The painting depicts a roiling blue sea and a man being pulled toward swirling waters of deep red. His head is turned to look over his shoulder toward a female figure. She returns his gaze from the upper right corner, where she is bathed in a golden glow. I studied the painting for a long time.

When I returned to the flat and checked my emails, I saw that Mr. Patel had set up a day trip to Agra and the Taj Mahal (*Image 16-2*). It didn't disappoint. Yes, it is a cliché of architectural beauty but for a good reason. It is a masterpiece. Shah Jahan built it in the mid-1600s as a memorial to his wife. Originally, it was encrusted with diamonds, rubies, and other precious stones, but over the centuries, they were looted. Nearby was Agra's Red Fort. Shortly after completion, Shah Jahan fell ill, setting off a struggle for succession between his sons, who imprisoned him in the Red Fort within sight of the Taj Mahal, where he languished for the next nine years.

Image 16-2: The Taj Mahal, Agra, Uttar Pradesh, India

I was also anxious to see one of Ashoka's pillars in Old Delhi. Ashoka was an emperor who ruled in the third century BCE. After conquering most of what is today India, he converted to Buddhism and renounced war and aggression. He issued edicts carved in stone or freestanding pillars throughout his kingdom. The inscriptions were in the local languages in the hope of teaching the morals and the ideals of civilized living. He hoped this would bring peace and stability to the kingdom. It lasted through his lifetime, which was shortened, ironically, when his brothers murdered him.

Later, when I sat for meditation, my mind wandered over recent events before finally settling.

> *The* Truth Seeking Man Caught in a Whirlpool of Temptation *spoke powerfully about the human condition. We seek truth but get caught in the sea of our desires. Both Buddhism and yoga see the source of humanity's problems as our temptation to fulfill our desires even when we know they will drown us in the long run. What an incredible Buddha moment it was to find that painting. My thoughts have drifted back to it often. It so aptly describes the*

117

dilemma we all face—how to live in the world without getting sucked into its darker aspects.

Shah Jahan so loved his wife and mourned her loss that he built the Taj Mahal to her memory, while his sons plotted against him and imprisoned him within sight of the incomplete memorial because they saw it as a waste of money and probably a diminution of their expected inheritance. Ashoka wanted to renounce violence and war. He tried to raise the level of civility only to be killed by his brothers—the whirlpool of temptation, of desire.

Then there was Old Delhi, once the home of wealthy merchants. It looked pretty shabby now. I thought about the inevitability of change and the beggar woman at the market. What put her there? Probably the death of her husband. In the old days, she would have thrown herself on her husband's funeral pyre. Today, she's often thrown onto the street to fend for herself.

And then there were the Harappans. Their civilization lasted for two thousand years before it vanished. There's speculation that their descendants are the so-called "tribals" of western India.

Nothing lasts forever, and like the Harappans, we have no idea when it will end or how.

By the end of this first week, the jet lag was behind me, and I was ready to travel around South India.

Chapter 17: Detached-Attachment

I took a taxi to the airport for my flight to Chennai on the Bay of Bengal. I was happy to swap Delhi's 40-degree weather for Chennai's 80s.

Indian airport security makes ours look like a joke. Only those with tickets are allowed in the airport. An armed soldier checked passengers at the door to the airport. There was an armed soldier at the security check and three at baggage. They didn't make us strip, but they took one man's carry-on apart completely. At the gate before boarding, another armed soldier again checked our papers.

My flight was on Kingfisher Airlines, owned by a beer company, and as the plane loaded, we were serenaded by ABBA's "Dancing Queen." Once airborne, ABBA continued reverberating through my head for the remainder of the flight. Meanwhile, the crew served inflight snacks with stainless-steel flatware and heavy reusable bowls, plates, and cups.

Chennai is the capital of the southern state of Tamil Nadu, whose language is Tamil. It bears no resemblance to Hindi, and I thought of the hours I'd spent trying to cram Hindi into my brain. Thankfully, English is one of the official languages throughout the country.

I chose to stay at an excellent Indian hotel with Wi-Fi in the room. The room itself was spacious. It had two twin beds, plenty of floor space for yoga, and a typical Asian shower where you pour warm water over your head from a bucket. The hotel was an easy walk to the beach and the St. Thomas Cathedral Basilica.

Saint Thomas the Apostle came to this part of India after Jesus's earthly life. He was eventually killed over his attempts to subvert local religious beliefs. In the mid-1500s, Portuguese explorers built a church on the site where the saint was buried. In the church, a sign directs visitors to the site of his original tomb and a reliquary.

As I entered the room housing the reliquary, I was met by a life-size statue of Santa Claus (*Image 17-1*). The incongruity of Santa dressed for the Arctic left me flabbergasted. But, as they say, "TII—this is India." The spearpoint said to have killed the saint was on display in the reliquary.

Image 17-1: Santa Claus at the entrance to the St. Thomas reliquary

An item in the *Hindustan Times* reported that Swami Aseemanand from Gujarat, near the Pakistani-Indian border, had confessed to a train bombing three years earlier that killed seventy people. According to reports in the Indian press, the Swami vowed to match the Islamists in India "bomb for bomb." A court later released him, agreeing with his claim that his confession had been forced. He was, however, reported to have forced some of India's western Christian tribals to convert to Hinduism. I guess the Swami hadn't gotten the memo about *ahimsa*, nonharming.

One evening, the Music Academy of Madras offered a dance performance featuring a style I particularly liked called Bharatanatyam.

The first series of dances were choreographed and danced by a renowned performer. She dressed in costume to address the audience, wearing a yellow-green bolero top with baggy green silk pants and a matching pleated front panel.

The first dance, she said, was an interpretation of the part in the Bhagavad Gita where Krishna reveals himself to Arjuna, representing Everyman on his spiritual journey. In the story, he is about to battle against his cousins (our lower nature) for the kingdom (our spiritual selves). Arjuna doesn't realize Krishna, his charioteer, is the supreme being there to guide him. When Krishna reveals himself, Arjuna is nearly blinded by what Krishna reveals to him: all of creation, all of his ancestors, all of his descendants, suns upon suns, the brightness of a thousand suns, and Krishna with more arms than can be counted, an indication of the vastness of his power.

The second dance, she said, could be taken either as the devotion of a lover for the beloved or as the devotee's relation to Shiva. "You are," she said, "the sun, and I am the lotus brought forth by you. You are the tree, and I am the creeper clinging to you as I ascend toward your upper branches. You are the ocean, and I am the river merging with you." Beautiful sentiments in any spiritual tradition.

She said her third dance would be an interpretation of a poem that dealt with loss, which she called "detached-attachment." A mother wakes one morning to discover her daughter has run off with a local no-count. So she sets off to find them. In her travels, she meets three sages who say they have seen the runaways, but they describe the man as a rich and handsome fellow and the girl as wonderfully adorned. The mother asks them to help her find the two, but they suggest otherwise. They tell her that sandalwood was intended to be used as creams applied to the body, not to stay in the mountain forests, and pearls were not meant for the ocean but to adorn your body, and as the notes on a musical instrument are not meant for the instrument but to be listened to, neither is the daughter meant for the mother. They tell the mother that she needs to acknowledge her attachment to her daughter but also practice

121

nonattachment and let her go. The daughter must find her own *dharma*, her own life, and not live her mother's *dharma*.

The Buddha lessons from the Bharatanatyam dances were several: the metaphor of the Bhagavad Gita and man's spiritual journey, the union of the self with Shiva or God, and the need to follow one's own dharma or path; these all spoke to me.

I liked the part of the Gita described in the dance. With this performance, I made the connection that God, in the form of Krishna, is by Arjuna's side throughout this existential struggle. God, in the guise of Krishna, is driving Arjuna's chariot. He is always at his side to help and advise Arjuna in his battle against his lower nature.

The poem behind the second dance could be a universal description of the devotee's love and commitment to God.

Many people struggle with yoga's concept of detachment, of letting go, particularly when applied to our children. However, the description of this dance dealt with the idea slightly differently, as detached-attachment. It acknowledges that the mother will always feel connected to her daughter, but she must learn to experience that attachment in a detached manner. We raise our children to let them go. The young bird must fly from the nest.

As I reflected on the story behind this dance, I thought about the mother describing her daughter as a ragamuffin, not as the well-adorned person the three sages encountered. These contrary descriptions reminded me of parents who denigrate their children's abilities as an explanation for their need to direct and control their children's lives when, in fact, the world may see them as well-functioning persons. There is a lot that could be unpacked in this story.

But also, in the mother's journey, she meets three sages. In the story of the origins of the term "serendipity," the king of Serendip (an old name for Sri Lanka) sends his three sons on a quest. And then there are the three wise men of Jesus's nativity. We do seem to have a fascination with the number three.

I tried to eat using my fingers, like the locals at the hotel restaurant. In India, the left hand is considered unclean, which meant I could only use my right hand. It was tricky to pull apart an *uttapam*, a thin pancake with thinly sliced tomatoes and onions cooked into the batter, and only use the fingers of my right hand like I saw the locals do. Because table space was limited, I often sat at a large family-style table. No one seemed to talk while eating, but one morning, when I had finished, one of my table mates turned to me and said, "You are very deft with your fingers." I thanked him for such a wonderful compliment.

Through the hotel, I arranged for a car and driver to take me to Puducherry, a former French colony known as Pondicherry, only about a hundred miles down the coastal road. The drive gave me time to reflect on my time in Chennai.

During these few days in Chennai, I had visited the site of Saint Thomas's martyrdom and the reliquary where his remains were kept until they were moved to the Vatican. I had seen what was purported to be the spearpoint that had killed him. At the Saint Thomas reliquary, I had been exposed to another Indian surprise: the presence of a life-sized statue of Santa Claus wearing sunglasses. And on one of my walks around the city, I had come across a larger-than-life portrait of Jesus and Ganesh (Image 17-2).

Image 17-2: Jesus and Ganesh portraits share
a wall in Chennai, Tamil Nadu, India

Not far down the street were several posters for an
upcoming convention of atheists. And the strains of a
saxophone version of Silent Night had been playing
throughout one of Chennai's large shopping malls. But high
on my list of memories were the Bharatanatyam dances and
being complimented for eating only with my fingers.

There were several other takeaways from Chennai. The first
was the complex tapestry of the spiritual and religious
aspects of India. Spirituality appeared to underlie
everything. It wasn't noticeable at first, but whether it was
expressed as Hindu, Buddhist, Christian, or atheist, it was
there. Granted, mine are superficial views, but it was
exciting and comforting to see what appeared to be respect
for a variety of paths to the same goal—finding ways to deal
with our human quest to understand life's big questions.

How could I forget the case of Swami Aseemanand who
confessed to bombing a train that killed seventy people?
That seemed to throw the concept of respect for the variety

of paths out the window. Communal tension does exist and is not far below the surface. Witness the destruction of the Babri Masjid by members of the Bharatiya Janata Party back in December of 1992, and the death of around two thousand in the riots that followed. Aspirations don't always translate into realities. My Indian friend was correct when she warned me, "Whatever you say about India, the opposite is also true."

Chapter 18: Man Proposes

I planned to spend a few days in Puducherry. It was close to where two of India's modern-day saints had lived and died, and I wanted to visit both. Sri Aurobindo was a philosopher, journalist, and fighter for independence from British rule. He became such a thorn in Britain's side that he fled to the nearby French colony of Puducherry, where he died in 1950. He was also a religious reformer. After his death, one of his followers, a French woman known as Dear Mother, established a utopian community she named Auroville. It was about a thirty-minute ride in a tuk-tuk, a three-wheeled motorized rickshaw.

The other local saint was Ramana Maharshi. He became spontaneously enlightened as a teenager and went off to the nearby holy mountain of Arunachala, where he lived in silence as a hermit for several years, only communicating by writing on a slate. An ashram was built near the base of the mountain by his supporters, and eventually, he took up residence there until he died in 1950. The ashram is near the town of Tiruvannamalai, about a two-and-a-half-hour drive from Puducherry.

After visiting Puducherry, I planned to go south to the Meenakshi temple in Madurai, visiting several other temples along the way. From there, I planned to take a train across southern India to Kochi on the west coast and then return to Delhi. It was an ambitious plan but one that seemed easily doable.

In Puducherry, I stayed at a small hotel in the old part of the city. The hotel was supposed to have a restaurant attached, but it was closed for remodeling. The room was comfortable, but the promised Wi-Fi didn't exist. On the plus side, it was a short walk to a couple of internet cafes; one was strictly computers and internet connections, and the other served chai and pastries with its Wi-Fi connections.

Some of the buildings in Puducherry were reminiscent of New Orleans, with black wrought iron balconies. The public display of statues of the Virgin Mary always amazed me, probably because I was not used to that sort of display.

On the walk to the waterfront, I discovered a delightful Indian-French cafe called Baker Street (*Image 18-1*). Its logo was the silhouette of a man in a deerstalker hat, a curved smoking pipe clenched in his teeth. Sherlock Holmes and a French bistro? But then this is India—TII. Once inside, who cared? There was a case filled with delicious French pastries, and their fresh veggies were washed in filtered and purified water. It was the safest place in town to eat. And the food was delicious.

Image 18-1: The Baker Street French bistro in Puducherry, Tamil Nadu, India

Down the street, Mohamed ran the Wi-Corner Internet Café (*Image 18-2*). The one that served no food. The place was easy to miss because the door to its second-floor location was poorly marked. Upstairs, three walls were devoted to computer stations—elbow to elbow. If you brought your computer or netbook, you could connect your machine for a slightly reduced fee. The cost was twenty rupees an hour, less than fifty cents.

I liked Mohamed. He had crazy hair that flew off in all directions and a longish, thin beard. He wore a long white ankle-length garment and a long-sleeved white shirt and told me he used to work for computer companies in Minnesota and the Boston area. One day, I asked him why YouTube was blocked. I told him my granddaughter had put a high school musical performance on YouTube but I could not access it. He promised I could access the site the next time I was in.

On my return, I saw the video as promised. She had written a piece for piano and trumpet; she played the piano, and her friend, the trumpet. Not realizing the poor trumpeter had to have pauses to breathe, she had written it basically for piano. It was about four minutes long, and the other kid seemed to gasp for air through the piece.

Image 18-2: The easily to missed Wi-Corner
internet cafe

Then I woke up one night with a fever and sweats. By morning, I felt only marginally better. I dressed and went down to the small reception area and just sat, thinking that if I were to die, it would be better to be in public view rather than hidden away in my room and not be found for days.

A couple of hours later, the clinic across the street opened. My temperature was 102, so they sent me to the hospital emergency room across town. I hailed a taxi and was ushered into the doctor's office after a short wait at the ER. As luck would have it, he had completed his residency in Australia, and his English was perfect. He examined me and gave me prescriptions that I filled at the hospital's pharmacy. At the checkout desk, I was presented with a bill for the doctor's services, about $2.25. I showed the clerk my prescription and was directed to a window outside the hospital's front door. I handed the pharmacist the prescription. He drew out a timeline for each drug on small brown envelopes and indicated with an "X" when I should take that pill during the day. He inserted the meds and handed me a bill for the equivalent of $3.40. The total cost was $5.65, but the best part was that within three days, I was back in the land of the living.

Image 18-3: The author at the Matrimandir at Auroville, Tamil Nadu, India

Feeling improved, I took a tuk-tuk for the short trip to Auroville, where the members of this intentional community had turned a bleak portion of the earth into a veritable garden in forty-three short years. Auroville's big attraction is its meditation hall, the Matrimandir (*Image 18-3*). The word combines *matri* for mother and *mandir*, literally an inner place of learning. But not just anyone can go there to meditate, or to use their term, to concentrate.

There were hoops to jump through to visit. I had to see a video and take a half-mile walk to view the Matrimandir. Then I went back to the office to make an appointment. But no, the office was only open for an hour in the morning and an hour in the afternoon. It was now closed. I would have to come back. I needed to make a proper appointment. "The first thing we have available is Sunday morning at nine o'clock." Okay then, it would be Sunday at nine.

On the bone-jarring tuk-tuk ride back to Puducherry, in the oncoming lane of traffic, a taxi hit a woman on a zebra crossing and knocked her to the pavement. With cuts and bruises, she limped to the curb with the help of her fellow pedestrians. A crowd gathered, in the way that only happens in India. As the taxi driver argued with the crowd, his two female passengers emerged from the back seat of the taxi. They were in their mid-twenties with long blond hair, and thank God for them, modestly dressed. They looked northern European and were about to intercede with the crowd on the driver's behalf. I recalled the traffic casualty in Madras on my first Indian visit, and I suspected their interference would not go well. My tuk-tuk driver seemed of the same mind, so we quickly skirted around the scene.

That afternoon, while sipping chai and munching on pastries at the other Internet cafe, I emailed a hotel in Thanjavur, my next stop, stating the two days I wanted a reservation.

Sunday morning, I went back to Auroville and sat in a small theater to watch another video, and because the tour was overbooked, they split us into two groups. I was in B-group. We waited while the guide told us what to expect and how to act in the Matrimandir. She warned us most emphatically not to display gestures of any religion inside.

131

When it was our turn, we walked the half mile to the geodesic dome, the Matrimandir. The structure was a giant golden globe, about a hundred feet high, that resembled a giant teed-up golf ball. Once there, we crossed a ramp over a huge lotus pond and climbed stairs leading to the entrance, where we left our shoes in little cubbies. We stopped at another station to put on special socks and to roll our pants legs up to keep the outside from entering the sacred space. Inside, the floors were covered in a soft, white carpet that followed a circular ramp up to the middle of the dome. The outer walls reminded me of Buckminster Fuller's triangular panels. Each seemed to glow with a bright golden light.

At the level of the concentration chamber, near its center, we entered into a vast open space. The entire upper half of the dome was an open space with a white marble floor. Twelve white marble columns reached fifty feet toward the top of the inner dome. Places were marked for meditators to sit between the columns. There were also several designated places around the outer perimeter for meditation.

In the center stood a solid crystal ball, maybe two and a half feet high, resting on a golden cradle of four six-pointed stars with a square in the center. A beam of light was directed down through the crystal from the ceiling. We were allowed to sit and meditate for about fifteen minutes; then we were ushered out.

> Close Encounters of the Third Kind *came to mind as I entered the Matrimandir. I also thought about kings building impressive structures to wow foreigners with the grandeur of their power. I thought about the Mayans and Aztecs leading their willing sacrifices up the stairs of their temples and how they were probably similarly wowed by what they saw from that height. I thought about what a great job these Aurovilians had done in bringing a barren landscape into productivity and hoped their wonderful ideals of human community would prevail.*

What our guide didn't explain, and I only discovered later, was that the entire structure represented the cosmology of Sri Aurobindo's Integral Yoga. It represented our spiritual ascent from the muck of the lotus pond to union with ultimate reality to the Supreme Cosmic Spirit of the Universe; the light source beamed down from the top of the structure. Each level we passed through on our climb to the meditation chamber represented what are traditionally known in yoga as the chakras, the seven energy centers of the body. The inner spiral stair was symbolic of the cosmic dance of Shiva and Shakti, the principle of the duality of matter and energy. The symbolism of the Matrimandir is so complex that every aspect of the structure seems to have meaning.

Image 18-4: Mount Arunachala, Tamil Nadu, India

When I felt well enough, I took a day trip to Tiruvannamalai and Ramana Maharshi's ashram at the base of Mount Arunachala (*Image 18-4*). It was a small ashram, where the saint was buried. Following tradition, I meditated, but I chose not to make the usual eight-and-a-half-mile walk around the mountain. I didn't feel well enough to do that, so I asked the driver to drive around instead. We agreed that under the circumstances, I would receive the same merit.

> When Ramana Maharshi was a teenager, he sat meditating on life and the loss of a close family member. Over and over, he asked himself, "Who am I?" and in a Damascene moment of enlightenment, he knew that he was not his body. Although his body might die, he realized that he was immortal consciousness. As I sat in his ashram, I recalled my experience at that rooftop theater years before and wondered what that moment was like for him as he saw the world he thought he knew in an entirely different way. He must have been stunned—as though scales had fallen from his eyes. He had seen a truth that turned his world upside down, and I imagined him dazed, trying to comprehend how his world now fit together.

After returning to Puducherry, I left the next morning for Thanjavur. With another car and driver, I headed south. En route, we stopped at several temples. At Kumbakonam, near Thanjavur, I hired a guide outside the temple. As he toured me through the complex, we encountered one of the resident priests, a young man probably in his thirties, who told me about the temple and its history, which I found very interesting. Later, my hired guide told me the priest's statements were completely untrue. "He's a part-timer only. He works at a finance office and comes here on weekends. He doesn't even know his own temple's history," he said scornfully.

At Thanjavur, we pulled up to the hotel entrance, where the receptionist politely told me she had not received my email reservation request. Not only that, tomorrow was Constitution Day, a national holiday, and not only did they not have a vacancy tomorrow, but in all likelihood, there were no vacancies at any hotel in any city in the country for the next few days. Constitution Day was that big of a deal.

I was stunned and could only stare in disbelief at the desk clerk. A national holiday had never entered my mind. And it seemed that here in India there could be a festival at any temple in any city that could disrupt my plans.

Chapter 19: But God Disposes

To say I was crestfallen would be an understatement. I managed to talk myself into the last room available for that night but only when I agreed to be out first thing in the morning. On the plus side, the hotel was directly across the street from a magnificent old temple. So, after supper, I crossed the street and wandered around its grounds. Bright lights around the temple attracted swarms of flying insects, which were dinner for the many bats that darted and dodged, snatching them out of the air. It was a quiet and peaceful place except for the slaughter of innocent insects. A few families strolled the grounds or sat in groups in the grass under the bright lights (*Image 19-1*). I wandered around, enjoying the evening and letting my current misfortune go.

India 19-1: Brihadishvara Temple at night,
Thanjavur, Tamil Nadu, India

Overnight, I made a plan. I would go to the airport in Tiruchirappalli and return to Delhi, where I would contact Mr. Patel's Pronto travel service to set up the rest of my travels. The best flight I could get departed the next day at half past ten at night. It wasn't optimal, but it was workable. Not having a clear idea of the geography of Tiruchirappalli and the airport, I planned to hang out at the airport until my flight left.

We got to the airport a few minutes after one o'clock in the afternoon, and to make a long story short, the airport closed from one o'clock in the afternoon until half past nine at night. The armed soldiers at the entrance informed me there was no access to the terminal until then. I pleaded my plight, and eventually, someone suggested I hire a taxi driver to tour me around town until the airport reopened.

Since the driver who brought me had left, one of the guards picked someone from the taxi stand to be my guide. And what a fantastic fellow he turned out to be. His English could have been better, but we could communicate and got along just fine.

Image 19-2: Sri Ranganatha Swamy Temple,
Tiruchirappalli, Tamil Nadu, India

We crossed the river to the vast Sri Ranganatha Swamy Temple (*Image 19-2*), a city unto itself covering a quarter square mile. From there, he suggested we have lunch at a workers' restaurant. While he negotiated with the owner, the patrons checked me over. It was dark and crowded, and I tried to remain out of the way and as inconspicuous as a six-foot-tall American could.

He pointed toward a sink with a single spigot where I washed my hands and dried them on a towel that should have been laundered last week. Then he signaled me to join him and several other men at a table. He ordered each of us a *thali*. A waiter came over, wet the table, and covered it with a banana leaf. On the leaf, he placed a helping of rice in the center and surrounded it with portions of dal, veggies, chutneys, and raita. This was a *thali*, a typical workman's lunch. I ate with the fingers of my right hand, with nods of approval from my lunch mates. When we finished, the waiter scooped up the leftovers in the banana leaves, which were probably destined for a bin in the alley that the cows would finish later.

Image 19-3: An elephant at the Rock Temple poses with a visitor, Tiruchirappalli, Tamil Nadu, India

Next, we went to the Catholic Church of Our Lady of Lourdes, painted in pink tones, then to the Rock Temple carved out of an enormous rock 272 feet high. Inside the entrance was a grotto cut into the rock wall, large enough for an elephant to stand. One stood stoically with a shackle around its ankle, while for a small fee, visitors had their photos taken with this poor creature (*Image 19-3*).

I walked past and climbed 437 steps to the top, where the view was amazing. Through smog, locally referred to as fog, I could see the Sri Ranganatha Swamy Temple we had just visited across the river.

Circling overhead were dozens and dozens of Brahminy kites. Spread below me was Tiruchirappalli, its houses brightly painted and cheerful looking, a stark contrast to the houses of the north. Directly below the temple, boys played cricket on a rooftop. Goats wandered freely around the observation area and seemed to prefer walking along the precarious ledges of the exposed rock.

As I prepared to leave, I paused and sat on one of the top steps out of the way of the steady flow of visitors. I noticed three boys in their early teens stop below me and huddle together, obviously planning something. They climbed up past me, and then two went back down below me. The third youth remained behind me, and I knew what this was about. He wanted his friends to take a photo of him with me in it. I turned, drew him toward me, and invited him to sit with me while his friends snapped the picture. He was embarrassed, and as soon as his friend had snapped the picture, he jumped up and rejoined his buddies. I could tell by their body language that they were scolding him for not thanking me. He turned back to me, hands in prayer at his face, and gave a slight bow, which I returned. Then they disappeared into the crowd below.

As the afternoon waned, we went to another temple called Ayyappan. I wasn't sure whether this was my driver's temple or if he just wanted to go there because they gave out free meals to all-comers, no questions asked.

This temple was unique. It was modern with single-story buildings, whereas all of the temples I had seen so far were built of stone and very ancient, some over a thousand years old. When I walked the path around the main building, I read markers and signs proclaiming the equality of all people with discrimination toward none. I liked Ayyappan.

Just before sundown, we ate a tasty meal of rice and lentils. I left a donation, then sat toward the back of the meditation platform to meditate. Suddenly, my driver was at my side, eagerly telling me, "They are putting God to bed." I followed him just in time to see a small procession of about eight attendants carrying the statue of the clothed god Ayyappan to his nighttime resting place. At sunrise, he would be dressed anew and returned to the place of honor.

It was time to go to the airport. My flight took me back to Chennai for a connecting flight to Delhi. I was glad Jack was out of town because it was very late when I got back to the house.

On the flight back to Delhi, I reflected on the past few days. It had been a great trip, and I was not being a Pollyanna about it. I had encountered several Buddhas in this part of my odyssey. Some offered insights. Some offered challenges.

I had seen some fantastic things in Chennai, like the dances, especially the detached-attachment of the Bharatanatyam dance. Sure, I had got sick in Puducherry and was almost ready to make it my final resting place, but there were some fun surprises, too. I had learned that apparent experts don't always have the expertise they would like us to think they have, like the temple priest who didn't know his temple's history. There was the Matrimandir in all its glory, even though I would have liked the guides to share details about its architecture. There was the surprise of the Australian-trained doctor and the Sherlock Holmes/French bistro in Puducherry. The lost email reservation resulted in experiences in Tiruchirappalli I would never have had: lunch with the workers, the Rock Temple and its goats, and the teen boys. The Ayyappan temple will always be a favorite memory. India may say the caste system is gone, but that is not true. At Ayyappan, they were trying to make a difference and welcome everyone. Is it any wonder that Ayyappan's followers are respected by Christians and Muslims across South India?

There were many instances where things could have gone badly off the rails but didn't. Partly, it was my positive attitude that had kept me open to possibilities. But through it all, Lakshmi, fortune, serendipity, had smiled on me. Fortune smiled when I woke up that night in a fevered sweat to a text from Kaitlin checking on me and offering to put me in touch with a physician she knew in Chennai if I didn't improve. She smiled again when the hotel clerk found a room. And again when the soldiers at the airport helped deal with the closed airport. And once more when the taxi driver took me under his wing for the day. My attitude had helped me in all of these situations. In all cases, I had tried to show respect, appreciation, and the expectation of help in my vulnerable position.

The big and humbling takeaway is remembering what Thomas à Kempis said in his Imitation of Christ, *"Man proposes, but God disposes." And then there's Alexander Graham Bell's corollary: "When one door closes, another opens; but we often look so long and so regretfully upon the closed door that we do not see the one which has opened for us." I will always try to walk away from the closed one and look for the newly opened one.*

This entire leg of my journey was one big Buddha lesson that mitigated against being judgmental. How could I think that it was bad that my reservation had not been received when I'd had experiences filled with such good memories? As

Ralph had said in the MBSR course years before, "Each moment of life is neither better nor worse than any other moment. Each is a constituent of life. Each has value, and each is to be witnessed and, in that way, each can be fully appreciated, dealt with, and acknowledged as appropriate."

Chapter 20: New Plans

The experience in Tiruchirappalli made me realize the need for professional help so that I wouldn't end up sleeping on the streets of some distant Indian city. I emailed Mr. Patel the morning I returned to Delhi. I told him I wanted to see Jaipur, the erotic temples of Khajuraho, and the backwaters in Kerala.

The morning's email also brought a message from Swami Shantiananda, the retreat leader at the Rishikesh ashram. He welcomed me to the retreat and sent contact information for two of the retreat participants who would be coming from the States. Both were women, and they would stay at a hotel he had recommended. I thanked him and sent the women an email saying I would meet them at their hotel when they arrived and would be happy to hire a car and driver to take us to Rishikesh.

While I waited for Mr. Patel to set things up, Jack told me a group from work planned to go to Amritsar toward the end of February. Amritsar is the site of the Sikh Golden Temple, near the Pakistani border in the state of Punjab. If I were interested, he said, he would get details. I told him yes; I wanted to go.

While Mr. Patel finalized my travel plans, I decided to sightsee around Delhi on my own. With recommendations from Jack and a travel guidebook, I chose the zoo, Purana Qila (the Old Fort), and a return visit to the National Museum.

There was a long line at the zoo, and I commented about it to my tuk-tuk driver. "Is it worth the hassle?" I asked. He said there was a special line for foreigners and also a special price.

The zoo was much better than expected. It was pleasant; the animals were well cared for. But observing the staff proved just as enjoyable: men clipped the grass with scissors; at a staff meeting, zoo workers sat outside in neat rows on blankets while their supervisor lectured them.

Next door to the zoo was the Purana Qila, or the Old Fort. It was the citadel of the old city, built in 1538 by the son of the first Mogul emperor. Archeologists think it was built on the site of the ancient city of Indraprastha, mentioned in the Mahabharata, dating back to around 1000 BCE. Delhi is a city with a long history.

As I strolled through rooms of Buddhist art objects at the National Museum, I came into one where a religious ceremony was in progress. The service was centered on a reliquary with a plaque announcing that it contained a relic of the Buddha himself. I lingered a bit and saw a young man in front of the reliquary display case with an older woman. Her beaming smile hinted that she was likely his mother. I decided he was probably a newly ordained Buddhist monk (*Image 20-1*).

Image 20-1: Buddhist ceremony at the
National Museum, Delhi, India

Later, Jack told me that the museums were filled with items looted from sites around India during the colonial era. Rather than return the religious relics, the government allowed them to be venerated in the museums.

That evening's email brought word from Mr. Patel that all was set for my next round of travels. A driver, Mr. Lalit, would pick me up early in the morning and drive me to Jaipur, where I would spend two nights. Then I'd go on to Mandawa, a small town in Rajasthan, famous for its old merchant houses called *haveli*. At six o'clock the following morning, we were on our way to Jaipur. As it happened, Mr. Lalit's English could have been better, but it was good enough that we could communicate our basic needs and wants.

Chapter 21: More Than a Tour Guide

On the outskirts of Jaipur, Mr. Lalit stopped at my hotel, where I checked in, had lunch, and met Sanjaya, my Jaipur guide. One of Jaipur's iconic buildings is the Hawa Mahal—the Wind Palace—built over 250 years ago. Here in the desert, the Wind Palace was designed with windows facing the prevailing winds (*Image 21-1*). Over each was hung heavy fabric soaked in water. The wind blowing through the wet fabric provided cool air for the women who lived there in seclusion.

Image 21-1: The Hawa Mahal, Jaipur, Rajasthan, India

We drove through the old part of the city, Sanjaya, pointing out things of interest. We stopped to explore the Jantar Mantar, a collection of nineteen astronomical instruments built by the wealthy prince Jai Singh II in the early eighteenth century. It is home to the world's largest sundial, accurate to within a fraction of a second.

On the way to the Valley of the Monkeys, we passed a man who stood in a doorway stark naked, his body smeared with a white paste. He just stood there watching traffic go by. Sanjaya identified him as a Jain guru. He said there were two kinds of Jain guru monks: the completely naked ones were referred to as Sky-Clad, and those who wore white robes were called Cloud-Clad. These monks and nuns, he said, practiced a very strict policy of nonharming, extending even to ants and mosquitos. Previously, I had seen Cloud-Clad Jain nuns dressed all in white, faces covered with masks to keep them from inhaling insects. As they walked, they used brooms to sweep bugs from their paths.

The Amer Fort, also called the Amber Fort, was a fantastic structure. Built at the end of the sixteenth century, its walls stretched for miles around the old part of the city. Today, besides its amazing view, one of its attractions was an opportunity to ride into the fort on an elephant (*Image 21-2*).

Image 21-2: The author astride an elephant at the Amer Fort in Jaipur, Rajasthan, India

Later, Sanjaya and I chatted over chai in the snack shop. He was curious about why I had come to India. I told him I was a yoga teacher and was going to a meditation retreat at an ashram in Rishikesh in a few weeks. He asked about the lineage of the ashram. I told him Swami Agrajananda founded it. Then we had a long discussion about yoga philosophy, and he told me there were five aspects of human nature we all need to control: sex, anger, ego, greed, and possessions. Then he said there were five things we should ask Ganesh for: health, wealth, a loving partner, children, and friends.

We talked about the need to control our negative thoughts. He said, "Replace negative with positive, but not trying to push away negative. Just say to yourself, 'I'm not my thoughts. Whatever I did in the past is past. It is done.' Now go and make good karma. Just say, 'I'm a good person who has done a negative thing.' But don't say, 'I do positive things.' Then you are taking credit. The most important thing is to surrender credit to Ganesh, to God."

Later, we drove past a hospital, which Sanjaya told me was private and very expensive. He said you needed "medical insolence" to be able to afford to go there. It took me a minute to realize he meant medical insurance.

At the end of our final day together, Sanjaya invited me to his small house. Once there, he asked me to join him on the *charpoy*, a frame with legs strung with light rope that functions as a bed as well as a couch for entertaining company. The room was small and sparsely furnished. In one corner sat a ten-year-old Mac computer on a wooden table scattered with his papers. We chatted while his wife prepared chai out of sight in the kitchen.

Our conversation turned to how easy it is to overgeneralize and project some judgment out into the future and how we are then ready to alter our lives to fit this projected and imaginary future.

Sanjaya said, "A long time ago, there was a farmer who lived near here. One day, his horse ran away. His neighbors said, 'Oh, what bad luck.' And they all felt bad for him. But he only said, 'Yes, you could be right.'

"The next morning, his horse came back with three wild horses. And his neighbors said, 'Oh, how wonderful.' He said, 'Yes, you could be right.'

"The next day, his son tried to tame one of the wild horses, but he was thrown and broke his leg. His neighbors gave him sympathy for his bad luck. 'Yes,' he said, 'you could be right.'

"The day after the accident, officials of the Maharaja of Rajasthan came to the village to take all of the young men for the army, but they didn't take the farmer's son because his leg was broken. And the neighbors all said how lucky the farmer was. But he just said, 'Yes, you could be right.'"

I told Sanjaya what a great story that was, at which point his wife brought in the chai. We chatted some more, and he told me that in the hot weather, he and his wife preferred to sleep on the marble floor of their house because it was so much cooler. I hated to leave Sanjaya. He was an extraordinary man and had been great company.

> *Sanjaya's story led me to reflect on Iris's encouragement years before to consider events and persons as Buddhas. I now realized that this exercise had helped me to begin letting go of my judgmental attitude. It's hard to be judgmental when a person or event might be giving me a valuable lesson. Likewise, Sanjaya's story of the shifting interpretations of the farmer's fortunes pointed out that our interpretation of events, not the events themselves, causes us problems.*

That night, I asked Mr. Lalit to suggest a place to eat, and at his suggestion, he dropped me at a vegetarian restaurant called Surya Mahal, the Sun Palace. For dinner I chose the chef's recommended *thali* which included malai kofta (dumplings in a cashew-tomato-cream sauce), paneer butter masala, vegetable pulao (rice with vegetables), dal makhani, mixed raita (a thin yogurt with veggies), a side of papadoms, naan, and for dessert gulab jamun (a sweet pastry in a clear syrup).

As I finished, a group of about a dozen American tourists, all men, came in and sat at a large table next to me. One guy presented the waiter with a note written in Hindi outlining his dietary restrictions: no wheat, no spices, no this, no that. Another told the waiter that if what he ordered came with spices, he would not pay for it. With that, I happily paid my bill and headed back to the hotel.

With Mr. Lalit at the wheel in the morning, we left Jaipur for Mandawa. The road north was good, with some light truck traffic. Then, at a small village in the middle of nowhere, we turned off into the bush. With each kilometer, the road became little more than a rutted path. Then, suddenly, we were on a paved road and almost instantly at our destination, the Sara Vilas [sic]. Mr. Lalit and I were both stunned by its size out here in the boondocks. I said to him, "I wonder if I'm the only guest?" This cracked him up, and for the first time, I saw him laugh. Dinner and breakfast were cafeteria-style, and I was the only guest.

Mandawa is a small town at the edge of the Rajasthani desert. Its main attraction is its *havelis,* large homes of wealthy merchants who made their fortunes as middlemen on the old silk and opium trade routes that passed through here (*Image 21-3*). The *haveli* is two stories high and built around a large central courtyard. A unique feature of the *haveli* is the way it is decorated. The walls are painted with typical Rajasthani motifs in bright colors and designs. Prominently displayed between windows or any place with a flat surface are portraits of the owner, hunting scenes, or whoever the owner chose to feature. Some of the paintings in the haveli we visited that day were interesting, like the one of a woman giving birth, another of a couple making love, several parades of elephants, and many dancers in see-through tops, the fashion of the day.

The road back to Delhi was much better than the one going to Mandawa— until when we approached the city and the traffic became so congested that we were reduced to a crawl.

Image 21-3: The interior courtyard of an haveli in Mandawa, Rajasthan, India

Back at the flat, I sat on my cushion and focused on my breath. I allowed whatever needed to bubble up to come.

> *The variety of spiritual traditions ... the religious ceremony in the Museum ... the Sky-Clad Jain monk ... sectarian tensions not apparent to the casual observer. The art of the havelis ... the stark contrast to America's Puritan cultural ancestors. Christianity's views on the human body. Sanjaya's teachings about controlling sex, anger, ego, greed, and possessions and about praying for health, wealth, a loving partner, children, and friends. He had it right, and I added him to my list of Buddhas. Especially powerful was the story about the man whose horse had run off. Was this event fortunate or not? The truth is that we don't know whether any event in our lives is "good" or "bad" until judged with hindsight. Events are just events that lead us along our path. It wastes and saps our energy to make judgments about them.*

Then thoughts and images faded, and I slipped into the dark purple of meditation . . . a point of light appearing . . . fading . . . scattering of star-like pinpoints . . . I concentrated on what was before me . . . let thoughts go . . . then drifted to focusing on my breath .

Chapter 22: The Treachery of Images

When I arrived in Delhi, people asked with a sly, knowing smile if I planned to visit the erotic temples at Khajuraho. The expectation was that I would. I waffled. I hadn't come to India to satisfy prurient interests. But finally, I decided I would see what it was all about.

At half past five in the morning, I stood at our gate waiting for Mr. Patel's Pronto service car to take me to the train station. When the car arrived, my driver handed me a packet with all the tickets and vouchers for the trip. His instructions were to take me to my seat on the train. At the station, he left me in his car while he went to find out exactly where I needed to go. When he returned, we gathered my things and made our way into the terminal under a banner proclaiming "Indian Rail—60 Glorious Years." Inside, people sat on blankets in family groups. Many slept on the floor. My driver explained they were country folk who couldn't afford a hotel. Overhead, a large tote board announced train and gate information. We found mine and headed toward our destination, stepping over sleeping travelers.

Within five minutes, the train pulled up. Then it was all elbows and nudges as everyone pushed for their reserved seat. I was by a window. A woman sat across the aisle clutched a cello between her legs; her husband sat next to me, attending to her every need.

At 6:14 a.m., we pulled out of the station. It was still dark, but the security lights along the tracks revealed high fencing around an industrial complex. We picked up speed as we moved into the countryside, where a pale dawn lit wheat and mustard fields. This was an express train, so freight and passenger trains waited on sidings as we sped past. We stopped briefly at the Mathura station for passengers to board and hawkers to peddle snacks wrapped in cones of yesterday's newspaper.

Rolling again, cabin attendants moved through the coach, offering chai, samosas, mango juice, and bottled water. Cello-woman's husband waited on her hand and foot.

At Agra station, home of the Taj Mahal, Cello-woman and her husband got off, and we picked up a tour group of Spanish senior citizens. They were loud and generally disruptive of our coach's early morning quiet. Their guide finally ordered them to sit down. Across the aisle, a woman read a guidebook entitled *Los Temples de Amora*, The Temples of Love. The English version I had seen in bookstores was titled *The Erotic Temples*. The two titles offered different perspectives on how our two cultures viewed the Khajuraho temples. Were the temples symbolic of love or blatant sexuality?

The city of Jhansi was as close as I could get to Khajuraho by train. I was met at the station by Raj, who would drive me to Khajuraho. The road was good through a rolling countryside. A few clouds drifted lazily across an otherwise bright blue sky. On distant hillsides, I saw small temples with red pennants flying from flagpoles that announced their active status. They reminded me of the country churches back home.

We passed women working road construction, wicker baskets of stones balanced on their heads. Then we passed through a teak forest and into a small country village where the road was covered with a violet powder. As we followed the purple road, we came upon a procession of decorated horses, women in colorful sarees, men banging drums, and blaring wooden trumpets. Raj lost his cool over the congestion, a rare reaction for Indian drivers, who are generally patient.

It was late afternoon when we were slowed once again, this time by a herd of cattle plodding down the road toward home at day's end. And then suddenly, we arrived at the parking lot of Clarks [sic] Khajuraho, a chain of five-star Indian hotels. It looked nice and more than adequate for my short visit.

In the morning, I found Raj at the reception desk, and we went into town to meet my guide for the day. Surindra was a young man with a young family. He told me he was a trained guide and a history major at one of the nearby universities. I said I wanted to understand what the temples were really about. Why were they built? What were their builders trying to tell us? He said he would do his best.

He pointed toward the temples across the street. "That one over there on the left," he said, "is an active temple. The ones straight ahead and to the right are not active. They are part of the UNESCO Heritage Park. We'll start there." Then he added, "Coming with me, please." Briskly, we crossed the street, dodging traffic, and across a nicely tended grass lawn toward the temples. As we did, Surindra gave me the local history of the temples.

"Around 900 CE," he said, "a local prince fought off attempts of a nearby king to capture this area. Our local prince's overlord rewarded him with land and his daughter in marriage. Temple building began as a way of thanking the gods and the goddesses for his victory, and at the same time, he was increasing his prestige in the area."

As we approached the first temple, I was overwhelmed by its scale. The temple sat on a raised stone platform, maybe fifteen or twenty feet high, decorated with carvings of men carrying all sorts of weapons. Some were on horseback, some afoot, forming a horizontal band around the platform at eye level.

Surindra kept talking. "Over time, to justify and enhance the prestige of the local ruler, a legend grew up about how the dynasty came to be. The moon god, Chandra, had an affair with an earthly maiden. The product of this happy coupling was a handsome boy. The earthly maiden was concerned her son would not have a good future since she and her lover weren't married. But Chandra comforted her by promising that if their son and his successors built eighty-five temples with erotic figures, she would be freed of the stigma of their illicit affair." *That's a long time to have to wait for exoneration.*

159

Then he added, "I guess that was the best he could offer her."

We stepped back a short distance from the plinth for a better view. Surindra pointed out the symbolism of the architecture. "You'll notice," he said, "on the right are stairs leading up to the entrance."

"Yes, I see."

"The stairs take you from our everyday world to a place of spiritual significance." Then, with his right arm sweeping upward to the left, "You see how the four sections of the temple gradually rise in height, each a bit higher until the one on the left is the tallest part of the structure."

Surindra turned toward me, "You see what I'm saying?" I nodded in agreement.

Image 22-1: The Vishvanatha Temple at Khajuraho, Madhya Pradesh, India

"Symbolically, it's a mountain (*Image 22-1*). It's called *sikhara* or mountain because that's what it's like. It's like a mountain reaching skyward toward heaven. The deity the temple is dedicated to is in that chamber. Let's go around to the front and go up."

When we got to the front, a wide stairway led onto the plinth. Then we approached another series of steps and, at the top, passed through an arched gateway adorned with mythic aquatic animals.

I followed Surindra into the interior chambers, each darker than the last. "We're passing through a series of halls used for gatherings of different sorts—maybe sacred dances." I thought of the Bharatanatyam dancers in Chennai.

Finally, we entered the deepest and darkest part of the temple. He said, "This is the womb chamber with the image of the temple's central deity, Vishnu, in this case." It was so dark that Surindra used his flashlight, slowly scanning the chamber. He continued, "This is not like your Christian churches, all full of light and such. For us, it's different. This is for individual worship of the divine. People might come through in lines to pause briefly and offer their prayers of thanksgiving to the temple's deity."

As we walked out through the three halls, Surindra pointed to the outer walls, which joined the three chambers to the *sikhara,* the mountain chamber. "When we go outside," he said, "this is where the so-called erotic sculptures are, at this point between the outer world and the spiritual world."

The entire exterior surface was filled with intricate designs and motifs interspersed with niches and nooks that displayed all manner of figures and images—figures on horseback, Ganesh the Hindu elephant-headed god, and all sorts of sprites and mythological beings. As we had approached the temple from a distance, it had appeared to be textured, but now, standing here this close, it was all deeply cut designs and motifs interspersed with near-life-sized statues (*Image 22-2*). In this portion of

161

the transition wall between the sacred and profane, we came face to face with the erotic sculptures.

I could understand how the casual observer would see these as erotic, especially in today's *Playboy*-influenced culture with its obsession with female breasts. All female figures, goddesses, nymphs, and humans were bare-chested. But then, that was how people dressed when these temples were built. It was the Muslim invasion, a few hundred years in the future, that would impose new ideas of modesty on this culture.

Image 22-2 A portion of the images form an exterior temple wall at Khajuraho, Madhya Pradesh, India

My eyes wandered over the surfaces: there was a dancing Ganesh, an elephant crushing the head of a prisoner, a dancer removing a thorn from her foot, and a couple making love with attendants at hand. One attendant looked discretely away while the other peeked over her shoulder and smiled. A man pulled a monkey toward a woman to frighten her into his arms. There was a group involved in sacred sex; one male figure had already ejaculated, which had taken him out of the action. There was a row of elephants facing outward, except one whose head was turned toward a couple in "sweet anal copulation," as Surindra described it. A

162

woman played a flute; another looked at a scorpion on her thigh (*Image 22-3 left*). Surindra explained that the scorpion represented her desire "for sweet copulation" as well as its probable outcome.

Image 22-3: Desire as a scorpion (left) and as a vyala (right) where it eats the one trying to kill it.

He directed his laser pointer toward a strange figure (*Image 22-3 right*). "This figure is called a *vyala*. It's a mythical creature. It's a composite of different beasts, reared up on its hind legs. There, can you see?

163

Underneath it is a man with a sword. He's trying to kill it, but also clinging to the *vyala's* back is this same man, and the *vyala* has turned its head to eat him alive." He paused for dramatic effect, then added, "This is symbolic of desire. Even though we may try and kill it, it still wants to eat us alive." Several *vyalas* were scattered throughout this section. "This," Surindra said, "is meant as a clear warning about the delicate balance that must be maintained to use sexual energy wisely and prudently."

As we turned to leave, Surindra directed his laser pointer to a sculpture on an outside corner. "If we look at her, we see she's looking at her reflection in a mirror. She seems pleased and smiles approvingly." Then he led me around the corner to view her from a different angle. "But from this vantage, we're not sure about the smile. Maybe it's a frown. We don't know." He paused. Then, "It wants us to think about our vanities."

On our walk back to the parking lot, I asked Surindra if there were any good books about these sculptures. He told me to wait outside while he went into a bookstore to find one. When he came out, he offered me a slim paperback by Devangana Desai, who he said was a leading expert on the temples.

With the book purchased, we were about to say our goodbyes when a little girl of about six years old ran up to him and hugged him around his legs. He introduced his daughter, a pretty girl with big brown eyes. I thanked him for sharing his knowledge and wished him and his family well.

Later, relaxing at the pool in Clarks Khajuraho, a beer in hand, I reflected on the day.

> *Again, there were many Buddha lessons from Khajuraho, and I almost chose not to go there. As we had toured, several small groups had wandered around in twos and threes. It was pretty obvious they were mostly intrigued and drawn to the more explicit sexual scenes, mistaking the metaphor for the reality. That's such an easy reaction. There are two*

164

groups of people: the ones who take things literally and those who take things metaphorically. I think we humans tend toward the literal.

The more I thought about it, the more I began to believe that if we looked at these two groups, the literalists, and the metaphoricalists, the literalists would be the larger group. I thought about poets who saw things metaphorically and poetically and how the ancients had conjured the gods and goddesses to explain human behavior. Then people began to take it all literally and search for hard evidence of the deity. We want Jesus or the Buddha to have been actual historical figures when we really should pay more attention to teachings that have been handed down.

I thought about a man who had joined my meditation group years ago. He was very interested in Buddhism and thought that if he could only get to the original words of the Buddha, he would learn the Buddha's unadulterated message. He didn't want the Buddha's words filtered through the lenses of those who passed along his lessons. He didn't seem to realize that since the Buddha didn't write down his lessons, they were already filtered through his followers. I had wondered if he was ready to learn whatever language the Buddha's early followers wrote his lessons in so that he could access the original thoughts. And the same could be said for Jesus's teachings.

For the builders of the Khajuraho temples, there seemed to have been a lack of shame or guilt at the public depiction of sexual themes, but they had also wanted to give the message that the sexual impulse, as powerful as it is, is best kept under control. The scorpion of desire carries a deadly sting. Sanjaya, my guide from Jaipur, would agree.

165

I especially liked the vyalas *and the woman with the scorpion. By its nature, desire can be deadly if we're not careful. I recalled the painting at the National Museum of Modern Art,* Truth Seeking Man Caught in a Whirlpool of Temptation, *depicting the drowning man reaching for* truth *in the opposite corner of the painting.*

Like so many things, the Khajuraho sculptures are what we make them—instructive or salacious. Once again, it's a case of seeing what we expect to see.

Chapter 23: God's Own Country

It was late when I got back to Delhi, and it was a scramble to be ready to leave early in the morning for Kochi in the southern state of Kerala. I had been to Kerala eighteen years earlier. This was where I had attended the Kathakali performance and my thinking about spirituality had been reoriented. I was not trying to recreate a similar experience. I only looked forward to relaxing and enjoying myself.

Kerala is an interesting place. For one thing, it is one of the more prosperous Indian states. The Communist Party of India has been a significant player in Kerala's political life since the 1950s, and it always felt strange to see the hammer and sickle prominently displayed. Kerala has the highest literacy rate in India at around 94 percent. It exports more medical doctors than any other part of India. An Indian friend told me she had wondered why this might be true and asked her friends for an explanation. The consensus was that Kerala is a matriarchal society. Whether true or not, Kerala works well.

Mr. Jameson, my Keralite guide and driver, greeted me at the airport. Going strictly by his name, I'd expected him to be from the United Kingdom, but no, he was a native of Kerala, the language of which was Malayalam. He had a full head of coarse black hair, and his dark skin contrasted nicely with his long-sleeved white shirt and light blue slacks. When we reached the hotel in Kochi, it was well after dark.

The next morning was a glorious seventy-five degrees, and sitting in the courtyard restaurant for breakfast was very pleasant. A single woman was finishing her breakfast when I arrived. Scattered throughout the courtyard were banana trees, date palms, jackfruit trees, and one fruit tree the waiter identified for me as a *chiku*. While the kitchen prepared an omelet and masala tea, I enjoyed the birds singing in the trees: the mynas and the bulbuls. High overhead, a small flock of green parakeets darted across the sky. When the woman left, two crows glided down to take her place at her table.

Mr. Jameson wouldn't pick me up for a couple of hours, so I decided to enjoy a stroll through the neighborhood. A plaque outside the hotel announced that it was built in 1633 and had been in continuous occupation ever since. In a nearby open field, a bunch of boys were playing cricket, and a sign announced a cycling race a few months earlier. I walked past Saint Andrew's parish hall and the Old Dutch Cemetery. Several signs read "God's own country." I would ask Mr. Jameson about that.

As we left Kochi on our drive to the mountain town of Munnar, Mr. Jameson drove through attractive neighborhoods on the bay's watery fingers. Kerala was green, a welcome change from the dull and dusty north. Local names and signs attested to the influence of Saint Thomas's Christians. We passed Saint Mary's Hospital and met a tour bus with the word "Mariya" in large letters over the windshield. We drove past a flower shop called the "Desent [sic] Flowers" and an Ayurveda center that advertised "freshness therapy." There was a "Flava Bakery" and a large billboard for "Angle Bras" with a normally endowed woman as a model.

When I asked Mr. Jameson about the "God's own country" signs, he said there were several explanations. According to legend, Parasuraman, an incarnation of Vishnu, had thrown his ax into the ocean to create a new land where his followers could live in peace and harmony. Another explanation said that all religions got along in Kerala without sectarian violence, so obviously, God had claimed the area. And yet a third said that Kerala was so lush and fertile that it must have been the home of Adam and Eve. However, a more prosaic reason was that it was the idea of an ad agency.

I had seen several churches as we'd left the city. There was a Syrian church that looked very Catholic to me, but Mr. Jameson said it was not. We passed one that was CSI, or the Church of South India. Again, it looked Catholic but wasn't, he said. Mr. Jameson was himself a Roman Catholic.

Kerala is a major food exporter, and it was evident as we passed farms and plantations growing cassava for tapioca, cashew trees, jackfruit (which Mr. Jameson said makes you fart), coffee, and all manner of spices, and then as we reached the higher elevations, we found bright green carpets of tea trees covering the hillsides.

Along the way, we stopped at a man-made lake surrounded by a eucalyptus forest of two-hundred-foot-tall trees. I wandered through the forest, enjoying the trees' scent and their size.

Image 23-1: The author's men friends at a lake in a eucalyptus forest in Kerala, India

Lakeside, I spotted a group of men on holiday taking photos of themselves (*Image 23-1*). When they finished, they came toward me. They wanted to know what I thought of India. Did I like it? Did I eat rice? Did I eat Indian food? Then, as we were about to part, someone suggested they get a photo of me with the group, and then I offered to take some of their entire group with their cameras.

Our destination was a comfortable Indian resort hotel just outside Munnar. From the hotel, I could look across the valley at several mountainsides of tea plantations. It was Valentine's Day, and the hotel restaurant was decorated with red hearts that evening. Several couples enjoyed a Valentine's dinner.

Mr. Jameson was keen to show me the tea bushes up close, and on our drive back out of the mountains, he had his chance. We encountered a group of women picking tea leaves near the roadway. They wore protective clothing against the sun and scratches from the bushes. As they picked the young tea leaves, they dropped them into canvas bags to be collected and weighed at the plantation. One woman (*Image 23-2*) picked close to where I could easily approach. She told me she had come from Tamil Nadu, the neighboring state, through sign language, gestures, and a few words as she pointed toward a distant mountain ridge. She told me her name, but being unfamiliar, it easily slipped my mind. When I told her my last name was English, she thought it was hilarious that someone would have the last name of a language.

Image 23-2: Picking tea leaves near Munnar, Kerala, India

From the mountains, we returned to the Kerala coast and a small hotel in Kumarakom. The Keralite manager, Thomas, and I hit it off, and he joined Mr. Jameson and me on an excursion to the nearby Kumarakom Bird Sanctuary. It was a fun experience as they identified the various birds whose names I would never remember. At one point, a swarm of dragonflies rose out of the undergrowth; their wings sparkled in the sunlight. I exclaimed, "Oh, look at all the dragonflies." Later, Thomas spotted another swarm, which he pointed out to me, saying, "There are some more little flying dragons."

Image 23-3: Boatman polling through a
Backwater canal in Kerala, India

That afternoon, I was going for a boat ride in the backwaters, a unique area in India. It's where the fresh water from five rivers meets the ocean water behind a narrow strip of land similar to North Carolina's Outer Banks. They have a system of flood control gates to flood specific areas with fresh water for rice farming. Then, after the growing season has ended, the fields are flooded with brackish water.

At the boat landing, I met the boatman and his wife. The boat was long and narrow but had a good freeboard. Before shoving off, his wife placed two red plastic chairs in the boat, one for me and one for Thomas. From the stern, the boatman poled us along with amazing skill. We slid through the canals and past attractive homes. Most had ghats (stairs leading down to the water) where women did laundry, washed cooking pots, and bathed.

We slid out of the canal (*Image 23-3*) and into a large, open paddy area that, in a few months, would be drained and planted with rice. Now it was full of floating islands of weeds and various water plants, offering food and protection to a variety of waterbirds.

The boatman poled us toward a cormorant tangled in an underwater net. Thomas and the boatman tried to free it, but it only snapped at them, and since none of us had a knife, we had to abandon the rescue attempt. As we pulled away, Thomas sadly announced that "He's going to lose his life."

Image 23-4: Elephants at a temple festival, Kumarakom, Kerala, India

When we returned to the boatman's landing, Thomas suggested I experience a ride on a local bus. We boarded the packed bus at the hotel and paid the four-rupee fare for the ride to the local Hindu temple a few miles away. When we arrived, a festival was in progress (*Image 23-4*).

It was the last day of a weeklong event. There were three performing elephants, a band, dancers, and all the kitschy little trinkets imaginable. I was fascinated by the band's wooden trumpets.

When we got back to the hotel, Thomas invited me to join him in the small lobby for chai. I thanked him for introducing me to his world. Then I asked him about all of the churches that looked like the Catholic churches of my youth but were not Catholic.

He explained that Kerala had a rich religious history.

"The Jews," he said, "came here hundreds of years before our Saint Thomas. Maybe it was only twenty-five years after Jesus left this earth. The Saint established seven church communities in Kerala before he went to the Chennai area. The people of these first Christian settlements are called Saint Thomas Christians. Over the centuries, those church communities grew, split, merged, split, and merged again. Today, there are eight denominations tracing histories of the Holy Saint."

"Plus the Roman Catholics and Anglicans," I said.

He wobbled his head in the affirmative and said, "Yes. You are right."

"And may I ask, which one are you?"

"I was raised in the Roman Church, but all coming from the apostles, so not much difference. One emphasizes one thing, another something else. All have truths. Have you heard that all roads lead to Rome?" he asked.

I told him I had, and he said, "Well, it's the same here. All roads lead to God, so each has truth, and any can get you to God." I nodded my agreement. I hadn't thought about it that way since I had been caught up in the struggle of which church had the right answer.

Then he said, "It's like the Hindus with Shiva or Vishnu. All have their followers and temples. But they all have the same truth about the Supreme Godhead."

I thanked Thomas for taking me to the temple earlier and told him what a grand experience that had been. He had truly made my visit to Kerala memorable.

> *On the flight back, I reflected on the past few days. Mr. Jameson and Thomas were good Buddha teachers, guides, and companions. Mr. Jameson had told me about the politics of the area, the ruling Communist party, and their work to improve the worker's lives.*
>
> *The woman picking tea had touched me, as always happens when I can communicate with someone even though neither of us speaks the other's language. The same was true with the men on holiday at the lake.*
>
> *But the experience of going to the temple festival with the decorated elephants, singers, dancers, and bands had been special. I appreciated Thomas's ecumenism and his comment about all roads leading to Rome. I had always understood that to mean that whatever our choices, they all lead to the same result. Thomas understood it metaphorically as all roads lead to the same source, i.e., to God: one truth, many paths.*

Chapter 24: With Charity Toward All

I met the Amritsar travel group in front of the train station, where our leader, Carol, passed out packets of information for the trip. She had planned well. She had someone to escort us to our assigned coaches and seats. Unfortunately, the twenty-eight of us were scattered in different coaches. The train was only seven minutes late leaving. I heard many stories about bad experiences with the Indian rail system, but in my experience, Indian trains were impressive, clean, efficient, and on time.

Amritsar is near the Pakistani border in Punjab, India's northwestern state. British India included what today is India, Pakistan, and Bangladesh. When the British pulled out after World War II, they split the former colony into separate Hindu and Muslim countries: Pakistan in the west and East Pakistan (now Bangladesh) in the east were predominantly Muslim. At the same time, the Hindu majority was given present-day India in the middle. None of these areas were either wholly Muslim or Hindu. So, when Partition happened in 1947, there was a population shift of several million people rushing to get from one side to the other. In the process, hundreds of thousands of people were killed in the chaos. Today, the border between these two nuclear powers remains unstable.

Chiranjiv, our guide, greeted us at Amritsar train station. He had a bus to take us to within a half mile of the Sikh Golden Temple. Buses were not allowed any closer for security reasons. Here, we switched to *tongas*, sort of a horse-drawn rickshaw, and with four people to a *tonga* we began the short ride to the Golden Temple.

Before we could enter the temple, Chiranjiv passed out head coverings. Then we exchanged our shoes and socks for a ticket from the shoe-check *wallah*, walked through a shallow water trough to clean our feet, and finally entered the temple grounds.

175

The temple is covered with a thousand pounds of pure gold and is surrounded by a large pool of water said to contain medicinal qualities. It is accessible only across a long, narrow causeway (*Image 24-1*). The Sikh sacred text is located in the Golden Temple, where, if it were a Hindu temple, the deity would be placed for worship. The line to view it was very long, so we were happy not to join the queue, leaving places for the faithful. The pool and temple are surrounded by a multi-story structure housing rooms for Sikhs who come on pilgrimage from around the world.

Image 24-1: Sikh Golden Temple at Amritsar, Punjab, India

Chiranjiv explained that charity is a cornerstone of the Sikh faith, and one of the ways it was practiced was by offering meals for all comers. Today, they were expected to feed only around fifty thousand people (*Image 24-2*). They were equipped to feed twice that number. The kitchen was huge, and men and women worked together to make the chapatis, dal, and rice they would serve the multitudes. The eating area was filled with several hundred men, women, and children at a sitting. Nearby, Sikh men and women worked together to clean and wash the stainless-steel plates for the next sitting. Chiranjiv pointed out that both men and women working together represented another tenet of the Sikh belief system—that all are created equal in God's sight.

Image 24-2: At the Sikh Golden Temple, every day thousands are fed a free meal.

As the afternoon faded toward sunset, we boarded a bus for the Indian-Pakistani border to witness firsthand the ceremonial lowering of the flags of these two competing nuclear powers. We found places in the bleachers and watched the highly choreographed precision of the military honor guards of the two sides prepare to lower their respective flags. Meanwhile, partisans for these two nuclear powers exchanged jeers and taunts. As the honor guard goose-stepped its way to their respective flags, it seemed a contest as to which side could kick their legs higher. Then, as the sun sank to the horizon, the flags of the two countries were lowered in absolute and precise unison to cheers of *jai-jai*, victory, from the two sides.

On the train ride back to Delhi, the coach steward moved up and down the aisle with water, chai, and snacks: spicy shoestring potatoes, taffy candies, and a cookie. Again, our group was split up through several coaches, which gave me a chance to review the weekend.

I was impressed and overwhelmed by thoughts of the Golden Temple and the charity of feeding upward of fifty thousand people daily. It staggered my imagination.

Sikh history has not always been one of only charity. There has been tension between some of the Sikh leadership and the central government in Delhi that has resulted in armed troops storming the Golden Temple, with loss of life on both sides. Then, in retribution, Indira Gandhi's Sikh bodyguard assassinated her. It's a complex history that I don't understand or feel I can comment on. What I saw of the Sikhs was impressive, and I will leave it at that.

Later, stewards came through the coach with a choice of veg or nonveg main course. I chose the vegetarian option: two naans rolled in foil, chana dal with paneer in gravy, rice, fresh veggies, pickles, and yogurt.

The show at the border had been unsettling to me. Knowing how volatile the Indian-Pakistani border is and how tense the nearby areas of Jammu and Kashmir are, it all seemed crazy to me, so crazy that it's hard to find the words to describe it—sophomoric comes to mind. It's just simply insane, considering the hair-trigger relationship these two countries have with each other. And they treat it as a cricket match.

This experience inclined me toward charity toward others and less aggression, whether for real or for play.

Chapter 25: On to Rishikesh

Once back in Delhi, I began serious preparations for the retreat in Rishikesh, which would focus on the Yoga Sutras and meditation. There were readings to finish, and I needed to coordinate travel plans with the two women arriving from the States later in the week.

Rishikesh is a small town about 150 miles north of Delhi located on a bend in the River Ganges as it exits the Himalayan mountains. The town was fairly isolated: the nearest train station was sixty miles away, and there was no air service. The easiest access was by car.

The retreat was scheduled to begin on a Sunday. Jackie would arrive late on Thursday and Esther late on Friday. The retreat being scheduled to start on Sunday morning dictated a departure early on Saturday. When I arrived at their hotel that morning for an eight o'clock departure, our driver, Rajiv, was loading Jackie's bags. Esther had yet to show up.

While we waited, I chatted with Jackie, who was probably mid-thirties, tall and slim, with light brown hair and glasses. Rajiv fussed with the bags and seemed anxious to leave with or without Esther. Luckily, she joined us before he did. He wanted to be back in Delhi before nightfall. When Esther arrived, I found out she was from New Jersey, just across the river from New York City. She was short, probably in her early sixties, with blond hair and glasses.

Because of Rajiv's extraordinary hurry to leave, he threw Esther's bags into the passenger seat while we three crammed ourselves into the back. I took him aside and warned him that good driving would be rewarded with a good tip while bad driving would not. In hindsight, I should have been more explicit in defining good driving.

On the road, I noticed Rajiv, like many other drivers in India, had an image of a god, saint, or holy man on his dashboard, not unlike Saint Christopher medals. His holy man of choice was Sai Baba, whose wild hair reminded me of an Indian Jimi Hendrix. Sai Baba's tagline was "Love all, Serve all." I liked that.

Our two-lane route took us north out of Delhi, across the Yamuna River. The traffic was lighter than I expected but increasing. This was my fellow travelers' first exposure to Indian driving. As the traffic picked up, the horn honking increased, and they became more and more jumpy. They didn't understand that honking was an essential part of driving in India. It's like a bat's echo-location ability.

With the slightest opening in traffic, Rajiv immediately sought to fill it, often without the courtesy of a honk from his horn. The other drivers considered this lack an insult, which earned him their scowls and scorn. Jackie and Esther shrieked in terror and constantly begged him to slow down. But Rajiv forged ahead.

Just as I began to relax, there was a sudden jerk of the wheel, and Rajiv veered into the oncoming lane to pass a bus. Dead ahead, a goods-carrying truck filled the oncoming lane. The truck didn't slow. The bus did not waiver. But somehow, Rajiv managed to pull in ahead of the bus with millimeters to spare. Surely, Sai Baba had protected us.

We sped along at a blistering fifty-five kilometers per hour, or thirty-five miles per hour, which was fast enough for our man. We slowed through a village, giving us a glimpse into rural life on a Saturday morning. There were women in bright sarees and salwar kameez with produce balanced on their heads. A bicyclist pedaled past with a couple of dozen large stainless-steel milk cans miraculously attached to his bike. Another bicycler hauled rebar to a building project to reinforce concrete.

Esther asked Rajiv, "Can we please stop for a few minutes?" But it was as though she hadn't spoken. "Sir," I said, "we need to stop." But he only picked up speed as we exited a village. Finally, I leaned forward and said, "Sir, please stop at the next place with toilets."

That got his attention, and we stopped at the next *dhaba* or lay-by. It was called the Big Bite Food Resort and seemed like a miniature Disneyland repurposed for India. The Big Bite looked brand new, like an oversized McDonald's or an upscale K&W Cafeteria. It was fully staffed, with steaming food trays for cafeteria-style selection. They were ready to serve busloads of tourists, but we were their only patrons.

Image 25-1: Saturday morning traffic on the road to Rishikesh, Uttarakhand, India

After our brief stop, we returned to the road, driving past sugarcane fields. Women cut, loaded, and hauled stacks of sugarcane on their heads to waiting trucks. Then suddenly, out here in the middle of nowhere, we hit a traffic jam. Of course. It was Saturday morning and market day. Trucks were parked on the verge to unload animals for auction. We crept along. Then suddenly, directly in our path was a truck with a broken shock absorber, five men in the cab and five more on the roof, headed directly at us (*Image 25-1*). And again, by some miracle, we avoided a collision, and no truck passengers slid off the cab's roof.

Through all this, Jackie and Esther berated Rajiv, who probably wanted to be rid of us as badly as my companions wanted to be rid of him. Jackie whispered to us in the back seat, "When we get to Rishikesh, if we get there alive, I'm telling the car company they should not use him ever again."

We approached the town of Haridwar and crossed a river. "This is the sacred River Ganges," Rajiv said. We were excited by this news. And then, halfway between Haridwar and Rishikesh, a sign cautioned, "Drive slow. Elephant corridor. Elephants have the right of way."

"Wow," we all said in unison. "Elephants." We were as excited as kids at Christmas. The ashram's website had warned us that crossing the Ganges to the mountainside was a quick and certain way to end our retreat. There was no mention of elephants on this side. Later, I heard a person had been seen on the other side being chased by an elephant. There were also rumors of tigers over there.

As we entered the outskirts of Rishikesh, Jackie said, "Look at that," pointing to sleek-looking, modern, multistoried ashrams on both sides of the highway. It looked like Club Med for the spiritually minded. Enlightenment was Rishikesh's primary industry.

Rajiv stopped and inquired about the location of our ashram, then circled back and almost missed the driveway again. The guard opened the gate, allowing us in. The wall on one side of the driveway housed dog kennels for the ashram's guard dogs that would be released onto the grounds later at night. They barked their greetings as we unloaded our bags.

Suddenly, our driver became obsequious in his desire to please. I gave him our collected low tip and sent him on his way. Meanwhile, the ashram staff whisked our luggage away.

Surrounding the ashram was a three-meter wall, about ten feet high, topped with embedded glass shards to prevent unsavory characters from entering the grounds at night. During the day, however, monkeys climbed on the wall at will and were peppered with rocks by the staff to keep them from entering the ashram.

We checked in at the office and were shown the library with its two Wi-Fi-connected computer stations that were available to us. The Wi-Fi was dial-up and slow. Beyond was a small courtyard and quarters for visiting swamis and swaminis, women committed to religious life. There were other quarters for families staying at the ashram.

The kitchen and dining hall were separate. There was a larger courtyard with crisscrossing walkways, flower beds on each side, and a lotus pond in its center. Scattered throughout were sculptures from some old, ruined temple. On one side of the courtyard, in the direction of the river, was a gated exit that led to a stairway to the top of the ghat.

On the far side of the grounds were our cottages and the meditation hall where our classes would be held. On its roof were lounge chairs offering a nice view of the river and beyond.

The ghat was a levy on the river's south bank with steps at various intervals down to the water. Its top was a paved service road used for maintenance access and exercise walks by the townspeople. At this point, the river was about a hundred yards wide. The waters here were calm, but further upstream toward the town center, large boulders created a turbulent flow.

Birds called from both sides of the river. Cormorants, ducks, and geese flew along the river. Cuckoos and crows were constant travelers back and forth. Brahminy kites circled overhead while terns skimmed the surface, and kingfishers hovered, dove, and emerged with small fish in their beaks. Near the far shore, I saw a large fish splash. For a badly polluted river, the Ganges seemed to teem with life.

For our little group, this was a learning holiday, but still, we were assigned no tasks, kitchen chores, or floors to scrub. Our only job was to do yoga, meditate, listen to lectures, and watch an occasional video.

The retreat would begin in the morning at nine o'clock. All meals were simple vegetarian fare. Lunch was our big meal. Our mornings were peppered with periods for yoga, breathwork, meditation, lectures, and study time. According to the published schedule, the afternoons were more of the same, with a break midafternoon. After supper, a final yoga session and meditation were scheduled. After that, it was quiet throughout the grounds until morning and a reminder that the guard dogs would be out.

I was happy to be at the ashram and looked forward to deepening my understanding of the Yoga Sutras and my meditation practice. The previous weeks had been good for me, forcing me to deal with a whole host of new situations: navigating Delhi, dealing with health crises, and making the best of derailed travel plans. It was all good. The drive to Rishikesh had been exhausting, not so much for Rajiv's driving as for Jackie's and Esther's reactions. It seemed unfortunate that, having come this far, they had not planned time to learn about India. They would take home a postage-stamp version of India based entirely on our drive to Rishikesh.

Part IV: "Future Suffering Can Be Avoided"

Pain is certain, but suffering is optional. We often think of pain and suffering as synonymous, but they are not. Pain is physical; suffering is mental. We might have leg pain, but our brain interprets it differently if we have been exercising or see it as a sign of a serious medical issue. The Yoga Sutras say that when we realize our thoughts are a source of our suffering, we can see a way out.

Yoga Sutras 2.16

Chapter 26: A Simple Mantra

That first morning, for breakfast, I had roti, a flatbread, and dosas, India's version of a crepe that is stuffed with vegetables and made from lentils. There were spiced potatoes and a variety of dips and chutneys. And, of course, chai, black tea with lots of sugar and milk. Meals were vegetarian and cafeteria-style. Lunch would be our big meal; dinner, light.

I nodded a greeting toward the others, sitting away from each other, eating their meal. I found an unoccupied table. Since my seminary days, when we had observed the *magnum silentium*, or the great silence, until after breakfast, I had been fond of quiet mornings.

I rinsed my tray and utensils in the cold water with soapy sponges when I finished. Then I placed the tray in a vertical drying rack, and the utensils went on a towel to dry. I wondered what our county health inspectors would think.

Next, I went to the computers in the library. I had told Louise I would check emails as often as possible but wasn't sure how regular I could be.

Afterward, I walked on the ghat, which became part of my morning routine. I headed upstream and noticed the carcass of a water buffalo slowly, languidly floating downstream. Occasionally, a fish splashed or geese flew low over the water, settling further upriver.

Back in my room, I jotted down some notes and readied myself for our first session. At the meditation hall door, I parked my shoes with those of others. Only socks or bare feet were allowed in the meditation hall, which was large and airy. Its windows offered a magnificent view of the Ganges and the mountains beyond. A mist hung over the river, and I could almost imagine Siddhartha as an old man poling his boat toward us from the far shore.

Someone had stacked cushions in a corner along with those ubiquitous cotton Mexican blankets, the ones used by every yoga studio I've ever been in. There were mats, blocks, and straps, everything required for practice. I collected what I needed, arranged my things next to Jackie's, and waited for others to arrive. We exchanged pleasantries as the rest of our group entered.

The staff had arranged a whiteboard, a small table with a water bottle, and a piano-style bench in front. We organized ourselves in a line facing front, all on cushions, which told me everyone had some kind of *asana* practice.

The door opened, and Swami Shanti walked in. He wore maroon pants with elastic bands at the ankles and a matching maroon sweater over a long-sleeved orange tee shirt.

A maroon knit cap covered his otherwise bald head. Maroon, orange, or saffron were the current swami colors.

He put his laptop on the table, pushed his cap back on his head, adjusted his glasses, and turned toward the whiteboard. At the top, he wrote "Good morning, *Sadhakas*," using the Sanskrit term for a spiritually adept person. Then he turned toward us, looked out over the room, and, in a soft tone, said, "Good morning. I hope you slept well."

We echoed his morning wishes.

Swami Shanti began by saying, "Most of us have met before, either in person or online, but before we get started, I would like to introduce myself formally. I am Swami Shantiananda. You can call me Swami Shanti or Swami Ji. I was born and educated in America and worked in marketing. I have meditated most of my adult life but only began formal training with Swami Agrajananda in my late thirties. I studied and trained with him and was ordained a swami about ten years later. I continued to work and study with him until he left his body five years later. Since then, I have tried to carry out his request that I teach and spread our tradition's teachings.

188

That is what I have tried to do through my books, my website, and these retreats. During these next three weeks, we will explore the teachings of Patanjali's Yoga Sutras, one of yoga's defining texts. I hope these next weeks will prove beneficial to all of you, as well as to me. And again, thank you for making the effort to be here."

His gaze moved from one of us to another. Then he said, "Thank you all for being on time. I know some of you have come a long way. I'm sure you're still very jet lagged." Again, murmurs in the affirmative. "It will take several days before you function at your usual level. When I travel back and forth between India and the States, I am forgetful and a bit spacey for several days, so try and take good notes, especially these first few days."

Swami Shanti said, "Well, let's start by going around the room and introducing yourselves. Please say something about yourself besides just your name."

There were eleven of us—three men and eight women, and we represented a wide range of backgrounds, countries, and languages. Jackie, Esther, and I were from the States. Julia and Carlos came from Argentina and Peru respectively. Ingrid and Hans had flown in from Denmark and Germany. Agung was Balinese, while Siti and Rajani were both born in Tamil Nadu and now lived in Kuala Lumpur. Angie was from South Africa.

We also represented a wide range of occupations: therapist, retired pilot of cargo planes, a wallpaper hanger, a yoga studio owner, a restauranteur, a shop owner, a computer programmer, a tour operator, a human relations director, a real estate broker, and a world traveler.

Then Swami Shanti said, "Now, tell me, please, what is it you each expect to get out of the next three weeks. Not something long and elaborate. Just a sentence, that's all."

Someone said, "I want to deepen my meditation practice." Someone else said that she wanted a clearer understanding of the Yoga Sutras. Another, that he hoped to achieve a degree of serenity. I just said, "I want to gain wisdom."

When everyone had finished, Swami Shanti thanked us and said that he hoped we all found what it was that we were looking for.

Then turning, he sat on the bench with one leg tucked under himself. He paused a moment before continuing.

"Meditation is a systematic practice," he said. "You must have a specific time and place to sit for meditation. Have a routine, like brushing your teeth. Meditate on the body, then on breath awareness—paying no more attention to the body—only the awareness of breath. Then move into the *So-Ham* mantra, letting go of the breath."

> *I had forgotten entirely about the* So-Ham *mantra meditation. I had been introduced to it years ago at that workshop at Swami Shanti's retreat center. I thought it seemed hokey at the time, so I never did it. We were told in the workshop that the sound* So *was the sound of the inhale, and* Ham *was the sound of the exhale. The presenter said that it meant "I am That." The word "That," spelled with a capital "T," referred to the universality of existence, of our connection to the All, again with a capital "A," in other words, God. But I had dismissed it.*

Swami Shanti continued, "So move from bodily awareness to breath awareness and into *So-Ham* mantra. Then just let your meditation take over and become deeper and deeper.

"With the *So-Ham* mantra meditation," he said, "you will move inward in a systematic way to a very deep meditation. That's the theory, anyway. But what usually happens is we plop down on our butts and say we're

190

meditating. Then there's a combination of things going on: memories come swirling around in the head, we're talking to ourselves, maybe there's a bit of breath awareness, and maybe we're counting breaths or something like that. What we end up with is a struggle going on inside.

"But if we take Patanjali and the Yoga Sutras very seriously, we start by paying attention just to the body, and then only the breath. And then we're exploring only the body for a month. And then, for a month, we are just focusing on the breath. Then we are aware only of the body."

His eyes scanned the room, resting on each of us as we dutifully nodded our assent. He noticed a bit of lint on his sleeve, picked it off, rolled it in his fingers, and flicked it into space.

"And then after that, for a month, you move to the *So-Ham* mantra, and you are only aware of the emphasis on the *So* with each inhale, with a tiny pause at the top, and then a long slow *Ham* going out on each exhale, with a tiny pause at the bottom. It's like a wave going up on the inhale, *So*, a little tiny pause, then a longer descent on the exhale, *Ham*, and then finally, a slide into silence as you lengthen the pause after the exhale. Then, when you allow the mantra to go to silence, you find that the body is not twitching and the mind is not wandering around the body. Now you are sitting in this meditative silence, and the mind is not talking. And if there were any irregularities in the breath before, they are not there now."

He paused for a moment. "This little pause at the top of the inhale and the longer one at the bottom of the exhale isn't like you did when you were a kid—when you tried to see how long you could hold your breath. You don't close off the glottis. You leave it open so you don't create pressures within the body. Do you understand?" He asked. We nodded back.

"Everybody up," Swami Shanti said. "We're going to do some practice. We're going to do some poses, some asanas."

As we rose from our cushions and arranged our mats, he continued. "Too often people just plop down on their butts, close their eyes and say they're meditating. Now, if you've ever done that--just gone from whatever it was you were doing and plopped down on your cushion, or on your mat and closed your eyes and started to meditate, what's your first thought?"

He paused and looked around at us. "Well?" He said. "What's your experience with that? Have you ever done that?"

There were a few murmurs of assent. "And what was your experience?" he asked.

Carlos said, "It's uncomfortable. Maybe even a little painful."

"Yes," Swami Shanti said. "It's a little painful. And why do you think that is?" And without waiting for a reply, he continued. "It's painful because your muscles have tightened up. You need to do some asanas, some posture work, first to loosen up your body. That's why Patanjali put the postures into the Yoga Sutras before meditation. He's trying to tell us that to have a proper meditation experience, we need to prepare ourselves first."

He surveyed our little group. We were all standing by this time, shifting from one foot to another.

"How many times," he said, "have you heard people say, 'Oh, I can't meditate, 'cause I can't sit like that'? Well, of course not. Unless you're Plastic Man, or Gumby, or unless you have some disease of your tendons and connective tissue, you're going to have to lengthen your muscles through the stretches that come from doing the asanas. Then you can sit correctly. But we have to stretch out first."

Swami Shanti stepped out of his sandals, unrolled a yoga mat and said, "Okay, let's begin with the simplest forward bend you know." We followed his direction with an easy forward fold—nothing strenuous.

"Now the simplest backbend. Easy. This is only about the spine. Now do it to the side. The easiest you know how."

We stood and dutifully followed his instructions.

"Now," he said, "fancy it up. Do it all more deeply. Each one." Again, we did as he directed. "Do a hip-opener. Maybe do warrior one and two or triangle." He wanted us to do these basic yoga poses. "First simple," he said, "then fancy it up. Do it easy, then a little deeper."

I did each one—first gently, then I stretched more deeply.

"Now do an inversion," he said.

Some people did headstands, others shoulder stands. I chose downward-facing dog. Any inverted or semi-inverted pose fosters relaxation and makes for easier entry into meditation.

After about fifteen minutes of posture work, Swami Shanti said, "Now on your back, a small cushion under your neck, not your meditation cushion—its too high—just something to support your neck and cushion the back of your head. We want to keep the spine neutral, all lined up the same way it would be if you were standing. You can use the blanket folded under your head with just enough to cushion your head on the hard floor."

He waited till everyone was in position. "Now tense every muscle in your body, and then release them all at once."

I followed his directions. Then he said, "Starting at the top of your head, tense and release the muscles of the face . . . of the neck . . . of the arms and

193

hands . . . of the back and buttocks . . . of the legs and feet. Now tense and lift the right leg from the floor, and gently lower and release. Now the same with the left leg. Tense and release the back and buttocks. Tense and lift the right arm and hand. Now gently lower. Then the left hand and arm. Gently lift the head an inch or two. Now lower. Tense and release the muscles of the face. Now relax the entire body. Go ahead and take two full diaphragmatic breaths, and when you're ready, sit up in easy sitting pose or whatever you use for sitting meditation."

I sat on the meditation cushion, back erect, with my ankles on the floor, one in front of the other, hands resting on my thighs, and my palms upward like Devika had taught me years ago. I placed my tongue on the roof of my mouth to help control the need to swallow.

"Close your eyes and be aware of your body. Only your body. This is only about awareness of the body. No mantra, no breath. Simply about the body. Hold your awareness on your body."

Nose . . . shoulder . . . leg . . . ear . . . . My awareness moved from one body part to another, each synced to one breath.

His voice was buttery smooth. "Now shift your awareness to the breath coming in and the breath going out through your nostrils. Air moving in and out through your nostrils."

I took a couple of breaths, maybe three, and then he said quietly, "Let the exhalation be just a bit slower. The inhale will take care of itself." After a few breaths, he continued, "Without changing anything else you're doing, allow there to be an awareness of *So* on the inhale and an awareness of *Ham* on the exhale. Let there be an awareness of the vibration of *Ham*. Allow the *Ham* part of the vibration to become slightly longer like you're stretching it out, and at the end of the *Ham*, let there be a silence before you repeat the inhale with *So*."

Swami Shanti's voice became even softer, "And at the end of one of these *Hams*, allow the silence to take over as if you've forgotten the mantra. Notice that the attention will come to rest somewhere, maybe in the heart, maybe at the third eye. If the sounds of *So* and *Ham* want to remain, let them stay. Eventually, let one of the *Hams* lead you into silence. The object on which you are meditating is the silence itself. A formless silence. The only thing that's left is a faint awareness of existence."

When his voice returned, I realized I had been in a different place altogether. Something was different. It was hard to describe. Empty? Open? Full? I wasn't sure; it was just somewhere different.

Then, very softly, he said, "Allow the *So-Ham* to actively return—become aware of the touch of the breath at the nostrils—be aware of the whole of the body. Now become fully aware of the body that you had forgotten about. While you're aware of the silence in the heart and the breath at the nostrils, and while you're still aware of the whole of the body, draw in a deep, full breath, and we'll chant OM three times."

Finally, he said, "When you're ready, open your eyes. Remember, we don't do meditation to be happy; it's the other way around. We create the joyous mind so we can have the meditation."

Swami Shanti stood and looked at us for what seemed like forever. Then he said, "We're out of time. The next session is at half past one," and he walked out, laptop under his arm.

> *I got his idea that we create a joyous mind so we can have the meditation. It is like cleaning the house before guests arrive. You don't have the guests and then clean the room. The idea from the popular press is that we meditate to be happy and less stressed. But that has it backward.*

Chapter 27: The Symbol of Consciousness

When we arrived for our next session, Swami Shanti had written the words *"Buenos días estudiantes"* on the whiteboard. Then he asked us to do a sitting meditation for about thirty minutes. I began the *So-Ham* mantra, centering on my breath, and let everything else slip away. At the sound of the bell, I opened my eyes and turned to Swami Shanti.

He asked, "Mantras, did you find the silence at the end of our meditation exercise this morning?"

I asked, "Do you mean did we experience anything from the silence at the end of our chanting each OM?"

"Yes," he said. "Those mantras are heading us toward one thing. They are heading us toward *Tripura*, the goddess—toward the silence. *Tripura* anthropomorphizes the silence at the end of OM into a goddess. But for many of us, this makes it easy to miss the point."

> *He was talking about the same thing the man had talked about all those years ago at the rooftop Kathakali performance. Artists anthropomorphize aspects of a formless and substanceless Being to make the concepts accessible to the ordinary person. You had to be immersed in this stuff to get its subtleties. It's so easy to take the poetic to be a concrete reality. And when that happens, when we miss the metaphor and get stuck in the literal, we miss the intended message.*

Swami Shanti continued, "In the OM mantra, we go from A to U, to M, and then to silence."

He took a remote from his pocket, pressed a button, and a screen lowered from the ceiling. He punched some keys on the laptop, and his diagram of consciousness (*Slide 27-1*) popped up on the screen.

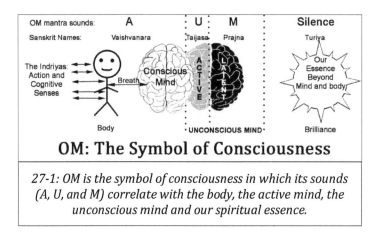

27-1: OM is the symbol of consciousness in which its sounds (A, U, and M) correlate with the body, the active mind, the unconscious mind and our spiritual essence.

"I've put a burst of brilliance on the right side with the words 'Our Essence Beyond Mind & Body.' If you give it a name, whatever you call it, people will argue about the term's meaning. We all agree we have senses," he went on, "we breathe, we have a mind, and we have an idea of an unconscious mind. And do we have some sense of something beyond all that? And most people will say yes. The brilliance represents that essence of us, if you will, of that part of us that is beyond our mind and body. Some may call it *atman*, soul, or Center of Consciousness. But what difference does it make what we call it? To avoid needless arguments about what to call it, I have chosen to use a brilliant sunburst. And in yoga, we say that is who I really am. That is essentially where yoga is trying to go—to the essence of who we are beyond mind and body. This sunburst helps to eliminate all of the debates about what to call it. We can all agree that who I am is not just my senses; it's not just my breath; it's not just my mind; it's not all the ways I describe myself; it's not my conscious thinking or my unconscious conditioning. But when we subtract all that, there is something left. And that's the brilliant sun. And that's who I really am. And that's essentially where yoga is trying to take us.

"It refers to the individual self, the little self, rather than the Universal Self, the capitalized Self. However, in the nondual tradition, our tradition, my tradition, they are both one; they are the same, the individual self and the Universal Self."

He paused momentarily and continued, "Yoga is the control of the modifications of the field of the mind. Then the Seer abides in Itself, resting in its own True Nature, which is called Self-Realization. If you, the Seer, can truly do that, control your mental fluctuations, then you rest in your True Nature—you rest in that brilliant sun. And that's yoga.

"Notice the three vertical dotted lines in the diagram. They divide the diagram into four chunks, and above each, I've included the sounds of the mantra OM. Over the section labeled 'body' at the left is 'A'; above the 'conscious mind' label is 'U'; over the one labeled 'latent unconscious' is 'M'; then at the far right is the brilliance under the word 'silence.'"

Then he seemed to veer off course. "Remember the first four words of the Gayatri mantra, '*OM bhur bhuvah svaha*'?" And he translated, "'Everything on earth, in between, and above arises from One Source.' The beginning, middle, and end are all from One Source—A, U, M, silence."

He continued, And all mantras have something to do with this—with this diagram—of moving from the gross to the subtle to the most subtle, and beyond, to the absolute reality. They're all saying the same thing. The words may be different, but the idea they want to get across is the same."

Oh my God, he blew my mind. I remembered the Kathakali performance nearly twenty years before and how I had reacted then. And that day in the ashram, it was similar. I was utterly and amazingly amazed by this subtle message and how easy it was not to recognize it. You had to attune to the correct frequency, or it would slip right past as it had with me.

Swami Shanti said, "Whatever we say about OM is representative of all levels of consciousness in the whole of the manifest and unmanifest reality, and in a sense, this is true of all other mantras."

I said, "In other words, it's everything."

"Yeah, it's everything. So, before we go too deep, we'll revisit what Patanjali said in the Yoga Sutras about OM. He said in the twenty-third line of the Yoga Sutras first chapter that OM is a shortcut to enlightenment. Even though it requires a lot of study and meditation, it's still well worth the effort to explore this route."

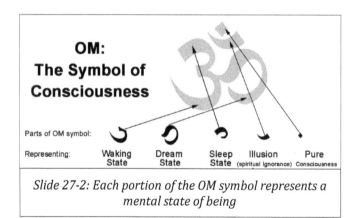

Slide 27-2: Each portion of the OM symbol represents a mental state of being

"This slide (*Slide 27-2*) dissects the symbol OM," he said. "It sort of looks like the number three with a tail behind on the right and a line and a dot on top. This symbol represents consciousness—individual consciousness, as well as the Center of Consciousness, Universal Consciousness. We're trying to describe something indescribable with the frailty of language.

"Now look at the bottom. Look at the sweeping curved line at the lower left. This represents the Waking State of our consciousness—everyday life. The circle on the right represents what yoga calls the Dream State— the play between waking and our active unconscious. And just so we're clear, this doesn't refer to the dreams you have when you are asleep at night. This refers to the normal condition where you may access things stored in your active unconscious. Things we can recall through conscious effort. Am I making sense?"

We all nodded despite the confusing names of the states of consciousness.

Swami Shanti continued, "That circle above on the left represents Deep Sleep or our latent unconscious. In other words, that part of our unconscious that we do not have access to, like traumas we've experienced but have repressed. But these things in our latent unconscious continue to influence our daily lives. Many people live in this state without conscious control of their behavior. They live reactively. Some are even proud of that fact. This is what Patanjali is talking about in the Yoga Sutras, what he calls the Deep Sleep State. Okay?" Again, we nodded like the bobbleheads on the dashboards of a tuk-tuk.

"That curved line above is called *maya*, the veil of illusion, that keeps us from seeing the dot above—*bindu*, the fourth state—the state of enlightenment—the state or condition of truly knowing." We nodded our understanding.

"Okay. Why don't we take a break here?" Swami Shanti said. This is kind of dense stuff. Let's take a short break and pick this up in about ten minutes." With that, he gathered his things and departed.

I was glad he had changed the slide because it helped confirm my decision to return to one of his retreats. I knew from the first retreat that he could be prickly in person, but I also felt he made some of these concepts easy to understand, and I was eager to delve deeper into the Yoga

201

Sutras. I had been to talks by Indian swamis and thought they didn't speak to me. I liked how Swami Shanti, an American-born swami, presented these ideas in more accessible ways for me. It took me a while to understand why this was true. The difference is that the Indian swami is speaking to an audience that already knows what he's talking about, so the teachings reinforce already-held beliefs. In the other case, the American swami is teaching an American audience new concepts.

Chapter 28: OM's Symbolism

We took a short break. Some of us did a few simple stretches, and others walked around the room a few times. Then Swami Shanti returned and called us back to order. "This next slide (*Slide 28-1*) pulls the first two together. Hopefully, this will give you a fuller picture.

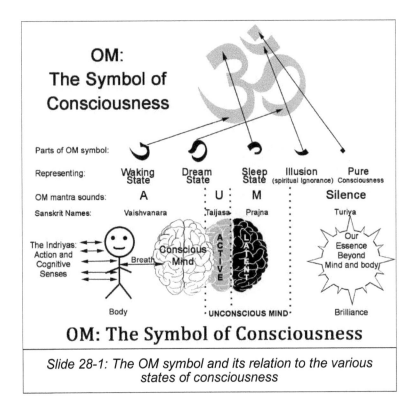

OM: The Symbol of Consciousness

Slide 28-1: The OM symbol and its relation to the various states of consciousness

"Both diagrams show the same things, just in a slightly different way."

After a short pause, he said, "Swami Agrajananda used to say the OM symbol was just the visual form of the sound of OM. It's a beautiful way to look at the symbol because it helps you remember A-U-M and the Waking,

Dreaming, and Deep Sleep States, that is, the gross, subtle, and causal. That's what matters.

"OM represents everything that was, is, or will be in the universe. So, in that sense, the whole universe is the symbol OM. All that transcends time, space, and causation is also OM. All of this, everywhere, is *Brahman*, the Absolute Reality—another way to say that any part is the same as the Whole. The little self and the Universal Self are the same. This very Self itself, *atman*, is also *Brahman*, the Absolute Reality. This *atman* or Self has four aspects through which it operates.

"The first aspect of *atman* is the Self in the Waking State, *Vaishvanara*." His laser pointer went to the lower left curve of the OM symbol (Slide 28-1). "In this first state," he continued, "consciousness is turned outward to the external world. There, it experiences the gross objects of the phenomenal world. And this is represented by the A of the sound of AUM.

"The second aspect of *atman* is the Self in the Dreaming State, *taijasa*." The pointer went to the open circle on the right. "In this second state, consciousness is turned toward the inner world, where it engages the subtle objects of the mental realm. This is represented by the U of the sound of AUM.

"The third aspect of *atman* is the Self operating in the Deep Sleep State, *prajna*." He pointed to the upper curve on the left. In this third state, there is neither the desire for any gross or subtle object nor any dream sequences. In this state, all such experiences have receded or merged into the ground of undifferentiated consciousness. This is represented by the M of the sound of AUM.

"The fourth aspect of *atman* or Self is *turiya*, literally the fourth." He pointed to the dot at the top. "In this fourth state, consciousness is neither turned outward nor inward. Nor is it both outward and inward; it is beyond cognition and the absence of cognition. It cannot be experienced through the senses or known by comparison, deductive reasoning, or inference. It is indescribable, incomprehensible, and unthinkable to the mind. This is Pure Consciousness itself, the real Self. It is serene, tranquil, filled with bliss, and is one without second. This is the real or True Self that is to be realized."

Then he said, "The Mandukya Upanishad says something like 'Everything, everywhere is OM.' I encourage you to read it for yourselves. It says all of this more poetically."

He looked around the room, then said, "In closing, this stuff is universal."

With that, he collected his things, tucked his laptop under his arm, said, "Till next time," and walked out of the room.

> *Later, I reflected on what Swami Shanti said about OM. At the beginning and end of my classes, I recite a short invocation and end with "OM. Shanti, shanti, shanti." An Indian woman had asked me after class one day if I knew why the word* shanti, *peace, was repeated three times. I knew that "shanti" meant peace, but I'd had to confess that I didn't know why it was said three times; I just did it. She said, "We're asking for peace in our body, mind, and spirit. And also," she added, to make the past, present, and future peaceful." There it was again, the beginning, middle, and end.*
>
> *Years ago, I had taken a couple of semesters of basic Japanese. Our teacher was from Mexico but had lived in Japan. In one of his early classes, he talked about sounds and used the OM mantra's A-U-M sounds as his example. He said we form the A sound in the back of the mouth, then move forward to the middle to make the U sound, and finally bring the sound all the way forward as we close the lips to make the M sound. He finished by saying, "A-U-M. The beginning, middle, and end."*

Again, I realized how these three are woven into the fabric of everything: the beginning, middle, and end, Brahma, Vishnu, and Shiva, A-U-M, shanti, shanti, shanti. It gets repeated in ways I never expected, like the stairs at Shravanabela Gola, the Jain temple, where the number of steps can be reduced to three—all reminders to the initiated, to the cognoscenti, to pay attention, to stay tuned in.

"Everything is everything," he had said. I love enigmatic statements like that. He meant that our small inner selves are synonymous with the larger Universal Self. In other words, atman, the little inner self, is the same as Brahman, *the Universal Self. Everything comes from* Brahman. *Everything is* Brahman. *All is* Brahman, *including* atman, *the little self.*

Back to the meditation on OM: the lower left curve of the OM symbol represents our consciousness in the waking, everyday state of being: going to the store, eating, interacting with others and our world. As our meditation practice deepens, it takes us into what yoga calls the dream state, the loop on the right side of the OM figure. We don't take up residence there; we visit during meditation. Our consciousness dwells in or engages aspects of our mental being, our active unconscious. Then, through meditation, our consciousness can move into a state of deep sleep, with the curve at the top left of the symbol, where our consciousness interacts with our latent unconscious.

As Swami Shanti had said, this is a state of bliss where clarity of vision makes all things apparent. Finally, as our consciousness moves into a state that we call enlightenment, represented by the dot above the curved line, consciousness experiences what is termed serene tranquility filled with bliss and awareness of Pure Consciousness.

OM represents everything, then. All states of consciousness, all states of awareness, all that ever was, is, and will be.

That's a lot to digest.

Thich Nhat Hanh, the Vietnamese Buddhist monk, had a meditation that helped me understand what was being said. He held up a piece of paper and said that all of the universe was contained in that one piece of paper. He went on to say that without the tree, the paper couldn't be made, and without the ground, the tree would not have grown, and without the rain, the tree could not have grown, and the cloud that gave the rain, and sun that shone, and the entire universe that created our sun—these are necessary for this paper to be. Then he said the logger was in the paper, so was his lunch, and his parents, and their parents. Everything that is and was resides in this one sheet of paper. And in fact, all of the future is contained in that paper. All is OM.

In other words, there is no independent existence. Everything depends on everything else. We live in an organic universe. That's one of the things that the environmental movement has been trying to tell us. Everything is related to everything. At some level, we know this, but our brains tend to slice the phenomenal world into discrete identities. It's a practical way to deal with the world. So I believe my eyes and ignore that it's all interconnected. But periodically, I need to come back to the realization that all is one.

The Buddhists have been so good at getting their message across. I think yogis could be better. Many yoga teachers, myself included, don't always see the subtle distinctions between yoga and Buddhist philosophies. Maybe someday, there will be a distinctively American version of yoga philosophy.

In his book Meditations from the Mat, *Rolf Gates says someone asked a Sri Lankan teacher what humanity's undoing would be. His response was, "The separation between you and me." We think we are separate and independent of one another, but in truth, we are not. We are all embedded in Indra's Web, which we call Life. And in that sense, the universe is alive.*

There's a Sanskrit poem that captures some of these ideas. A free translation goes like this: That, meaning the All, is Wholeness. This little aspect here is also Wholeness. From the Wholeness of the All comes this little aspect of the Whole. Wholeness comes from wholeness, and Wholeness remains unchanging.

Chapter 29: Barking Dogs

After breakfast and a walk on the ghat, we were all in our places, waiting for Swami Shanti to come through the door. He was already ten minutes late, and we began to mutter among ourselves. Could we leave after fifteen minutes, like in college, or were we stuck here until he showed up? Then someone suggested he was testing us to see how committed we were. Would we sit there like lumps or use our time wisely and meditate? Which was what we should have done. Instead, being unenlightened, we sat and gossiped.

Finally, he showed up in a pair of orange pants, an orange sweater, and, of course, his maroon knit cap. He opened his laptop and placed it on the table. Then, on the whiteboard, he wrote in Malaysian *"Selamat pagi, pelajar."* As he finished and turned toward us, he said, "Good morning, students. Somebody posed the question: To do this stuff and have direct experience, do you have to have burned up all of your *samskaras*?" I didn't remember anyone asking in class, so I guessed someone had asked him privately.

He continued, "You know what *samskaras* are." It was a statement. "They are the negative subtle impressions of our past actions that are stored in *karmashaya*. That's Sanskrit for our unconscious. We'll talk more about *samskaras* and *karmashaya* another time when we talk about karma."

He walked over to one of the windows, looked out toward the Ganges, then turned back to us and said, "So the question is: Do we have to have burned up all of our negative subtle impressions that we've accumulated as a result of actions throughout our lives before we can have the direct experience of the Self, of Self-Realization? And the answer is absolutely not. No, this is one of the myths that's been floated around by some of these so-called experts, by some of these people who call themselves gurus.

"If you look at the end of chapter IV of the Yoga Sutras. In lines 27 and 28, Patanjali talks about what you do with breaches or breaks in enlightenment. The mere fact that he mentions this in the Sutras is good news because he wouldn't give an instruction if it wasn't going to happen. His answer is, like the modern twelve-step program, go back to basics and restart. It's as simple as that."

He paused. Looked at his left arm. Adjusted his watchband. Then he continued.

"Imagine you're sitting on the edge of a farmer's field. On the other side is a huge diamond and that diamond is enlightenment. If you get to that diamond, you reach enlightenment. But there's a problem: There are thousands and thousands of sleeping dogs guarding the field and the diamond. Now, the field and the sleeping dogs represent all of your karmas and *samskaras*. All of your actions and all of the negative consequences of those actions are stored in your unconscious, in *karmashaya*. But all I have to do is carefully tiptoe through this field without waking up those dogs. And if I can do that, not wake up any of the dogs, I can get to the diamond on the other side of the field. I then instantly awaken to *atman*, or *purusha*, or *Brahman,* or the brilliant sun on the right side of the diagram of consciousness. Remember that from last time?

"Here's the problem. If I go tippytoeing out into the field and just barely get into it when I awaken one of the dogs, and this dog jumps up and begins barking, and he awakens others that begin barking. What do I do? I run out of the field with dogs barking at my heels."

> *I thought of all the dogs I had encountered in India—some half-starved, ribs showing. Dogs sleeping on sidewalks and in vacant lots, but none seemed particularly friendly. Many showed signs of past fights. Crossing a field of sleeping Indian dogs would be a daunting task.*

Swami Shanti continued, "And in meditation, all of those thoughts that come into our awareness are like the barking dogs. So what we need to do is: We train our barking dogs. We purify them.

"What we do is begin with the most noisy and troublesome dogs and begin training them to be nice puppies that sleep all day. I don't have to train all of the dogs; I only have to train the most active and noisiest dogs, and then I can go tiptoeing through the field around this dog and that dog. All I have to do is get through the field without waking up the dogs. Then I can touch the diamond, get my experience of enlightenment, and when I need it again, I can come back through the field of sleeping dogs.

"And returning to the metaphor of meditation, the larger, more troublesome things that we have going on in our lives, we have to deal with them. We have to deal with some of those big troublesome issues in our lives, like maybe a nasty divorce, or a death, or anything that grabs our attention over a long period of time."

Swami Shanti paused to adjust his glasses and decided they needed cleaning. He pulled out a lens cloth from a pocket and polished each lens before continuing.

He replaced his glasses and said, "In the middle of some life issue, we say, I can't meditate—what do I do? Well, be honest. In all likelihood, is that distraction going to go away tonight for that person so that person can have a nice *samadhi*-like experience? I think not. So what does that person need to do? I think what that person needs to do is to review the *yamas* and the *niyamas*. Reflect on nonviolence, commitment to truth, maybe that person's commitment to the truth of whatever it is that is causing the distractions. Reflect on self-study and surrender. Then work with the body, work with the breath, work with the mind as best as possible. Take a walk, do some Hatha Yoga, eat some good food, and take a nice shower. Take care of yourself and just accept that tonight's meditation just might not bring *samadhi*. But you do go on with your regular meditation, just accepting that it may not be the best meditation ever. Gradually, you deal

211

with the aftermath of that relationship, or whatever, and you allow yourself to heal. Then that big growling dog doesn't cause trouble for you anymore. And it may take a year or two or three. But these things have to be dealt with one way or another before you can cross that field and reach the diamond.

"When we do that, there are other thought patterns that come forward from the mind-field. And if we gain the ability over time to sit there quietly, just as we've been practicing, and be aware of the breath, maybe following a mantra like *So-Ham* like we've been doing, and follow it into silence . . . if we are reasonably able to do that without waking up the other dogs of the unconscious mind . . . and if we can do that, well, then there comes a point where we can get glimpses of *samadhi*."

Swami Shanti looked at us, first one, then another, as if deciding whether to continue with his thought. Finally, he said, "When it happens to you— and words don't really describe it, that's why I'm saying this because what I'm going to say is a pale reflection of the experience—you see the world with clear eyes for the first time, and you wonder how you could have existed and not seen it with such clarity. It's like you've lived your whole life seeing through cloudy lenses, and now it's all clearly seen. You feel yourself simply disappear into the vastness of the universe, and you are the tree, the moon, the person next to you, and you experience the immensity of all creation, both past, present, and future, and you realize that there isn't really any past, present, or future, but an all-encompassing All. And there are no differences, no separations. Everything is a manifestation of All. Time is an illusion. Separation is an illusion."

Then he quietly said, "Till next time," picked up his things, and walked from the room. No one moved for a good five minutes.

> *When he explained it like he did, it all seemed possible. I had always thought you had to tame all the dogs or reach perfection before slipping across the field to the diamond.*

212

But what he'd said made sense. Deal with the most annoying distractions, with the immediate stuff.

Before, he had talked about the diagram of consciousness and how meditation moved things from the latent unconscious into the active unconscious, where we could deal with them. That goes along with some of my previous readings about things bubbling up from the unconscious during meditation. When something comes up, then you can deal with it. We can begin work to tame that particular barking dog.

A key to some of the more advanced meditations is to begin by recognizing thoughts simply as things that the idle mind generates, much like clouds floating in the sky. They come, and they go. Another essential practice is to begin to hear sounds simply as sounds without the mind interpreting them. See without categorizing the image. Let the thought come up and view it simply as a thought passing through awareness. It's a thought, and thoughts come and go like clouds. Don't obsess over the cloud because it's changing even as we observe it. During meditation, don't hang on to them. Let them change and let them go. And quietly slip across the field without waking the dogs.

What Swami Shanti had said at the end was very moving and very personal. I appreciated what he said, even if it sounded a bit woo-wooish. I respected what he said and the simple fact that he related something so personal to us, which I found very touching.

Chapter 30: The Nature of Guru

In one session, Rajani asked, "Can you practice without the guidance of a Guru?"

Swami Shanti stopped pacing, turned, and riveted his eyes on her. Then he said, "Yes, of course you can. And the part of what you just said I would challenge—what came out of your mouth—is quote without a Guru unquote. That's what you said, right?"

She answered, "Yes," in a timid voice, and I knew from her tone that she felt challenged, and I thought, *Here he goes again.*

Swami Shanti continued, "There's no such thing as a Guru in this tradition. What I just said is a universal truth. And it was an attempt to be respectful of other opinions and other traditions, even though they are not accurate, because some may say Gurus do exist.

"In our tradition," he said, "it is very accurately said that if a person says 'I am a Guru,' that person is not worthy of being called a guide because guru is not a person. And just because our tradition says there's no such thing as a Guru doesn't make it true. I'm not asking you to believe our tradition and reject everybody else. Listen to what I say and decide for yourself what makes sense. Don't ever mindlessly surrender yourself to anything or anybody unless what they say and do makes sense to you. And run from anyone who claims they are a Guru." To emphasize his point, he stepped forward a couple of steps.

"Over and over," he continued, "you read *gu* means darkness and *ru* means light. And *guru* is the light that dispels the darkness of ignorance. Then if that's what it's about, how is it we're so quick to turn this light that expels darkness into a Guru with a capital "G" into a person?

"'Oh, your Holiness,'" he said mockingly, "'You are a Guru.'" Then, with disdain dripping from his voice, he said, "No, you are not; you're a fraud."

"The force of guru, the light of guru, the consciousness of guru can operate through a person, but if that person claims to be 'a Guru,' then it's all a big lie."

"You're confusing me," Esther said.

He ignored Esther and continued to direct his remarks to Rajani, "And so can you do it without a Guru? I'll give you two answers, both of which are accurate. Can you do it without guru? No. Can you do it without a Guru? Yes."

Everyone in the room shifted around, obviously uncomfortable for Rajani, and I wondered what was coming next. Where was he going with this?

Swami Shanti said, "I'm going to explain how there is no conflict between those two comments. Can you do it without a human being? Yes. Can you do it without the force field of guru? No, you cannot, because guru is the force field within. There's ascending force, and there's descending force. There's the effort we put into a thing, and then there's the grace that comes and pulls us the rest of the way.

"This is how guru operates. If you do your work, you've heard it said: when you're ready, when you are prepared, guru will come. When you need it and when you're prepared and ready, guru comes from within and pulls you the rest of the way.

"So can you do it without guru? No. It is not possible. Can you do it without a Guru? Yes, of course, because you don't need a human being. But what seems to work out well for us is if we're having help and guidance from someone who has already trodden the path and through whom the gift of guru operates, then you have the best of both worlds.

"But it must be remembered that guru is operating through that person. That person is not a Guru. You still have to do the work. You still have to be prepared."

There was silence in the meditation hall. Rajani sat with a blank expression, just staring at Swami Shanti. After a long pause, he said, "And that's why you were wrong, Rajani, when you asked if you could practice without the guidance of a Guru."

Swami Shanti pulled off his cap, thoughtfully scratched his head, and, placing his cap back, continued. "Guru is a force field that operates from within. There's the effort you put into a thing, and then there's the grace that comes and pulls, or in some cases pushes, you the rest of the way."

Again, he paused, rolled up his sleeves, and placed his hands on his hips before continuing. "Those multistaged rockets that they use to fire astronauts into orbit. How do they get them up there? It takes the flaming effort of one of those huge rockets to get almost out of the earth's gravity. Then another stage gives them the final push to break free of gravity. And this is the way that guru works. If you do your work, if you have the fire of *tapas*, if you've done your work and the work's done and you think you can't do anything more, that's when guru comes from within and pulls you the rest of the way."

The room remained quiet. Then I broke the silence. "This sounds an awful lot like what I grew up learning about God's grace. Is that what you're saying? Guru is the gift, not the giver."

"You could put it that way, I suppose," he said almost begrudgingly.

"Let me tell you a true story about Gurus. There was a man at one of the famous temples on the upper Ganges, high up in the mountains from here. A group of Americans had gone there searching for enlightenment. And they met this man at this temple who seemed full of wisdom, and they brought him to the States. He was supported by these people, and he gave all sorts of talks and lectures. He became more and more well-known. At some point, someone had given me one of his cards he'd had printed with a picture of himself in the Himalayas with a pious look on his face. I showed it to a well-known swami and asked if he recognized the man. And the swami laughed and said, 'Oh yes, of course. He is the maintenance guy at a temple in Uttarkashi.' This man was not known for any spiritual accomplishments or study. And he certainly wasn't an expert on scriptures or Sanskrit. But he was passing himself off as a Guru."

After lunch, I used my free time to find a secluded spot on the ghat, where I sat and mulled what Swami Shanti had said about the distinction between Guru with a capital "G" and guru in lowercase, about Guru as a person and guru as a "force field" from within.

> *Swami Shanti was correct in what he'd said about guru and people who put themselves forward as Gurus or allow that to happen. However! Rajani had unknowingly found his Achilles heel. I felt bad for her because she was stunned and, from her demeanor, quite taken aback by his response. I talked with her later, and she still felt hurt "by his rudeness." Her friend Siti was angry with him. It was sad but understandable.*

> *I felt embarrassed for him because he seemed unaware of how he came across to the others. Or perhaps he didn't care. Only three of the eleven of us in the retreat were from the States. I wondered to what extent his behavior reinforced their ideas of a stereotypically overbearing American.*

> *However, what Swami Shanti had said about not trusting people who put themselves forward as a Guru resonated with me. It's so important to learn to trust your intuition. The MBSR teachings had said the same thing. All of these teachings should empower a person to learn to trust*

themselves and not surrender to the machinations of a supposed Guru-person.

I've always been suspicious of people who have come to India or found some person at home they begin to revere as an enlightened person. The world is full of frauds. Khushwant Singh's book Gods and Godmen of India *details some of these false Gurus. Swami Shanti's story is also a case in point. I was reminded of the weekend priest at the temple in Kumbakonam who didn't know his temple's history, and then there was the swami who confessed to bombing the train, killing seventy people. There had also been an instance when I was with Mr. Jameson in Munnar. We'd stopped at a popular tourist site, and a man dressed like Shiva with wild hair and a faux tiger skin wrapped around his shoulders had approached me. Mr. Jameson had run him off, telling me he was a fraud who leeched off gullible tourists. India may be the home of many enlightened individuals, but it is also home to a number of frauds.*

Swami Shanti had said guru was the power moving through the teacher. That guru was the power that nudged a person toward trusting their intuition. He described it as an inner awakening, an inner push. And that made sense.

I got this distinction between having a Guru as a personal teacher and guru as an awakening to an insight or a teaching. It can seem like a minor point, but it is extremely important because a lot of people get sucked into the concept of needing a Guru as a physical person. This has caused many people to turn over their lives and fortunes to an individual or an ideology and get hurt. There are several instances where the founding Guru of some yoga center got run out because he preached celibacy but had sex with his followers.

Thinking about what Swami Shanti had said, I realized there were many instances where the power of guru operated. These were turning points in my life: some were minor, but many were major ones.

The power of guru had certainly moved me out of that affair. It's easy to say the affair awakened something in me and let it go at that. But in a real sense, I came to feel capable of being loved, as much of a cliché as it sounds, and that changed the trajectory of my life, moving me toward Diana and yoga.

All of the Buddhas in my life had moved me along my path. They were bringers of light, my gurus. They were the bringers of gifts, of serendipitous discoveries. They were the bringers of grace that helped guide me along my journey. I have had teachers who have said something to the effect that if I found what was said to be true and relevant to my journey, well and good, but if not, then that was okay too. In other words, if it fits, wear it; if not, don't.

A lot of things had flowed from the hitchhiking trip. The power of guru had worked through many people, situations, and circumstances on that trip. I was touched by the kindnesses of strangers, their rides, the salmon dinner, and the casual remark about a book that had helped me make meaningful connections. There was the Vietnam vet who'd got me thinking about my experiences and how they fit into the depression I'd experienced. And there was the comment by the long-haul truck driver about whether Castaneda's books were fact or fiction—what difference does it make; it's the meaning we give it that counts. Years later, when I watched the Bill Moyers series with Joseph Campbell, Moyers asked, "What is the meaning of life?" And Campbell answered, "What is the meaning of a peanut? It's the meaning you give it that is important."

But it's easy to forget the other part of what Swami Shanti had said this morning about being open and ready, which circles back to serendipity. I must be open and ready; otherwise, I miss it entirely. I see serendipity as the power of guru. I need to remain open and attentive.

Chapter 31: More Than Closing the Eyes

Each morning in the meditation hall, my fellow retreatants and I went to the same tiny piece of real estate we had claimed as our own that first day. We set up our mats, cushions, and blankets the same way each morning. We were so territorial, so possessive, so habitual.

We sat quietly until Swami Shanti entered the room, his orange robes flapping. He went to the whiteboard and wrote "*Howzit.*" Angie laughed at his use of this South African slang greeting.

Then Swami Shanti asked, "Does everybody know about the *indriyas*? The *indriyas* and *pratyahara*, the fifth limb of the Yoga Sutras' eight limbs."

There were mutterings around the room. Someone said something about *pratyahara*, the withdrawal of the senses. But no one said anything about *indriyas*.

Swami Shanti pressed on. "*Pratyahara* is the fifth limb of yoga's Eight Limbs of Practice. It means withdrawal of the senses. Some people think all they have to do is simply close their eyes. Maybe jam earplugs in or something. These people have completely missed the point.

"The *indriyas* are the five incoming senses and the five outgoing senses," he said. "The incoming senses are the five cognitive senses, the ones that bring in knowledge through *manas*. Remember, *manas* is your lower animal intelligence as opposed to your higher functioning intelligence. In other words, *manas* is the more reactive part of your brain.

"Anyone? What are the five cognitive senses?" he waited a beat or two, but when no answer came, he pressed on. "Hearing, smelling, tasting, touching, feeling. Now, what are the outgoing senses?" he asked.

He pushed back his knit cap and ran his hands over his bald head before continuing. No one stepped in to fill the momentary silence. He slid the cap back into place and then continued. "The outgoing senses, the senses of action, are eliminating, procreating, moving, grasping, smelling. Information comes in through one of the five cognitive senses, and it's up to *buddhi*, the discriminating mind, to process information and send it out to one or more of the proper senses of action.

"Think of the *indriyas* as doors—five entrance doors and five exit doors to *manas*, the mind. Our job is to train *manas*, the keeper of our *indriyas*, our entrance doors and our exit doors. And how do we do this? We do this with our *buddhi*, with our higher functioning mind. *Buddhi* first has to know what's going on. Then it has to learn to control what comes in and what goes out the doors through the senses. And who's the one who's going to do the training—me or someone else? That's the big question you have to answer for yourself. Is your higher-functioning mind going to be in charge? Or maybe your lower mind, *manas*, is going to be calling the shots, and you're just along for the ride. Maybe you're going to let your ego, *ahamkara*, run the show. Or maybe, like so many people, you let *chitta*, your unconscious mind, be in charge. It's your choice. You could even decide to turn it over to another person. Maybe somebody who calls himself a Guru."

I didn't want to take his last comment as a slam against Rajani for her question the other day about the need for a Guru but rather to see it as a reminder that each of us needed to control our own lives. But before he continued, I caught his glance in Rajani's direction.

"But," he said, "to be able to make the right decision, you have to learn to watch the mind's functioning through its actions, and a good way to do that is to begin by observation of gestures and body language. We are pretty good at reading other people's body language. We have to get good at reading our own.

"There's a lag," he said, "between the conscious and unconscious mind. Neurological tests show the unconscious mind 'knows' before it passes on to the conscious 'mind.' Have you ever had something just pop out of your mouth before you realized it?"

My mind went back to that evening years before when my daughter Anne and I had been talking about our day at that yoga convention. Then suddenly, the words "I've been thinking about doing a teacher training program" had popped unbidden from my mouth.

Swami Shanti continued, "This shows how the unconscious mind is the controller of actions, even though we like to believe our conscious mind is in charge. There is also a lag between the conscious mind being aware and the actions it directs. And this lag is where we need to do the work to train the mind.

"And maybe we don't exert control over our senses. Maybe we are unwilling to withdraw our incoming and outgoing senses. That is the dividing line between those who will experience the depths of meditation and those who will merely achieve some degree of mental relaxation, which is fine if that's what you really want. Only those who are willing to do the work will experience the true depths of meditation. And that work involves sense withdrawal, *pratyahara*. Some even write books about meditation but have only experienced the surface levels of physical relaxation. In the current popular culture, I'm afraid to say, but it's true, meditation and relaxation have become interchangeable terms.

"A good place to begin is to close the doors of the senses of action. You've got an itch? Withdraw the sense of action that wants to scratch the itch. Have the urge to move? Let it pass. Don't move."

Swami Shanti surveyed us, making sure he had our attention before continuing. "As you begin the cultivation of *pratyahara*," he said, "you may hear sounds around you but you will learn to hear them simply as sounds.

Don't say, 'Oh, that's a robin outside,' or, 'Oh, who slammed that door?' What I'm telling you is the sounds may come in, but we don't engage with them. We don't interpret them. We learn that they are simply sounds, nothing more. What you don't want is to let your mind get on that thought-train, because when it does, your mental-conductor punches the ticket, and your mind goes off on a holiday journey.

"We have to teach our senses so that we can do this thing called withdrawal of the senses, *pratyahara*. The thing that makes it difficult is not trying to do it. The thing that makes it easy is actually doing it."

> *What he meant was once I've trained my mind not to react immediately but to give myself a brief pause beforehand, it becomes easier. But if I don't do that, it causes me a bunch of hurt. I think that's what he meant when he said, "The thing that makes it difficult is not doing it." So I mentally substituted "makes problems for me" for "makes it difficult." Another thing he said was that sitting around and thinking about it makes it seem difficult, but once I jump in and do it, it becomes easier. It's easy to think myself right out of doing things like that. And again, I thought of the woman meditating at Shravanabela Gola with the fly on her face. If she could do it, I certainly could learn to do it, too.*

Rajani raised her hand and said, "My husband won't support me in my practices."

Carlos nodded his agreement and said, "That was why my wife and I split up. She couldn't understand my need to practice either."

"I don't want it to come to that," Rajani said.

Swami Shanti just said, "Be aware."

Thankfully, he didn't let their remarks turn our session into a Dear Abby moment. But I did wonder why they brought this up in the first place because neither of them followed up on it.

Diana had been convinced I wanted to go live in an ashram, and nothing I could do or say seemed to change her view. When I finished this retreat and returned home, I could apply what yoga had taught me to build a solid and meaningful relationship with Louise.

Then he was back to his topic. "*Pratyahara*, the fifth limb of yoga, is about withdrawal of the senses. What it's trying to tell us is that for meditation to move us in the direction of *samadhi* or enlightenment, we must begin to close the doors of the *indriyas*—the senses. Our eyes may be open or closed. Our ears may be plugged or unplugged. We are breathing, but the sense of smell is not registering. Our skin is not feeling. Our tongue is not tasting. *Buddhi*, our discriminating mind, has closed the doors to these sensations.

"You know," he said, "most people close their eyes to meditate, but you don't have to. Some teach you to sit with eyes half-open with a soft focus. Then, from the start, you are working to let go of the sense of sight."

Swami Shanti scanned the room. "Okay. It's time for meditation," he said and rang the meditation bell.

I readjusted my cushion and spread a blanket on the hard floor to cushion my ankles. I pulled myself into an erect posture, opened my chest, and breathed fully and deeply as my eyelids closed off that sensory doorway.

Letting go of the senses was a form of nonattachment. Swami Shanti had said earlier that some people rebel about letting go of sensory inputs. I knew that if Shravanabela Gola woman could do it, so could I.

227

Chapter 32: Who's Piloting Your Ship?

One morning after breakfast, I let my walk on the ghat be a walking meditation. On their way to town, I nodded to a couple of women in colorful sarees and was startled by a flock of green parrots that erupted from a nearby tree. I had work to do with my *indriyas*. When I got to the meditation hall, someone had opened the windows wide, and the room was filled with a chorus of bird and monkey sounds. What a great way to begin a day.

At the previous session, Swami Shanti asked us to start on our own that morning and do about thirty minutes of yoga postures. Half of us were teachers, so we helped the others with little mini-classes.

We finished and sat on our cushions, waiting for Swami Shanti to arrive. When he did, he wrote the day's greetings on the whiteboard: "*Bonjour les étudiants.*"

"Good morning," he said. "I hope you all had a good practice this morning and are feeling ready for a guided meditation."

A murmur of approval was his answer.

"We'll do the Sixty-One Points meditation," he said.

We arranged our places for a reclining meditation. The floor was hard, so I rolled my blanket to provide a cushion under the back of my neck and head, then stretched it out on my mat.

When we were settled, Swami Shanti said, "Now close your eyes, let your tongue rest on the roof of your mouth, teeth slightly apart." He paused for a breath or two. "Now let your awareness come to rest on the forehead. Be aware of the forehead. You may experience it as flesh, bone, or as a sensation, as an awareness. You may see it, or you may not." He paused for a few breaths. "Now remind yourself of your ability to move but that you are choosing not to move. You can move but choose not to move."

Then, in his smooth, buttery voice, he said, "You may see light, a glow, or a firmament of stars. Whatever you see is alright. Be aware of your throat. You may experience it physically, or you may experience it as an awareness or as a sensation.

"You may see a light, a glow, or a constellation of stars, or you may not. However, you experience it is okay. Now be aware of your right shoulder—flesh, bone, a sensation, or an awareness."

Then he moved through the body, matching one breath with each of the next fifty-eight points in the body. Each breath was a new point in the body. My attention followed his voice around my body, ending back at my forehead. When he finished, he brought us back into a sitting pose.

Swami Shanti walked slowly back and forth in front of the room. He paused a moment and looked down at the floor, lost in thought. After a breath or two, he turned toward us and said, "Earlier, we talked about the *indriyas*—the senses of knowledge and action. The incoming senses of knowledge are smell, touch, hearing, seeing, and tasting. Remember? Information comes in, and something has to be done with it before we take action. Yoga philosophy has five senses of action: movement, holding, speaking, reproduction, and elimination. Think of these senses as doors. Five doors coming in and five doors going out."

Outside, a monkey screeched. The gardener had probably thrown a rock at it.

Then he said, "Yoga divides the working mind into four. A part of the mind yoga calls *manas* takes the incoming senses in. Then there's conscious and unconscious memory, and yoga calls this *chitta*. Next, there's what yoga calls *ahamkara*, literally, the I-am-ness, or the ego, if you will. Finally, and most importantly for the purposes of this discussion, there's *buddhi*, what we call the executive functioning part of the brain. This is the part that knows, decides, judges, and discriminates."

He used his remote to put a diagram up on the screen that showed the four functioning parts of the mind according to yoga (*Slide 32-1*).

"Now," he said, "let's look at this diagram more closely. We'll look at *manas* first. Its job is to direct the senses of knowing, the incoming senses, and the senses of acting, the outgoing senses. It does this by kicking the incoming information from the senses up to *buddhi* for a decision on which action-sense will react."

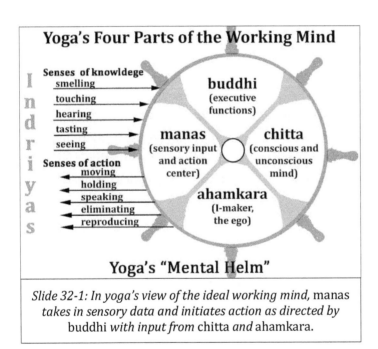

Slide 32-1: In yoga's view of the ideal working mind, manas takes in sensory data and initiates action as directed by buddhi with input from chitta and ahamkara.

"You're with me so far?" He paced back and forth as he talked. "Let's imagine for a moment how these four working parts of the mind might work if Hans were to decide to go for a walk. Hans' legs might send a message to *manas* saying, 'Let's go for a walk.' *Manas* might send the request to *buddhi*, where it's considered; then *buddhi* might send word to *manas* for Hans' legs to take him for a walk or maybe not to take him for a walk.

"Let's look at the process in a more refined manner. Let's suppose when *buddhi* gets the request from *manas* to go for a walk, *buddhi* checks with *chitta*, the conscious and unconscious mind. *Chitta* considers the request and sends up to *buddhi*. 'Hey, last time we went through the woods on our walk, we fell, so this time, let's walk on the sidewalk.' *Buddhi* agrees and sends the okay to *manas* for the suggested walk but on the sidewalk. Then *manas* sends the appropriate action messages to the legs, and Hans is ready for his walk down the sidewalk."

He paused at this point, his attention momentarily caught by a cuckoo that landed in a tree just outside the window. It called once, then flew off.

"Wow. That was nice," he said, glancing toward the sound. Then he continued. "Now let's imagine *ahamkara* says, 'Hey, I don't like that way. It's too dark. Let's walk past Susie's house. Maybe she'll invite us in.' So *buddhi* scratches *buddhi's* head and comes up with a route that's favorable to the three other parts of Hans' mind, and off Hans goes for his walk."

We murmur agreement.

Then he said, "So what happens if the conversation completely bypasses *buddhi*? *Chitta* just jumps in and says directly to *Manas*, 'We're going to the ice cream store the third time today.' And maybe *ahamkara*, the I-maker, says, 'Maybe Susie will be there this time.'"

He stopped in the middle of the room, turned to us, and said, "You can see if *chitta* is calling the shots; the unconscious mind is promoting its own agenda. And the same is true for *ahamkara*, the ego. Each has its own agenda, which may run counter to the general overall good."

His eyes moved to each of us until he finally said, "Let's look at how this works from a different angle. Let's imagine that our body is a ship that is underway through the Ocean of Life to deliver precious cargo, our True Self, safely to a distant port. The ship's captain, *buddhi*, must navigate through treacherous waters to get to port. To do that, the captain, *buddhi*, must direct his commands to *manas*, represented in our story by both the helmsman, who controls the direction of our ship, and the lee helmsman, controlling its speed."

He paused a moment, then continued. "Now, the seas are stormy," he said, "it's raining hard, and the ship's rolling badly. Memory (active and latent unconscious), *chitta*, who's on the bridge with the captain, says, 'Captain, the last time we were in this kind of weather, we all got seasick. Maybe it would be good to change course and speed to accommodate for the weather and seas.' But I-maker, *ahamkara*, says, 'Captain, you're a good seaman. You can easily get us through this by taking a shortcut through that area of shoals. That will get us out of the bad weather. Just change course and kick it up to full speed. That might even get us into port a little quicker and save some money, too.'

"And our captain, *buddhi*, says, "I think, for now, I'll hold course and speed. But I'll check the barometer regularly to see what the weather's doing. Then if I need to, I'll decide whether or not to make adjustments."

Swami Shanti paced back and forth across the room before he continued. "But let's suppose the captain, *buddhi*, has had a few too many and maybe is dozing off in the Captain's chair. So *chitta* makes the suggestion to change course and speed to accommodate for the weather and gets no response from the captain, *buddhi*. Then *chitta* and the I-maker, *ahamkara*, get into a shouting match and, on their own, give contradictory orders to *manas,* helmsman and lee helmsman."

He stopped pacing and looked each of us in the eye before continuing. "I'm giving you tools here to monitor your own behavior and to help you decide who's going to pilot your ship. It's up to you. Do you want to protect your Self and your ship and get safely to port or not? Your choice," he said. "It's up to you. You decide how *buddhi* is going to navigate your ship through the Ocean of Life. It's entirely up to you.

"Now let's take a short break."

I sat for a few minutes to let it all sink in. I would have to go over my notes to fully digest what he had just said.

> *What Swami Shanti had said about piloting my ship made sense. For much of my life, I hadn't put* buddhi *in charge.* Chitta, *my unconscious, pretty much ran the show. I realized awareness was vital. Paying attention and being present and focused were the keys to taking charge and piloting my ship. I needed to check whether I was letting my ego or my unconscious choose the course of my life. They needed to be advisors, not the ones giving the orders. There are times when* buddhi *needs to let intuition or gut instinct take the reins, but only under supervision.*

> *Years ago when my father taught me to ride a bike, I'd exhaust myself by riding as fast as I could, which prompted him to ask me which one of us was in control—me or the bike. The sidewalk in front of our house sloped slightly downhill to the corner. At the corner, the side street was gravel with a wide ditch between the street and its sidewalk. One day, riding as fast as I could down the sidewalk in front of our house, I was going too fast to negotiate the turn at the corner. I had a choice: hit a tree or a ditch and land in the gravel. I chose the tree and bent the fork. While a welder fixed the fork, my father cautioned me first to learn to ride and control the bike at a slow speed, then to work on speed. It was a hard lesson.*

I think something similar works here. Taking charge of my ship means I start small, just get the practice started, and then refine the practice. It's all about being present. Baba Ram Dass wrote a book on the subject: Be Here Now. *Those three words encapsulate the idea completely. But it's also about remembering where the ship is going and what the goal is. Suppose I want to control my weight. Do I unconsciously let* chitta *go ahead and eat another cookie at lunch? Do I listen to* manas *(sensory input) and say, 'Oh, that last one tasted so good, "I'll have another"? Or maybe I let* ahamkara *(ego) decide, "Having this other cookie supports my idea that I can eat anything I want without consequences." But then I should let* buddhi *(my higher intellect) collect those messages from* manas, chitta, *and* ahamkara *and decide what's in the best interest of the goal to keep my weight under control.* Buddhi *needs to ask, "Does this thought, word, or deed move me toward my goals or away from them?"*

Seeking perfection is a sure road to failure because it's easy to quit when I see that I am a long way from perfect and because perfection is an unattainable goal. Transformation happens when I change a habit, which only occurs when I value persistence over perfection.

Chapter 33: Avoiding the Barking Dogs

After the break, and before he had a chance to begin, I raised my hand to tell Swami Shanti that after the Sixty-One Points meditation, I had been completely unsure about my identity—who I was, where I was. I had never experienced anything like that before.

"That gives you an idea," he said, "of what it's like to be conscious without the identity of what it is to be Don. When you came back, the characteristics stored in *chitta*, your unconscious, didn't come along right away. And the sensory inputs to *manas*, your lower, reactive mind, that would have tried to fulfill its desires by awakening from *chitta*, by awakening the active and latent unconscious mind, hadn't awakened yet. But there was enough *buddhi* intelligence there, enough of the executive functioning part of the mind there, but the intelligence at that moment was not linked to the personal traits that define Don. This is a bit like what *samadhi* is. There's no Don in the fourth state of *turiya*—in *samadhi*.

"Remember when we talked about *turiya* in connection with OM? *Turiya* represents that fourth state of silence after the sounds of A-U-M. Remember?

"Everything that defines Don is still asleep. Remember when we talked earlier about the mind-field and the sleeping dogs? A big part is not just the fact that those dogs represent our attractions and aversions, but they are ready to snap at us. They can also be our identities and our personalities.

"Swami Agrajananda said our habits are our personalities. Who am I at this conscious level? I am a composite of *manas, chitta, ahamkara,* and *buddhi*. I'm a composite of my reactive, animal mind, my unconscious, my ego, and my executive functioning mind. You need to establish a friendship with your mind. Who's talking? And who are you talking to? Well, it's the conscious, Waking State of yogi Don. Yogi Don is talking to

Don's unconscious. Yogi Don is not talking to the conscious Waking State Don or Don, the wallpaper man. When Don, the wallpaper man, plans a job, the latent wallpaper man comes forward. When Don sits down to meditate, the wallpaper man recedes behind the veil between the conscious and unconscious Don. Don, the wallpaper man, recedes back across the dotted line in the symbol of consciousness chart (*Slide 33-1*), and the meditative Don comes forward. It's like folders on your hard drive. You pull up the folder you need for that particular occasion. And with each one, there is an associated *manas, chitta, ahamkara,* and *buddhi*—each folder is a composite of the working mind."

Swami Shanti listed several identities for a person on the whiteboard and asked, "Which one of those clusters of identities does not involve the use of *manas, ahamkara, chitta,* or *buddhi*?" What is the job of the person as a parent? To raise kids. Et cetera, et cetera. What is the task of Don, the Seeker, the *Sadhaka*? It is to be aware of all those things—the four parts of the mind—on both the conscious and unconscious levels. That's the job of Don, the Seeker.

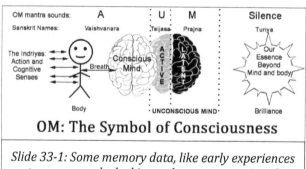

OM: The Symbol of Consciousness

Slide 33-1: Some memory data, like early experiences or traumas, are locked in our latent unconscious but can be retrieved and moved into active unconscious, where it becomes accessible to the conscious mind, and can be dealt with.

"Now, in this slide (*Slide 33-1*), you can see that there is an overlap of the conscious mind and the active unconscious mind. There's a dotted line between the conscious and active unconscious mind—between the grayed part of the brain and the black protion. In other words, we can pull up things from our active unconscious and bring things into conscious awareness as needed. Things in our latent unconscious are more or less housed there. Things like early childhood memories and traumatic events are all things that drive our unconscious behaviors. Sometimes, in therapy or deep digging, these memories may move into consciousness, but mostly, they stay there, driving behavior in ways we don't suspect. Things do move back and forth. Nothing is static. Memories are recalled and repressed.

"And as memories are recalled, the boundary line between the active conscious mind and the latent unconscious will expand. Don's active unconscious will get bigger, and gradually, the unconscious becomes conscious. So Don the Seeker becomes more aware as the active unconscious expands.

"Simply experiment with yourself. There's an experimenter experimenting with somebody called yourself. You are talking to your Self. Don, the *Sadhaka*, the Seeker, is having a conversation with the totality of Don. Because at that point, he is, in all likelihood, not aware of Don, the parent. All of this totality of unconsciousness, the totality of *antahkarana*, that is, the whole of the mind, as a nonspecific identity, is being talked to. Therefore, Don, in the Waking State, can say, 'Mind, why are you this way or that way?' The Seeker is having a conversation with the totality of the selves.

"Let's say Don wants to go to the park and learn to play cricket. What he does is carve out a new little file folder on his mental hard drive, and he gives it the name 'Cricket Player.' And over time, he fills up that file. For the last few days here at the ashram, we've been adding to our 'Meditation File.'"

Julia asked: "Is it the role of the *Sadhaka* to make sure they don't wake up?"

"Yeah. Eventually, that's what makes you a Master. The word 'master' means master of your own inner process. However, the term 'Self-Realization' does not mean total mastery. It means you've mastered enough of this so you can traverse the mind-field without waking up those dogs. You're allowing the *indriyas*, the *manas*, *chitta*, and *ahamkara* to recede back into the latent unconscious.

"And in so doing, all of the barking dogs are asleep, and you can slip past and cross the mind-field to reach the diamond on the other side. That's the realization of the Self, but it's not mastery yet. And what do you do after you've reached the other side? You do the laundry and wash the dishes. That is, you keep on doing what you were doing before. Life goes on. Swami Agrajananda was admonished by his teacher against his singing, painting, and playing the *vina* on Indian radio—it's a dissipation of energy. It was a distraction for him at that point in his life.

"And this is the same with relation to sex. The admonition in the Yoga Sutras is really against the dissipation of energy, of the sexual energy. It's not a prohibition against sex as such. The trap is that you realize or acknowledge you have a talent, and then redirect your energies, and end up dropping your *sadhana*, your practice. Don't lose sight of the fact that the energy, the force, the *shakti* is working through you—these aren't powers you own, but you are a conduit, a channel for the energy. And it's easy for that channel to get blocked.

"So who's talking to who? You're training a little part of the mind to talk to the rest of the mind. I—the conscious waking-state me—am talking to the rest of the totality."

> I continued to mull Swami Shanti's question about who was piloting my ship. Back in the 1970s, spontaneity had been all the rage. We were urged to be more spontaneous and let it all hang out. In retrospect, that's turning the ship over to a drunken helmsman and a drunken lee helmsman. It also

runs counter to what Jung said about taking conscious control of our lives, moving the unconscious controllers into conscious awareness. Otherwise, we continue to undermine our own best efforts and go where the wind blows us.

The way to begin that process is to start small, with the easy things. Keep the goal in mind, and let buddhi *captain the ship. Am I going to have an extra dessert? Am I going to continue smoking, drinking, taking drugs? What do you think,* buddhi*? Unconscious* chitta *says to go ahead and have it.* Ahamkara, *the ego, says nobody's going to tell me what to do.* Buddhi *has to decide whether this action leads to my goals or not.*

Even getting close to samadhi *never seemed like a possibility, but apparently I had touched it with that meditation when I'd thought I was disoriented. His file-folder metaphor made sense. The Everyday-Don mental file folder didn't open right away.*

I understood that whatever role I was engaged in in the conscious world, that "file folder" would open with its set of unconscious inputs, ego structures, and demands to help me function in that role. Each one would call up what was needed from the active and latent unconscious. And then, when I sat down to meditate, all of the working or waking-world identities would slip into the background, those "file folders" would close, and the "me" folder marked "meditator" would open.

As I do the work of meditating, of allowing things to move from the latent unconscious to the active unconscious where they are accessible, I'm doing the work that Swami Shanti is talking about, which is the same thing that Jung talked about when he said that until we make the unconscious

conscious, the unconscious will direct our lives, and we will call it fate. Yoga is helping me move memory data from the latent unconscious to the active unconscious, where it is accessible to my active conscious mind.

An example of that process, though not particularly deep, does show how the process works. The first time I gave blood, I fainted and fell to the floor. I forgot about that incident, and the next time, the same thing happened. Then I stopped giving blood. One day after meditation, I made a connection to an experience I'd had in the second grade. I was hospitalized with a life-threatening, systemic infection that involved swollen lymph nodes in my neck. After two weeks of penicillin injections, the doctor came to my room to lance and drain the swelling in my neck. He applied a large bandage, which broke soon after he left the room, soaking my bed in blood. Once I brought that traumatic experience into my conscious awareness and connected it to fainting as a blood donor, I was able to give blood without fainting. I changed my apparent fate. I had moved memory data from the latent unconscious into the active unconscious, where it became accessible to my conscious mind. This is exactly what Jung was talking about: I made my unconscious conscious.

I was glad to hear Swami Shanti say the Yoga Sutras didn't prohibit sex. What it talked about, he'd said, was the dissipation of energy. The wise use of energy, as Donna Farhi put it in Yoga Mind, Body & Spirit. *Today's times differ from when Patanjali wrote down the* Yoga Sutras. *Then, yoga was practiced only by men who lived in caves as hermits. For them, it would have been a binary choice: sex or no sex. And if we remember that* yama's *major teaching is a prohibition against harming, then it's natural that this would also be true when it comes to sexual energy. Use it wisely, not to control others, but as an energetic exchange between adults whose consent has been mutually and freely given.*

Thinking about sex this way reminded me of my visit to the temples at Khajuraho and the erotic sculptures. Instead of thinking about sex as procreation, if I thought about it as energy and the interaction of energy between adults, I could better understand the depictions at Khajuraho. They were displayed to extol the energy aspect of sex, whereas the woman with the scorpion on her thigh was a warning about how it can hijack me from my spiritual path.

Chapter 34: Spiritual Ignorance

When Swami Shanti entered the room, he wore his usual maroon pants, matching untucked long-sleeved maroon shirt, and a Mandarin collar. The usual maroon knit cap sat atop his head. He looked sharp. Slung over his shoulder was a large cloth bag in a matching maroon color. On the whiteboard, he wrote, "Good morning, students."

"Today," he said, "we're going to talk about ignorance—spiritual ignorance. Ignorance as in ignoring, not paying attention, being without knowledge, or being unaware. This ignorance is not synonymous with being stupid."

"I'm talking about *avidya*, Sanskrit for spiritual ignorance. Ignorance in the sense of turning our attention away from knowledge."

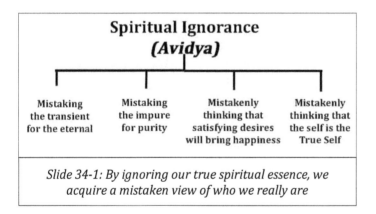

Slide 34-1: By ignoring our true spiritual essence, we acquire a mistaken view of who we really are

He put a slide on the screen (*Slide 34-1*). "The Yoga Sutras," he said, "identify four types or sources of spiritual ignorance or *avidya*. Because of our human ability to forget who and what we really are, we mistakenly confuse the ephemeral with the everlasting, the temporal with the eternal. We are confused and see perfection and purity where there is only imperfection and impurity. We mistakenly think that by satisfying our desires, we will live happily ever after. And finally, we mistake our lowercase self for our capitalized True Self. This spiritual ignorance, *avidya*, causes us to be shortsighted and make poor life choices.

"The first one is pretty easy to understand. Everything changes. We all know that, but do we act that way? We all know the answer to that one. The answer is a big NO. Everything changes. Nothing lasts. But we act like it will and make life decisions based on that assumption.

"Nothing in this world is pure—there are no absolutes—everything contains some sort of flaw. Some Japanese artisans intentionally put an imperfection in their work as a reminder that nothing is perfect and there is beauty in imperfection.

"We think that our desires will lead us to happiness, when in fact they only lead us to misery because life is change. What we thought was absolute and immutable today changes tomorrow and is no more."

Then he turned his back to us, bent over, and fiddled with something in the bag he'd brought. When he turned back to us, he was wearing a Richard Nixon Halloween mask. Holding his arms up overhead, his fingers in a "V," he said, "I am Richard Nixon."

From behind the mask, he repeated, "I say to you, 'I am Richard Nixon.'" He dropped his arms and said, "And what do you think? At first, you might smile and wait for the punch line of the joke. What if I said it again and again, 'I am Richard Nixon.' What if you came to discover that I *really* believed I was Richard Nixon? You would probably think I was crazy and want to have me locked up. Yet this is exactly what we do with many aspects of our lives and our relationships to the world's objects. We identify with them and mistakenly think this role is who I really am."

He took off the mask and laid it aside.

246

"This is a form of *avidya*, a veil that keeps us from seeing what really is. Spiritual ignorance prevents us from seeing clearly. We come from a country, and we say we are that country. We say, 'I am American,' or 'I am Indian,' et cetera. We follow a certain path or teacher and say, 'I am Buddhist, Christian, Hindu, Jew, or Muslim.' We say, 'I am a daughter, son, father, mother, sister, or brother.' We say, 'I am the doer of this or that action; I am good or bad; I am happy or sad.'

"None of these are ultimately 'who' I am. One who intuits the true meaning or idea of 'who I am' is beyond all of these. That person has begun the journey of seeing beyond the spiritual ignorance called *avidya*, and that person is on the journey to the realization of the True Self, by whatever name you call that, whether *purusha*, *atman*, Self, soul, or something else. It is a journey of yoga meditation and contemplation that leads one from ignorance or forgetfulness or *avidya* of the not-self to know who we truly are. An eternal being, a spirit dressed up in a body, as the author Mary Oliver puts it."

Swami Shanti asked, "What's the *avidya* trap we fall into about the body? We know it's a false identity, but what's the mistake we accidentally made?"

Esther said, "We think we'll live forever."

Swami Shanti said, "We simply forget that the body's temporary. We all know it, but we pretend otherwise. When you go to a funeral—when you were young, and your first grandparent died, and you went to the funeral, did you think that was going to happen to you? Isn't this what young people think only happens to old people but not to them? That's *avidya*.

"Do any of you enjoy romantic comedy? I do. And what does the couple always do at the end of the movie?"

I said, "They get together."

And everybody chimed in and said, " . . . and they live happily ever after."

Swami Shanti asked, "Is it true?"

All, "No."

"How do marriages end?" Swami Shanti asked.

All, "Various ways—in separation of one sort or another."

"By divorce or death," Swami Shanti said. "I don't think there are any other options. Are there any? The marriage is temporary, but on your wedding day you think, and what you see in the happily-ever-after movie is, everyone lives happily ever after that. Let's be honest with ourselves. Isn't it true that when you watch that movie or experience that in life, or watch one of your friends get married, or watch one of your children get married, isn't there part of you that sees what is going on and thinks this is not really going to end?"

Jackie interjected, "I never have seen it that way. The day I got married . . ."

Swami Shanti interrupted her, "Can you not find . . ." Jackie was about to interrupt him, but he cut her short. "I'm asking you a question. Can you not find in yourself any inclination towards what we're talking about?" His voice dropped, and his eyes seemed to narrow. I thought, *Oh my God. Here he goes again.*

Jackie looked straight at him and said, "When I was a child, I watched the fairy tales . . ."

Swami Shanti cut her off again. "You're the exception, Jackie. And I sincerely . . . I sincerely invite you to explore within because I think you will find that you, like the rest of us, are subject to *avidyas*. I think you will discover that."

248

Jackie stammered as she once more tried to interrupt Swami Shanti, "...uh, well, but..." But once again, he cut her off. I could tell she was fuming inside and wanted desperately to lash out at him, but she held her tongue.

He continued, "...but if you simply say, 'Oh, no. I've always known that it ends.' That, of course, is a true statement. But is anyone in here actually so deluded that you literally, yes, literally, think that a marriage is eternal? That it's going to last forever? Intellectually, we know it won't. Here, what *avidya* is talking about, what it's asking, is that we look at ourselves and at what we call our autopilot—our automatic response in life. And if we're going to seek Self-Realization, we have to find this autopilot thing in ourselves. We have to find this tendency, like it or not, because it's there."

His eyes drilled into Jackie's, and he continued. "This is just one example of temporary and eternal. The day that you moved into your house, did you literally sit there ... I mean, did you actually sit there and become aware of the day that house was going to burn down or the day a bulldozer was going to flatten it to the ground and put up a new building? Did you think of that? Or were you looking at how you were going to set up your living room and bedroom and kitchen and all that? I'm not saying this to be mean; I'm really not. I'm really just saying these things so you can think about this and give yourself an answer. And if you are so clear of *avidya*, if you are so far advanced spiritually that you don't see these things and you don't experience these things, then we have no business being here together because you're already an enlightened sage. Your journey is done. Really, truly, if you see life in that way, there's nothing left for you to do. There is no *sadhana*, no practice. Then you've become enlightened. You're like Ramana Maharshi; you've become spontaneously enlightened, and you should open your ashram and begin teaching these things to others."

I could tell that Jackie was quietly fuming. She held her tongue, but I was sure she was very close to a real outburst.

Swami Shanti said, "*Avidya*. Now, what *avidya*, spiritual ignorance, is talking about is our tendency to live life on autopilot—our automatic response in life, letting *chitta,* our unconscious, take over. And if we're going to seek Self-Realization, we have to face this in ourselves. We have to face this tendency to bury our heads from the reality that nothing is permanent, nothing is perfect, that fulfilling our desires will not bring ultimate happiness."

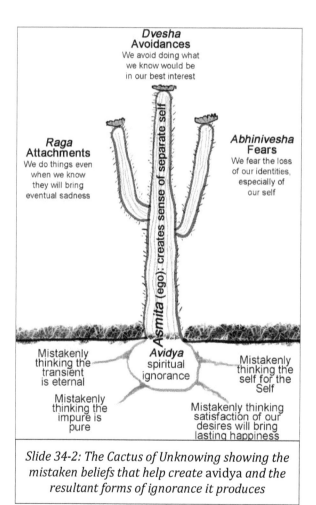

Slide 34-2: The Cactus of Unknowing showing the mistaken beliefs that help create avidya and the resultant forms of ignorance it produces

He paused, looked around the room, and sat on the bench in easy sitting pose, legs folded one in front of the other. He unbuttoned his shirt sleeves and rolled them up two turns with what seemed to be total concentration.

"And if any of us think we are so free from *avidya* that we do not experience these things, then we have already become an enlightened sage. Then, for you, the journey is done. If we see life in that way, there's nothing left to do. There is no *sadhana*, no practice.

"And the only place any of us can do this kind of exploration is internally. It's our own *sadhana*, our own practice. Your *sadhana* is not my *sadhana*—my *sadhana* is not your *sadhana*."

He stood as if to close out that subject and open a new one. "So we live in the world," he said, "and try not to be of the world. We try to remember to see things as we know they really are and remember change is inevitable—our desires are only going to bring us temporary happiness because satisfying our desires is what I call the Hamster Wheel of Life. There is no such thing as perfection in this world. We need to remember nothing is permanent—everything is in a state of flux. Our desires will eventually cause us pain, and we constantly think of ourselves as some false identity. Like Richard Nixon or some other false identity."

He put a new slide up on the screen (*Slide 34-2*). "I call this the Cactus of Unknowing. Remember, this thing called *avidya*, this spiritual ignorance, is the source of our suffering. *Avidya* creates a sense of an independent self that gives rise to *asmita*, the ego, the sense of separation between you and me. It says I'm different. I'm special. It gives rise to *raga*, our attachments because it deludes us into thinking that our desires will bring us everlasting happiness when, in fact, satisfying desires is only a temporary high. And it gives rise to *dvesha*, our avoidance of the things we know somewhere deep inside us will be to our benefit if we would only do them. But instead, we continue to avoid doing them. And *avidya* generates a sense of fear of *abhinivesha*, a sense of fear at the prospect of losing our false identities, our sense of an independent self. And when we

251

lose one of those identities through a death, job loss, or the like, we go into a depression.

"There's a short Japanese poem I would like to leave you with. It goes like this: 'Though their hues are gay / the blossoms flutter down. / And so in this world of ours / who may live forever? / Having this day crossed the mountain vastness of existence / I have seen but a dream / but I am not enraptured.'"

He got up from the bench and said, "That's a lot of very heavy stuff for you to absorb. Let's leave it there for now. Next time, we'll talk about how to deal with all of the negativity in life.

> *After that session, I needed to sit and just be. Maybe it was just having lost Diana, but that experience had made me acutely aware of the temporary nature of life and everything around me. And I certainly would never have considered myself enlightened, but that loss caused a shift in perspective. It wasn't that I felt mournful over her loss. No, I accepted that a long time ago. The ten months after her diagnosis gave me time to prepare myself psychologically, but for me, the sense of the temporary nature of existence has brought things into a clearer and sharper view. It will end for me at some point, and the world will continue as it has for billions of years.*
>
> *I knew that satisfying desires would only bring temporary happiness, and I was okay with that. I realized that it was important to check my attractions, those things that I am obsessively drawn to, just like it was essential to look at all those things that I avoided but were good for me. I needed to check these things periodically. That periodic checking needed to be part of my practice.*

I felt bad for Jackie. Swami Shanti had treated her poorly. When I talked to her later, she was still furious. "That bastard," she said, "he's just a conceited asshole." I knew he had been trying to make a point, and it seemed apparent that he did not like women challenging him. But still. He could have dealt with the situation better.

And there was the way he had dealt with Rajani's question about guru. Both women had felt hurt and belittled by his reactions to their questions. I was surprised that they hadn't walked out on him. He was touchy and thin-skinned, but he did have a way of simplifying some complex concepts and making them accessible. In that respect, he was a good teacher, but dealing with him on a personal level was like handling a frightened porcupine.

I tried to pull my thoughts away from these negative experiences. Swami Shanti had said we think we are the wave and forget that the wave and the ocean are one. It's good to remember that. Thich Nhat Hanh's comment about a piece of paper containing the tree, the sun, the rain, the logger, and all of the universe reminds us that everything is related and dependent on everything else. All is All.

I liked Swami Shanti's Japanese poem. In the scheme of the universe, we are short-lived, and just like the beautiful blossoms, I will eventually wither and fall from the cherry tree. Life seems beautiful as I live it, but as I see it, when it's over, it's over. It's like pulling my computer's electrical cord from the wall. What happens to the electrical current that is me? I don't know. The electrons may get reassembled and reused. Again, I don't know about that. But the electrical current that runs me isn't me. When it's over, it's over. I have one chance to get it right.

People have asked me if I believe in reincarnation, and my answer is no. Maybe I don't understand the concept, but reincarnation seems like a prescientific explanation of how a person today displays a trait of a long-dead ancestor. Today, we know how genetics passes along some traits and how a familial or cultural environment can pass along others.

The idea of a heaven to reward good behavior and a hell to punish bad conduct seems like an attempt to extend the parental reward and punishment techniques used to correct and direct small children's behavior. So some ask, 'why should they be good if they won't be rewarded in heaven or punished in hell.' The answer seems simple. My good behavior will be rewarded by being able to live a stress-free life, and my poor behavior will only bring me stress and more anxiety. And isn't this, after all, what yoga is trying to point out? Isn't it trying to tell me that by controlling my thoughts, words, and deeds, I will have a more rewarding, less stressful life?

Chapter 35: Countering Negativity

We were in our places, perched on our meditation cushions, quietly chattering with our neighbors. The windows of the meditation hall were open; a slight breeze moved through the room, offering a hint of warm spring days ahead. Even so, several of the women had wrapped their yoga blankets around their shoulders. Bird sounds filled the room.

At a few minutes past nine o'clock, Swami Shanti briskly walked into the meditation hall. That morning, he wore maroon pants drawn tight around his ankles and a yellow-orange tee shirt. Over his shoulders was thrown a maroon shawl, and, of course, perched on his head sat his maroon knit cap. Under his arm, he carried a folder, which he placed on the podium at the front of the room. Then he turned to the whiteboard, picked up a marker, and wrote, *"Guten morgen Studenten."* To which we responded, *"Guten morgen Herr Swami."*

He replaced the marker and asked, "What is yoga?" It was a rhetorical question because he continued, "Yoga is the control of the modifications of the mind-field."

He paced across the room, "And once we pull off this 'letting go' business, what's the result?" He stopped and turned toward us.

"Samadhi," I said. "We've reached *samadhi*. The identification and connection of the Seer with what is seen. In other words, subject and object become one."

Swami Shanti nodded, still pacing. Then he said, "Then the Seer abides in Itself, resting in its own True Nature. That is Self-Realization. Now, here in Sanskrit, the word means 'Seer,' but I'm going to ask what we mean by that. Soul, witness, *atman*, Self? So then the text goes on to say, 'Then the Seer is in its own nature.' And when the Seer, the consciousness, is not in its own nature, whose nature is it in?" He turned to us for an answer.

255

And I said, "The Seer is in the Waking State."

He began pacing again. "Yeah, and our unconscious takes on the shape of those colored thought patterns. Then it incorrectly thinks that's what it is itself—those colored thought patterns. It gets mired in *avidya*, in spiritual ignorance. And what do we mean by colored thought patterns?" He paused and adjusted his shawl.

"So that's the basics of the first four lines of the Yoga Sutras," he said. "A lot of people say these first four lines contain all of the knowledge of yoga, but I say to understand the sweep of the Yoga Sutras, you also need to understand the next line. I think it's significant to talk about witnessing colored and uncolored thoughts because I may not know what it means, this 'letting go,' but we have an understanding of colored thoughts—of attachments and aversions—and unclouding means letting go of them. Letting go of our attachments and embracing the things we've avoided that will help us move forward in coming to terms with *avidya*. So now we have a bunch of lines that come next and what are they about?"

I chimed in, "They're about how to do it. How to uncolor those thoughts. How to uncloud our thoughts. How to get desires and aversions under control. In other words, how to do 'the letting go' you talked about earlier."

"Yes," he said. "And when we're ready to do that . . . when we're ready to work on unclouding our minds, we can begin using the power of *Kriya Yoga* to do just that. But we'll get into that a little later."

Swami Shanti took a deep breath and turned slightly to look out the window toward the Ganges, where a flight of geese honked as they cruised just above the water's surface. He turned back and said, "What a person in their first yoga class or their first meditation class wants to know is: How am I going to stabilize and clear my mind so I can maybe do this 'letting go' thing? And so, for practical purposes, I'm going to say to that person, 'Skip over the next several verses of the Yoga Sutras and go to the thirty-third line of the first chapter to what is called the Four Attitudes.'" He put a slide up on the screen (*Slide 35-1*).

He was pacing again, lost in thought. Then he turned and said, "So Patanjali tells us, he goes right into the heart of this thing and tells us, there are four ways to deal with negativity in ourselves and other people. The Sutras' suggestions are a distillation of the wisdom of the ages," he gestured back with his arm to some imagined distant past. "If you do this, you will purify the mind."

The Four Positive Attitudes for Peace of Mind

Peace of mind is gained by cultivating:

* **Friendliness toward the joyful**
* **Compassion toward the sorrowful**
* **By celebrating the goodness of others**
* **By disregarging the negative acts of others**

Yoga Sutra 1.33

Slide 35-1: Patanjali's method of maintaining a positive attitude in the face of negativity

---

He walked to the whiteboard, and underneath his morning greeting, he wrote the words "1) THE JOYFUL ONES" in big block letters.

"When Patanjali says to be friendly toward the joyful, it sounds like no big deal. But stop and think about that person in your life who maybe seems too perfect, too happy, too up all the time. Aren't they sort of annoying? Don't those people kinda get under your skin? And don't you sometimes just want to push them out of your life? Sometimes, these people aren't easy to be around. We want to brain them, don't we? Sometimes, we just want to be moody, or withdrawn, or whatever; isn't that right?

"Well, Patanjali tells us to be happy toward these sorts of people. It's a good practice. It's an essential practice. You become a better person."

Back at the whiteboard, Swami Shanti wrote "2) THE CRANK." He replaced the marker and turned back toward us.

"What do you do with mean, rotten, nasty people? We try and keep a neutral attitude. It doesn't mean approving of that person's behavior. We're not buying into their behavior, and we're not reacting to their bad behavior. So what do we do if we're yogis? We meditate and cultivate a sense of neutrality toward that person or that event.

"We can sit down and quietly allow ourselves to be aware of our sense of seeing, of hearing, of tasting, of touching, of smelling. If we do that, then the mere act of sitting there and being mindful of the senses can bring calmness, stability, and tranquility. It doesn't mean listening to the chirping birds. It means just sitting and being aware of hearing itself, of hearing sound as sound but not interpreting that sound and saying, 'Oh, that's a cardinal, or that's a robin,' or whatever, because then your mind forms a train, a train of thought, and before you know it, that train has left the station with your mind onboard.

"So we need to come to our cushion and contemplate a mind free from desires, from attachments, from aversions. This stabilizes and tranquilizes the mind. But that might be hard to do. One way to experiment with it is to conjure up something like what you imagine the mind of the Buddha would be like, or the Dalai Lama's. So let me just sit here and pretend my mind is as clear and calm and free from desires as the Dalai Lama's mind or the Buddha's mind. And you will find that something happens. It works."

"That sounds like daily life," I say, half under my breath.

"Yes, that's daily life," he said, turning back to the whiteboard; he wrote, "3) CELEBRATE GOOD" and "4) IGNORE FAULTS." He turned back to us and slid the marker through his fingers a few times, then said, "Be friendly toward the joyful, compassionate toward the suffering. Celebrate the good in others and ignore their faults and imperfections. Look for the positive. Ignore the negative. How much simpler can we say it?"

Swami Shanti looked around the room, then said, "So OM is a shortcut to enlightenment. We talked about that a few days ago. Working with the Four Attitudes is a shortcut to dealing with negativity, yours or the negativity around you. When you meditate on these Four Attitudes, keep in mind that the socially disadvantaged, the immigrants, the poor, people who begin to move into a more affluent place in society, when those already above them in social standing feel resentful of the success of others, what we're seeing is the negativity of that first Attitude. By telling us to be friendly toward the joyful, Patanjali's also telling us to be supportive of other people's success, the success of the underclass."

Then Swami Shanti said, "Let's take a little break. Be back here in about fifteen minutes.

Chapter 36: Caution, Bumpy Road Ahead

When we reassembled, Swami Shanti jumped right in.

"I've got a new slide for you," he said as he took the remote from his pocket and put another slide on the screen (*Slide 36-1*). Then he sat down on the bench like he did sometimes, one leg tucked under himself. "It's all quite natural," he said when comfortable. "Patanjali goes on to say there are nine kinds of distractions: There's illness, mental distractions, and doubt; we lose focus on our goal, become lazy, and become trapped by our desires. We experience faulty thinking or failure to advance our practice, or we backslide. And as if those nine things aren't enough, they trigger four other things: mental or physical pain, sadness or dejection, restlessness or anxiety, and breathing irregularities. And that sucks and throws a lot of people off, and they quit. That's why I call them the Thirteen Road Hazards.

Thirteen Road Hazards
Predictable Obstacles

illness	dullness	doubt
negligence	laziness	cravings
misperceptions	failure	instability

Companions to the Obstacles

mental & physical pain   sadness & frustration
unsteadiness of the body   irregular breath

Yoga Sutras 1.30-1.32

Slide 36-1: On yoga's journey, Patanjali notes thirteen predictable obstacles, to which should be added anything that takes us out of our routine.

"So what do we do about it? How do we deal with all these road hazard things? We sit down on our cushions and work to make our minds as one-pointed as possible. We work to train our minds in meditation to focus on a single object. Even if we focus our attention on rum-raisin ice cream, we begin to pull ourselves away from those hazards. But at the same time, it is useful to focus on cultivating the Four Attitudes: be friendly toward the joyful, be compassionate toward the suffering, celebrate the good in others, and overlook the faults of others. Cultivating these Four Attitudes will overcome negativity."

And with that, he picked up his things and walked out of the meditation hall. I sat and processed the things he had talked about.

> *Swami Shanti had begun by saying that yoga was letting go of our mental disturbances and our ruminations. Then he'd said we might have difficulty "letting go" of our attachments and aversions. But suppose we use our* Kriya Yoga, *the combined practice of* tapas, svadhyaya, *and* ishvara pranidhana, *or desire to practice, self-study, and surrender. We may feel like crap, but if we sit down on our cushions and try to be with whatever it is that's thrown us off . . . in that way we can neutralize those obstacles, those attractions and aversions, through meditation. Then he'd said we could jump ahead to the Four Attitudes to help deal with negativity. He'd also suggested that the best way to deal with the Thirteen Road Hazards is to work the Four Attitudes—be happy at the good fortune of others, be compassionate at the misfortune of others, celebrate the good in others, and overlook their faults.*

> *When I had first started to do yoga, a woman in my class came across as Mrs. Perfect Suburban Mom. She had a perky demeanor and wore snappy little yoga outfits. Always up. Always chipper. Then one night, she came in and confided that one of her teenagers had been arrested on a drug*

charge. And this little devil part of me just jumped up and down with delight. I was so happy to see even a small smudge of imperfection in her life. I tried to fake compassion and offer sympathy, but my response was probably stilted and artificial.

Fortunately, others were there to give her the support she needed. I knew my response was wrong, and I sort of felt my heart shrink a little bit, like the Grinch. It wasn't until I studied the Yoga Sutras that I understood my reaction to Mrs. Suburban Mom. And when I did, I incorporated the Four Attitudes into my closing words at the end of class. May I be friendly toward the joyful and compassionate toward the suffering. May I celebrate the good in others and remain impartial to their faults and imperfections.

I liked what he'd said about applying the Four Attitudes beyond individuals and applying them to groups like migrants. His talk that morning had made me think about my position on the negative-positive continuum. I am more on the positive side. When faced with challenging experiences, I felt that I could successfully get through whatever it was.

As an eleven-year-old, I became gripped by the fear that someone was trying to poison my food and drink. If I was offered a plate of cookies, I never took the nearer one. Instead, I randomly chose one at the back or side. I avoided taking the glass in the cupboard that was nearest, instead I chose one at random. Around this time, I also developed an intense fear of riding across a bridge in a car—walking across was no problem, but put me in a car about to cross a bridge, and I was on the floor of the backseat covering my head and crying in terror. My family could hardly have been unaware of my bridge phobia, but I was able to conceal the poisoning issue. I dealt with it silently. I knew it was irrational, even as it began to drive my life. Finally, I told myself that things couldn't continue the way they were going and forced myself to take the first glass, the nearest cookie, the closest piece of candy. The first few times were agonizing. Then, with each choice, it got easier and easier until it became natural and I no longer thought about it. But amazingly, the fear of bridges melted away almost without my realizing it. At some deep unconscious level, I felt empowered knowing that I could overcome almost any difficulty.

Two months shy of my sixth birthday, I started first grade and later skipped the eighth. So when I boarded at the seminary in my third year of high school, I was fourteen years old, two years younger than the rest of my class. It was a very difficult year, as I struggled with my social position and grades. There was a saying at school that the doors opened out easier than in. Each spring, the faculty met to determine who would stay and who would be asked to leave. I was determined that I would succeed and that if I did leave, it would be on my terms.

At OCS, everything was new and different from anything I had experienced. The curriculum was compressed and fast-paced. I was also in another situation where I was evaluated on an ongoing basis. At OCS, our motto was "Cooperate to graduate." Dropouts were packed off to the fleet as enlisted seamen with a note in the service record that they had been rolled out of OCS.

As a newly commissioned ensign, I was posted to my first duty station, a troop transport. Our mission was to land US Marines on a beach Normandy-style. An early assignment was as a wave commander. In that role, I led eight or ten boats full of US Marines to the beach. In one training exercise conducted in a dense fog, my wave was the only one to land on the beach. I had oriented with the dim sun, and I looked backward at my boat's wake to keep a straight course, plotting my position with a grease pencil on Plexiglas over a map of the beach. All the other waves got lost. I hit the beach. That experience was a key factor in being moved to a place of leadership ahead of my peers.

As I have reflected on this and similar experiences, I've considered how these sorts of positive experiences can stick in the memory and affect our actions much like their negative twins, the stress caused by traumatic events. While strong positive experiences may propel me forward, they can also limit options if I obsess over them. They are the mirrors of their stressful counterparts.

However, these early successes helped to cultivate an overall positive attitude that helped me deal with many life situations, especially the snafu with my hotel reservation in Thanjavur.

Sometimes, noticing the experiences of others can offer insight into our behavior and an opportunity to make changes. One such opportunity presented itself when three of us went to the other side of the Ganges upstream from Rishikesh.

We were spending most of our days in class, with only enough free time for a quick trip to the nearest Daily Necessities shop. But as our time at the ashram drew toward its end, we were given an afternoon of free time. At our orientation, the ashram director had reiterated that we were not to go to Ram Jhula or Laxman Jhula, a couple of footbridges over the Ganges upstream from town that led to a small commercial area on the river's far shore. It reminded me of God's prohibition to Adam and Eve, "Thou shall not eat from the Tree of Knowledge of Good and Evil."

Image 36-1: Rishikesh shopping area on the opposite bank of the Ganges from the ashram

With an afternoon free, Jackie, Julia, and I were feeling defiant of authority and decided, despite the prohibitions, to take a tuk-tuk to Ram Jhula, the northernmost bridge. When we arrived, the footbridge was crowded, and monkeys played tag in the bridge's suspension cables. On the other *side, we found a vibrant commercial area only a few blocks deep, nestled between the river and a steep hillside. Bookstores, ashrams, temples, and eateries were interspersed with souvenir shops. Mostly, everyone was on foot (Image 36-1). Occasionally, a motorbike inched its way through the pedestrians as they often did in India, where people were forced to walk in the streets. Indian motorbikes hardly make any noise at all. Still, their presence annoyed Julia to an extreme. With the passing of each one, her anger seemed to increase. Finally, it boiled over, and she told us in no uncertain words these motorbike riders would never be tolerated in Argentina. Someone would kick the shit out of the riders. I thought maybe she'd slept through Swami Shanti's lesson on negativity.*

Chapter 37: The Karma-Go-Round

Swami Shanti came through the door a few minutes late, saying, "The word 'karma' means action." At the whiteboard, he scribbled "Good morning, students," and continued. "It is the playing out of our actions that are the result of the latent habit patterns or *samskaras* that are stored in the depths of our unconscious minds."

He put his things down and repeated, "Karma means action. It refers to all of our actions, and by that, I mean every one of our thoughts, words, and deeds. Each one creates an effect out there in the world as well as in here." He pointed at the center of his sternum. "The Gita," he continued, "tells us that even when we choose not to act, that is in itself an act. So all of our actions, real or imagined, create *samskaras*. So does our approval of another's actions. Our refusal to act creates *samskaras* or deep impressions in the depths of our unconscious. In turn, each one of those *samskaras* is capable of generating further thoughts, words, and actions, which will create new *samskaras* in the depths of our unconscious.

"Meditation helps to keep the channels of the river of our consciousness open and clear, but there are other ways, too. Practices that stabilize and clear the mind are good river dredges."

Rajani asked, "What are some practices to clear the mind?"

Swami Shanti said, "Look at your Yoga Sutras, please. Book one, line thirty-three. What does it say?"

While he waited, she fumbled for her copy of the Yoga Sutras and the reference he'd given her. "In relationships," she read, "the mind becomes purified by cultivating feelings of friendliness towards those who are happy, compassion for those who are suffering, goodwill towards those who are virtuous, and indifference or neutrality towards those we perceive as wicked or evil."

"So there you have it," he said, "the Four Attitudes we talked about the other day. He stood with his hands on his hips as though addressing a recalcitrant child.

"How about a loving-kindness meditation?" I asked in an effort to defuse a potentially volatile situation.

He replied, "That's Buddhist, but sure," and before anyone else could interject, he continued.

"Back to karma. By our actions, karma builds up a storehouse of *samskaras* that drive further actions, often in undesirable directions."

He scanned our group and said, "You are bright people, so I think you can see where this is going. Our actions, including our thoughts and words, as well as our deeds—and when I say actions, what I mean is not just the acts themselves but the thoughts and words, whether or not they lead to physical actions out in the world. They all produce *samskaras* that eventually lead to new actions, often without our conscious awareness. So a cycle is created. The action that I take produces two things: something out there, but also something in here." He pointed to his chest.

"There are three kinds of karma. First, there's what's called *sanchita*, which is the vast storehouse of old impressions—these are stored in your unconscious and will metastasize, creating more actions and more *samskaras*.

"Then there's *kriyamana*, those potential actions that are in front of us—actions that we could take but haven't yet. We've thought about them and maybe talked about doing them, but we haven't acted on them yet. Still, even the thought and word are creating a *samskara*. Maybe not as deep and as permanent, but still, thoughts and words create *samskaras*. We all know that the mere thought of doing something makes it easier to eventually do it."

270

Swami Shanti picked up a water bottle and took a long, slow swallow. He replaced the glass, picked up a napkin from the table, and wiped his lips before continuing.

"Finally, we have *prarabhda*, which are those actions that are already playing out. We've done the act, maybe years ago, and its consequences are still playing out in the big, wide, wonderful world.

"So, suppose I do something that is not nice to another person. That negativity, that *samskara*, ends up getting deposited in the murky depths of my latent or active unconscious, and at some point, it will influence my actions, creating another round of actions or karmas and then depositing more *samskaras* that have been created.

"A nice analogy is to compare the mind to a river and *samskaras* to the sandbars or rocks that are deposited on the river bottom. The *samskaras* then alter the course and direction of our river and our future actions. The trick, then, is to stop that whole business—break the cycle. Dredge the river."

He slid the knit cap from his head and took a moment to rub the top of his head with both hands. Replacing the cap, he walked to the nearest window and slid it open.

He turned back to us and, leaning against the windowsill, said, "The consequences we must deal with are also those in here. These are the ones that clog our unconscious, both the active unconscious and, more importantly, our latent unconscious, because these are the ones that are driving our actions without us even realizing it. These are the consequences that often shoot us in the foot and cripple our best efforts to do good.

"In much of life, we didn't choose; we just acted. We're running on automatic, and then we have to ask who's piloting our ship. In many cases, autopilot is running the show, which is to say, the habit patterns that are set by the *klishtas*. They are emerging from storage in *chitta*, in our latent unconscious. If we can't see this in ourselves, maybe we can sometimes see it in others."

Swami Shanti told a story about two women going to a retreat. They'd planned to go together. One of them had a small fire in her house and couldn't go with her friend. She felt really bad about not going. Later, she found out that her friend had been killed in a car accident on the way to the retreat. We can't make our karma go away. It just is what we've made it for better or for worse.

> *After the session, I just sat and thought about what Swami Shanti had said about karma, how every thought, word, and deed creates* samskaras, *or deep impressions in our unconscious, and how those* samskaras *generate actions. I thought about brain plasticity and how even mentally practicing something causes changes in our brains. I wondered how actors' brains get reorganized when they assume roles involving positive and negative emotions. Does it become easier for them to act out these emotions in the outer world? I've never seen any research that directly addressed this question, but I have seen some that might imply that this is true.*
>
> *I thought about how differently the West and the East view transgressions. In the West, our sinful acts are punished by God—sort of the lightning bolt approach to punishment. While in the East, our sinful acts themselves punish us.*
>
> *His story of the woman being upset about being unable to go to the retreat as planned with her friend reminded me of Sanjaya's story about the man whose horse ran off. When it happened, his friends were sad for him at the loss of his horse. But then it came back with other horses. What*

272

happened to the woman who had the small fire and what happened to the farmer whose horse ran off were just events—neither good nor bad. They were actions playing out.

Swami Shanti went on about using buddhi, *the executive functioning part of our intelligence, to deal with* kriyamana karma, *the actions that we haven't performed yet. He said that we need to be aware, and if we're not going to be aware, if we're not going to explore our unconscious, we're going to continue to do the same old things over and over. Then we'll never get off our gerbil treadmills. If we do, if we work to cultivate discrimination in our actions, and if we make our actions as conscious as possible, then we will reduce the* samskaras *in our unconscious and make our actions less harmful to ourselves and others. So future suffering is thereby avoided.*

It all sounded like a very tall order. But it would be a beginning if I tried to consciously change things in my life one thing at a time. It was, after all, what I had preached to my classes all along: yoga teaches us to be present and to focus. Begin with little things. Change the easy ones—things that are easily accessible in the active unconscious. Then as things tumble from the latent to the active unconscious, address them.

I felt balanced when I left the meditation hall. I walked through the garden where a visiting swamini knelt in the grass with her camera, taking close-up photos of rose blossoms (*Image 37-1*). They were beautiful but would soon fall to the ground, as in Swami Shanti's poem. I walked on through the garden to the ghat. As I passed a pond, I noticed a giant bullfrog on its edge, catching the last of the sun. On the ghat, several of our group sat in the grass observing an elephant on the other side of the river that had come down from the mountains. It was the first one we'd seen. It was exciting to see this harbinger of summer.

Image 37-1: Swamini photographing a rose blossom

Chapter 38: Dealing with Karma's Fallout

The morning was cool as I walked through the flower garden and past the lotus pond. Lotuses are amazing plants. The first one I saw had been grown by a friend. It stood on a stem five or six feet tall, and at the top was a blossom the size of a dinner plate. Its leaves were about the same size but on shorter stems. I would be gone before it was hot enough for these lotuses to bloom.

At the meditation hall, I slipped out of my sandals and arranged them neatly with the others parked at the door. I was a few minutes early; Rajani and Siti were already at their places. I nodded toward them, arranged my cushion, and sat. Someone, the staff, I supposed, had opened the windows wide, and a light breeze moved across the room. I always enjoyed the birds chattering in the trees just outside.

The others came in ahead of Swami Shanti, who wore maroon pants, a long-sleeved tee shirt, and the ever-present maroon cap atop his head this morning.

He placed a file folder on the lectern, walked to the whiteboard, and wrote "*Godmorgen elever.*" "Did I get my Danish correct?" he asked Ingrid.

"Yes, thank you," she said. "*Og godmorgen til dig også.* And good morning to you, too."

Back at the whiteboard, he wrote the words "*Kriya Yoga,*" underlined them twice, and then turned back to us.

"I was mentioning this thing called *Kriya Yoga* the other day," he said. "*Kriya Yoga* is used to minimize the *kleshas*, the gross colorings, or clouding of the mind."

He continued, "In other words, it helps to minimize the effects of our attachments, our desires, our aversions or negative desires—think back to the Cactus of Unknowing (Slide 34-2). Our attachments and avoidances need to be eliminated on the road to *samadhi*, or deep absorption.

"But where to begin? We begin on the gross level. Start with the easy stuff—with the most obvious things. Now, if you look at what Patanjali says, he makes this leap into how you get rid of all of those colorings or cloudiness of mind. Then he says if you can't quite do this, can't quite make this complete jump and eliminate all of these *kleshas*, we have this thing called *Kriya Yoga* that we can apply to the gross levels. We do this through *tapas*, *svadhyaya*, and *ishvara pranidhana*, through our determination, study of ourselves, and then surrendering its fruits. That's *Kriya Yoga*. The combined power of those last three elements of the niyamas. So if we work them, it knocks off the rough edges of attachments and aversions, and they become attenuated."

Outside there was a ruckus in the trees—a monkey screeched and there was a flurry of wings as a flock of something or other retreated to a safe distance.

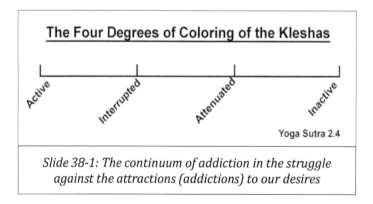

Slide 38-1: The continuum of addiction in the struggle against the attractions (addictions) to our desires

Swami Shanti continued, "What do the Sutras say when there is still some coloring but it has been attenuated? They say there are four stages or degrees of colorings." He walked back to the whiteboard and drew a horizontal line with the words "active," "interrupted," "attenuated," and "inactive" at equal points on the line (*Slide 38-1*).

Turning back to us, he repeated, "active, interrupted, attenuated, or inactive. By inactive, we mean they are dormant. Let's use smoking cigarettes as an example. I'm a regular smoker. My habit is active. Then I decide I want to quit smoking, and I do for a while, but periodically, I have one or two, maybe after meals. My habit is interrupted, but it's still very much there, isn't it? But then, I'm able to go without a cigarette after meals. But I still think about having a cigarette after meals. And this may be the way it is for months, maybe years. My smoking habit is now attenuated. At some point, I stop thinking about smoking. Maybe at some point, I even find that the thought of smoking is distasteful. At that point, we say it is inactive or dormant.

"Sometimes, it's referred to as a seed, but more often in English, it's translated as being dormant or inactive. So with the one, you very definitely have the idea it's still there, and this seed could easily regerminate and come back in full force. But when we talk about it in English as being inactive, our tendency may be to think, 'Oh, it's inactive, so I don't have to worry about it anymore.' And it would make it easy to miss the fact that inactive carries the idea of activity for something that is not now active. Saying that it becomes a seed carries the idea that it could easily regerminate and grow again."

He paused, removed his glasses, and, with a lens cloth from his pocket, carefully cleaned one lens, then the other. Next, he placed them on the table and rubbed his temples before replacing them and continuing.

"We all know that habits are strong," he said. "Attachments and aversions are strong. It's the nature of desire that habit gets its way. Why do some people quit smoking or give up alcohol, and a week later, they're right back into it?

"The coloring is so strong. And what very often doesn't happen is it doesn't get attenuated. We don't realize it. We say, 'Oh, I don't have willpower, and I ended up back in the ice cream store once again.' What we failed to do was to complete the attenuation phase. We need the willpower, the determination, in other words, *tapas*, to stay with it.

"Otherwise, all we did," he said, "was deal with the gross level of coloring. I thought about the ice cream. I read John Robbins's book about nutrition and the evils of ice cream, but I never did anything more with it. So I ended up back in the ice cream store."

Under my breath, I said, "And I hate myself for it because I'm a weak person."

Swami Shanti nodded toward me. He kept going. "And I hate myself for it, and the whole cycle keeps going. This is common sense we already know. First, there's dealing with the gross level of coloring. Then there's going past the part that's active, or we've succeeded in attenuating it a little bit by training our senses, by doing things like having a conversation with your mind and saying, 'Mind, you can want that thing, but I'm not going to give you a hand to pick it up.'

"What do you do to attenuate it further once that process has already started? If you were doing a style of meditation that says," and then his voice went falsetto, "'Oh, teacher, teacher, teacher, how do I get rid of these troublesome thoughts?'" Then, back to his normal voice, he continued, "Are they going to be further attenuated by suppressing thoughts, by pushing them back down into the latent unconscious? No. So we have to be willing to allow them to come so we can see with discrimination what's going on. Make sense?

"Then by witnessing it neutrally in meditation—the ice cream example— you're sitting there meditating on *atman*, or the Self within, and then along comes a bowl of ice cream."

Then, maybe it was a dramatic pause, I wasn't sure, he said, "Let that all sink in while I take a quick break and we'll continue."

Chapter 39: From Clouds to Trees

When he returned, Swami Shanti arranged himself on his bench in lotus pose, removed the knit cap from his head, and rubbed his head vigorously before continuing.

"Through meditation, you bring the *kleshas*—those desires that generate attachments and aversions—down to seed form. You bring them to a mere potential. That list of the four stages of lessening the coloring or intensity of our desires—the slide we looked at before the break (*Slide 38-1*)—is a continuum with those four stages as points along it. But to lessen the intensity of our desires, of our attractions, and our aversions, we must first do *Kriya Yoga* and its threefold process of dealing with them (*Slide 39-1*). We need to allow our *tapas*, our determination, to lead us, so we

---

Kriya Yoga

Tapas: Determination or ardor
Svadhyaya: Self study
Ishvara Pranidhana: Surrendering the
   fruits of your practice

Yoga Sutra 2.1

Slide 39-1: The threefold practice of Kriya Yoga

---

can engage *svadhyaya*, that special study of ourselves, and then we do the *ishvara pranidhana* part, the surrender of the fruits of our efforts to that power that is greater than us. Doing that knocks off the rough edges. And then Patanjali, the codifier of the Yoga Sutras, goes on to say, 'Oh, by the way, you need to know there's a process to this.' It's someplace along the active-dormant continuum. And now he says, 'Oh, there's still something left, there's still some *klishta*, some coloring, some residual desire, which means it's not dormant, it's just attenuated.' So if you don't want to do the quitting-starting thing, then you're going to do the *Kriya Yoga* thing."

Swami Shanti took a sip of water before continuing. "Now I've relieved things somewhat, but there's still more to do, what then? You do meditation. And I don't mean sitting there saying, 'I'm going to sit here and finger my mala beads and chant, *'Hare Krishna'* or *'Hare Ram.'* That's magical thinking. And magical thinking is not going to block or eliminate those *kleshas*.

"What comes next is *samyama*, the application of the power of concentration, meditation, and enlightenment. And some may say, 'I don't know how to do *samyama*, I don't know how to do *samadhi*. Putting all the fancy words aside, what do you do? What do you suggest?"

At this point, Swami Shanti just sat there scanning us, expecting an answer.

Then Siti finally said, "You engage your attention."

"Yes. Attention. Just let it simply be attention. Let the bowl of ice cream come in front of you. And then sit there with it. And you want to get up from your meditation seat and get some, but you don't. You just sit there. And if you'll sit there and meditate on the bowl of ice cream—and this may sound very, very strange . . . still, it's the principle of inspecting within, of introspection—if you can meditate on the bowl of ice cream, through discrimination, through *buddhi*, your higher mental process, your brain's executive functioning, you'll disassemble the ice cream and see it for what it is: a minimal amount of flavoring and fats, basically junk and fillers. You will see it as the distraction from your goals that it is. And this process will attenuate it even more.

"What thoughts arise in meditation? What kinds of thoughts? Neutral thoughts?"

Carlos said, "Disturbing thoughts. Colored thoughts."

"Yes, the ones that are colored. The ones that are *kleshas*. The ones with a little bit or a lot of attraction or a little bit or maybe a lot of aversion. Neutral thoughts don't come to mind. How many times have you walked on the ghat and walked by a whole bunch of trees—the ones that are planted along the ghat? How many times sitting in meditation has one of those trees popped up in your meditation? None. Because they're neutral. They're just trees. They are not the sweets somebody put on the counter at lunchtime. There's a reason."

I said, "They have no meaning."

Swami Shanti said, "They don't relate to me. And who is it that made them relate to me?"

Everyone answered in unison, "*Ahamkara*, the I-maker, the ego."

"Then an alliance, or a connection, has not been formed with *ahamkara*, the ego, to make the trees into *kleshas*. It's all a process of turning the *kleshas* into trees. Into neutral trees that don't pop into your awareness to disturb your meditation."

> *I reflected on how Swami Shanti was sometimes all over the place. Eventually, though, he would get his point across, but he seemed to go in fits and starts, one direction, then another, before finally coming in for a landing.*
>
> *Later, I thought back about how hard it had been dealing with some of the major colorings of my mind. Alcohol wasn't that big of a problem. I drank quite a bit in the navy, and Vikki and I drank a lot while we were together, but when we split up, I had bought a bottle of whiskey to celebrate my new apartment. When I moved out over a year later, it was still at the level it had been at that first night's celebration.*

Smoking, on the other hand, was different. I had tried several times to quit. Once, I went for several months, maybe even over a year. Then I began dating someone who was a smoker, and within a few months, I was back smoking again. After a bad cold, when I hadn't smoked for a week, and I went out with Diana, a nonsmoker, it was so much easier not to start again. Those experiences helped me understand what Swami Shanti had said about the continuum of the colorings of the kleshas: active, interrupted, attenuated, and inactive. I had worked through all of those stages in becoming tobacco-free. And I realized how important it was to associate with a like-minded person. I remembered Sister Mary Richard in my first-year high school religion class who had periodically reminded us that "by their fruits, you shall know them" and that "birds of a feather flock together."

I realized that to deal with those kleshas or any issues, I had to work constantly toward the goal. I didn't realize it then, but I was doing the Kriya Yoga thing on my own: I needed to keep the commitment up, constantly examine myself and my motivations, and surrender the efforts; knowing that Diana and I were birds of a feather helped.

Chapter 40: A House of Cards

Swami Shanti sat in lotus pose for some time, then shifted and placed his other leg on top. He continued. "It has been a good three weeks for me, and I hope it has been for you too."

Everyone responded positively. There had been some tense moments. I had learned a lot about the Yoga Sutras and, more importantly, about myself. Still, it would take time to integrate it all thoroughly.

"Before we all go our separate ways," he said, "and I know some of you have to leave this afternoon, and others will be leaving throughout the day tomorrow, so before those things happen, there are a few things I want to share with you.

"Remember," he said, "the clouds we've talked about are made up of all of my false identities and the fears that come with them. When you're able to transcend all those clouds, those *kleshas*, then you get an expanded view. We lose that state when *ahamkara* pops back up, and eventually, you'll conclude that all emotions are attachments. *Ananda*, bliss, is a state of being. It is not an emotion. It is the innermost layer of ourselves, what you're used to thinking of as your 'soul,' your core self. When all else has been let go of, when we reach that state of bliss, of *ananda*, there is an extreme expansion. But then our lower nature kicks in and knocks us out of our state of bliss, out of *ananda*.

"Every emotion is caused by either getting or not getting what I want. It is best to stay with and ride out an emotional issue. We can say, 'Oh, it's only *maya*, it's unreal, it's an illusion, so I'm not going to be attached to whatever it is.' But does that get you freedom from it? No, that's magical thinking. Only by riding with and dealing with the issue do you let it go."

I thought back to Swami Shanti's slide of OM (Image 27-2)
with the curved line between the main symbol and the dot

above it. That curved line was the veil of maya *that kept us from seeing the truth. I thought of the loss of a naval career, the loss of my first marriage, the loss of Diana. All part of the path that had led to where I was. Sitting in an ashram in Rishikesh, India.*

"This is one of those places," he continued, "where we can get ourselves into trouble. Sometimes, we can say, we're supposed to be doing nonattachment, that I'm just going to stomp on it, I'm going to put a stop to it. I'm going to block it. It's unreal; it's *maya*, and it's an illusion. It doesn't mean anything, so therefore, I'm going to stop it.

"Well, that doesn't get you freedom from it. What does get you freedom is paying attention. Pay attention. Pay attention. And another way of saying 'pay attention, pay attention' is to sit with it, be with it, ride it out, but do it attentively.

"And when you're in the process of riding through that thing, it's not a comfortable process. The word in yoga teachings that matches this idea of riding through these issues is *tapas*, or our burning desire to succeed. It's the third *niyama*—it means fire. It's a particular type of fire. It's the fire that comes from riding through the emotional storm. Why does it come? It comes because of attachment. Why? Because I'm either not getting what I want or I'm not able to avoid what I'm trying to avoid. So that attachment leads to my emotional responses. What this is saying is that for each emotion, we are either getting or not getting what we want. It's either an attachment or an aversion. It depends on how we are riding through it, though.

I interjected, "They're sort of the flip side of the same coin, aren't they?"

"Yes," he said. "If we're just riding through it with no awareness, then we get pulled this way and that. But if we're riding through it with awareness, then it can be a positive experience if the starting point is that I've done some of these experiments, and I've discovered for myself that what the yogis are saying is accurate. And it seems to me to be generally true that there is *sukha/dukkha*—there is a pleasure and pain aspect to it. This happens because of falling into the trap of *avidya*, which is called attachment. If I like it, I'm attached. If I don't like it, I'm still attached because I'm putting energy into pushing it away, but that's called attachment.

"If we've experimented with ourselves enough, then when we ride through the emotion, we're doing it with awareness, and we're not too likely to fall into the trap of liking it and staying stuck in it. In such cases, we let emotions become just emotions without the storyline. It's just anger. It's just a sense of loss without the storytelling. And I know it's not easy to stop the storytelling, but it's that storytelling that supports the emotion and keeps it going. Remember, it's just life's pain.

"And what's the pain of life? It's the emotional response to attachment. It's the emotional response to forcefully being pried from an attachment. It's *klishta vritti*—memory traces that are colored. Mainly, they're colored with the fear of anybody messing with them. I've got my ten million attractions and ten million aversions, and I've got them all neatly bundled together—like a house of cards, and I don't want them knocked over.

"My house of cards, my false identity, is pretty fragile, and *ahamkara*, the I-maker, wants to protect it. That's natural. It can naturally kick off a flight or fight response or a faint or freeze response. And when you're riding through the emotions, you're sitting there quietly, experiencing the death of those attractions and versions. It's just the pain of life, the pain and suffering of living. I don't want to minimize it; I want to offer an understanding.

"Okay," Swami Shanti said. "Let's take a short break, but please be back here in fifteen minutes. We have something special, so please don't be late."

287

Swami Shanti hit the nail right on the head when he said we need to deal with attachments, aversions, likes, and dislikes without the storyline. They are simply fluctuations of our mental activities, what the Yoga Sutras call vrittis. *They are mental disturbances, monkey-mind chatter, clouds, and mental colorings. I cling to them because I see them as defining who I am. They are backed up and supported by the mental stories I tell myself. I perpetuate them, and only I can sweep them out. Meditation is my broom.*

Thoughts of attachment and detachment swirled around in my head. We deal with attachments in all sorts of ways. We have attachments that arise from our desires, and we have attachments that arise from our aversions. Dealing with these is important if we are to free ourselves from a life driven by them.

Esther raised a question that people often ask about how to reconcile yoga's detachment and a parent's attachment to their children. The question she raised was: How can you reject your kids? And I thought how the dance in Chennai answered that question with the story of detached-attachment. You raise your children to be fully functioning adults who will leave the nest.

Swami Shanti's analogy of the house of cards helped me recognize and understand the depression I had fallen into in the years after I'd left the navy. The roles we assume for ourselves are houses of cards. And when they inevitably are blown down, we are left with a sense of emptiness and a loss of identity. It was what I'd experienced with my resignation from the navy. I'd had the beginnings of a promising career. I'd demonstrated initiative and leadership and been rewarded with early job advancement. I'd chosen to let that go for the benefit of the family. Things might have been

288

different had I achieved that goal, but things had only gotten worse, and we'd divorced. Then there was the loss of my feeling of security after the break-in and fire, the loss of my job. In each of these cases, a role that I'd implicitly felt was me had been easily swept aside like a house of cards. In hindsight, it was apparent that I had been depressed but I hadn't seen it at the time. And most recently, Diana's death had presented me with a similar loss. This time, however, I'd understood things more clearly.

I thought back to Yoga Sutras' discussion of avidya, spiritual ignorance, and how it generates our sense of self, spawning our desires, aversions, and fears. The fears it talks about are the fear of loss of self, of loss of our identities, of our roles, of having our house of cards blown down.

Chapter 41: Do It

For once, everyone heeded Swami Shanti's admonition not to dally. My walk to the dining hall to refill my water bottle refreshed me. We were all back in our places when he returned.

"I've got a little surprise for you today," he said. "But first, I'll explain some things so you can appreciate what you're about to see.

"A friend of mine, here in town, is a teacher of Bharatanatyam. Do you all know what that is?"

Maybe half of us raised our hands.

Swami said, "Yoga was originally restricted to men only. Instead, women learned and performed various dances, mainly in a temple setting. These dances were grounded in many of the same texts as the male yoga practices. A big difference is that they were visually expressive of these texts. The dance style is called Bharatanatyam, and it originated in the southeastern state of Tamil Nadu.

"It uses a complicated gestural language of exact body movements—eyes, hands, head, and feet. The dancer usually dresses as a bride, wearing colorful sarees and jewelry.

"During the British occupation of India, these dance forms were suppressed, as was yoga."

Then the door opened, and a woman dressed in an all-white saree walked in. "I hope we are not too early," she said to Swami Shanti.

"No, no, no. Please come in." Then he said, "This is Lakshmi," indicating the woman in white.

Lakshmi stepped through the doorway, and Swami Shanti said, "This is my friend Lakshmi, who teaches the Bharatanatyam dance here in town. And she has . . . well, I'll let her do the introduction. Lakshmi, these are my current students just finishing their study of the Yoga Sutras." He indicated us. "Please, go ahead."

Lakshmi told us she taught young women Bharatanatyam dance. Then she said, "One of my youngest students will dance for you. Anjali, being six years old, is performing her first recital very soon. Even at this young age, our dancers learn to let go of *asmita*, their pride, because *asmita* only steps on their feet, so they are not dancing from the heart. Like you, she is engaging *tapas* and *ishvara pranidhana*. Anjali works most diligently and surrenders to her divinity.

"But," she said as she walked to the door, "let me ask Anjali's mother, Anika, to bring her in and dance for you."

Anika came into the meditation hall wearing a deep red saree and trailing her was young Anjali in a kid's version of a salwar kameez with yellow-gold pants and a deep red kurta, or overshirt.

With a short introduction, Lakshmi called Anjali to the front of the room. The little girl seemed very self-possessed as she stepped forward with all the confidence of a seasoned performer. I expected she would dance to some recorded music, but instead, she began singing, struck a pose, and started her dance. Our young dancer displayed all of the gestures of head, eyes, hands, and feet one would expect of a more seasoned dancer. When she finished, we applauded her enthusiastically.

> *As she danced, I remembered the dance I'd witnessed in Chennai, when the woman danced the story of detached-attachment, with its caution to the mother that her daughter needed to follow her own dharma, not the mother's.*

But on a deeper level, the lesson was that attachments are the clouds that obscure our realization of that deeper Self. Swami Shanti had described it as a house of cards, built through spiritual ignorance, a significant part of the human condition. Ignoring our True Nature creates a sense of separation, generating desires, aversions, blessings, and curses. A blessing in that we can't function in the real world without them, and a curse in that they are the source of our woes, of the vrittis *that produce monkey mind, that constant mental chatter. These are the fluctuations of our mental state referred to in the first lines of the Yoga Sutras. But to live the Path of Yoga, we must let go of those attachments and live this sense of detached-attachment.*

After the dancers left, Swami Shanti said, "These dancers must learn many of the same things you are learning here. They apply it differently, that's all. But back to our lesson.

"When an action occurs," he said, "it causes an effect that goes into the latent part of the mind, and it sits there waiting for this next opportunity to arise, and then it goes back into the basement of the mind a little bit stronger than the last time. It could be called anger. It could be called frustration or pride, pride at getting my way. 'See, I'm a winner in life. I'm not a loser. I used to be a loser, but now I'm a winner.' There's a setup. If you think you're a loser, you're a loser. If you believe you are a winner, you're a loser, in terms of what we're talking about, because both are *avidya*. Both are spiritual ignorance.

"And you think, 'Hey, I'm not either one of those. I'm not a loser. I'm not a winner. I'm *atman*. I'm *Brahman*. I'm consciousness. I'm the pure awareness that has been here all the time. I fell into the trap of thinking I'm a loser or I'm a winner. How did I fall into these traps?'"

Julia answered, "That's the ego."

"Yeah," Swami Shanti said, "that's ego. And remember, we're talking about the yogic ego—*ahamkara*, the I-maker. And what is it that the *ahamkara* does? What is its one mistake? It keeps saying that this has something to do with me or that it's mine, I possess it, or I am it. Wrong on all counts. I cannot possess it, and it's not who I am. Boo-hoo, *ahamkara* made a mistake. That's not who I am—a small mistake with huge implications.

"Once we realize that, we say, 'I have attachments. Of course, my mind will want to convince me that I don't have any desires.' Our minds will do that, even though we know they are phantoms. All they are is some mental head-trip, some sort of mental gymnastics.

"So what are we going to do? *Tapas*. We engage *tapas*, our desire to push through this thing, whatever it is. We're going to sit and ride it out. Let our determination for practice help us to ride through it. What do we do? We get over it. It washes off, and we keep going. There's a tendency to let it take over, to surrender to it, to crumble in the face of it. And there's something comforting about wallowing in it. And we wear it and feel terrible."

He paused as if in deep thought, slowly walking to the windows facing the Ganges and opening several. Turning back, he came back into the center of the meditation hall.

He removed his knit cap, tossed it to the bench, and said, "It's not about stopping, blocking, or suppressing. It's just about sitting with it and riding through it. I'm sitting in a meditative stance, but it's not meditation. Right now, where I am is *saucha*, purity—the first of the *niyamas*. I'm attempting to allow this mind to purify itself. How do I do that? I sit here and try to find *santosha*, contentment. I accept it and fall back on my determination, my *tapas*, not to wear it and wallow in it. This is just the way it works.

"Paying attention to my inner voice that's asking, 'What do I want?' I then decide to do what my heart wants, doing my practice, even if it means doing it by myself. I'm just going to do it. *Tapas*. Nothing's going to get in my way. I'm just going to DO IT!

"As you return to your everyday lives, remember to continue practicing the *yamas* and *niyamas*. Cultivate the Four Attitudes to combat negativity. Keep your body fit and healthy by doing your *asana* practice regularly so you can sit comfortably for meditation. Your breath is the connective tissue to meditation.

"When you're ready to sit, blow your nose, clear your mind. Focus on the body for a month. Then a month on the breath and a month using the *So-Ham* mantra. Work to lessen the *samskaras* and quiet those sleeping dogs so you can tiptoe across the field and reach the diamond of *samadhi*. Practice regularly and without attachment. Let go, and let it be. Just do it.

"Safe travels to wherever you go next," Swami Shanti said. "Keep the fires of *tapas* burning brightly, and keep up your practice, but remember that if you slip, just restart and keep going.

"OM. *Shanti, shanti, shanti.*"

With that, we ended our three-week retreat. Hugs and well wishes went all around as we prepared to go our separate ways. Our next practice was to pack for the return trip to the world of bills, mortgages, work, demands of relationships, and the big question: Could we sustain what we had learned?

By dinner, Siti and Rajani had left. Immediately after, Esther was on her way to Dehradun airport and her flight back to Delhi. Jackie and I decided we would take the train to Delhi, but that involved the ashram securing a driver who would pick us up at half past five in the morning to drive us to the train in Dehradun. With that settled, we thanked Swami Shanti for leading us through the retreat and thanked the staff for their help and support.

I had liked Swami Shanti's recap of practice after the dancers had left. With that and all of the background he had given us over the past three weeks, I felt the surge of tapas.

I had made an excellent decision to go to India after Diana's death. The whole experience had been good. I understood some of the issues that drove my life and looked forward to continuing to put the lessons into practice.

I appreciated the first-class coach's comfortable seats and the breakfast it offered. Our return to Delhi was a far cry from our journey to Rishikesh. The journey to the retreat had been harrowing and crazy. The retreat had brought insights and a new commitment to practice. The train to Delhi seemed a perfect way to bring the experience to a close and summed up the whole thing.

But I was curious to know how Jackie felt about Swami Shanti after they'd crossed swords. As expected, she was pretty vehement in her response. "Asshole" and "bastard" were the first words to come out of her mouth. Then she said, "I think he's on the spectrum. He's bright. But his social skills are zip, nada, and zilch. In one-on-ones, he doesn't make eye contact. Did you notice that? And the way he just came in, almost without preliminaries, jumped right into his topic. He just wrote on that damned whiteboard some cute greeting in German, or Danish, or whatever. And then when he just ended it and walked out. Very strange." She let her voice trail off. Then, turning directly toward me, she said, "Very strange. Don't you think so?"

She told me she had gone to him privately and asked for a mantra. He refused. He told her those personal mantras were gimmicks, and he wouldn't do gimmicky things.

She was probably correct in her evaluations. I found his writings much different than his personal teachings. His written materials were clear and concise. In person, he could turn on a dime—making perfect sense in his rambling way one minute, only to make a person feel belittled and foolish the next. These attitudes were never directed toward me, and I wondered if it had anything to do with the recent loss of my wife, since he had recently lost his mother.

I got a copy of the *Hindustan Times* from the coach steward and learned for the first time about the earthquake that had caused the nuclear disaster at Fukushima and the Arab Spring that was sweeping the Middle East. The train's rhythm made my eyes heavy as I read the paper, and I soon drifted off to sleep.

We were in Delhi by noon, where Jackie and I said our goodbyes. She'd fly out in the morning. I would spend a few days saying goodbye to Delhi, where I had begun to feel very much at home.

On the taxi ride back to the flat, I felt a lift seeing flowers in bloom throughout the city; it was, after all, nearly April. When I got to my neighborhood, I couldn't believe how beautiful it looked, with the blooming bougainvillea cascading over walls. While I would miss Delhi, I also looked forward to an in-person relationship with Louise. Emails had kept us in touch. Now I would see if we had a basis for a continuing relationship.

Chapter 42: Breathe for Health

After returning to Delhi, I had a few days to prepare for my flight home and reflect on my experiences.

As I thought about them, I realized that none of the participants had said they had a positive intimate relationship with another person. They were all either struggling with a strained relationship or had given up and were now living alone. No one had said they had a positive relationship in which they were practicing the deeper yoga principles.

I had met Louise just before I left. We'd connected immediately and had kept in contact over the past three months. Now I was ready to see if a long-term relationship was possible.

I would use my practice as a tool to foster this new relationship. Being a swami was not a life goal. I would never reach the level of practice of the Dalai Lama or one of his monks, but I had already gone deeper in a couple of the meditations at the ashram. I didn't need to obsess over it. I would do my practice and let go of the results.

What I knew was that over the last several years of practice, yoga had already made me a better person. I was more present, more attuned to those around me, less egotistical, less stressed. Being a better person in a positive relationship was what I chose as my goal. Baba Ram Dass's words resonated with me even more. "Be here now," he said. How much simpler could it be stated? That was the key. Be present and focus on living each moment as it comes. *Plan for the future, of course, but experience and live each moment.*

It sounded so simple, but as is often the case, putting it into practice is where we often fail. Rishikesh had helped me understand that. I am a big fan of starting with small baby steps and building from there. Courses, workshops, and books are often designed for people at all levels of practice, and it's easy for the beginner to focus on the end product and forget about the steps to get there. I know I've done that in the past. We see the goal, forgetting about the work we need to do to get there. In today's fast-food culture, we expect things to happen now, so our thinking skips over all of the hard work to the goal. Then it's easy to become discouraged. We expect perfection quickly and with ease. As Devika had said many years before, when she taught me about meditation, we should strive for persistence, not perfection, in our practices.

Over the years, several things have moved the needle for me—my loving-kindness meditation, the Four Attitudes, and a sense of gratitude for everything—everything, not just the seemingly good stuff but also the seemingly negative stuff. The negative stuff may be hard to embrace, but it is essential to do so.

After my return, Louise and I continued to deepen and expand our relationship. We eventually bought a house and married. For me, losing a spouse through death had made me appreciate life and our relationship in ways I had never experienced before. Swami Shanti was correct in one way when he asked us at the retreat if when we got married, we thought that it would end. That thought had never occurred to me when I married Vikki, nor when Diana and I got married, nor had I considered it when I lost my parents or *siblings. It was Diana's death that had made that clear to me. I don't obsess on the subject; it's just that I realized life should not be taken for granted. Even if it's only leaving the house on an errand, I know it could be the last time we see each other. And that knowledge, by itself, keeps me grounded and focused.*

Once back in my routine, I continued my practice. I felt comfortable with the postures, meditation, and yoga philosophy, but my weakest area was with the breath practices.

While doing research years before for the yoga pilot study, I came across a research paper on breathing practices called Sudarshan Kriya Yoga, or SKY. The paper was vague about the technique but specific about the results. The authors reported great success using the technique with victims of post-traumatic stress disorder (PTSD). A search of the literature turned up nothing about the technique itself, only that it was developed by Sri Sri Ravi Shankar, founder of the Art of Living Retreat Centers.

Some months after I returned from India, the Art of Living Center began teaching an introductory course in the SKY breathing technique. When I took the course, I was able to experience the effects of various breath exercises that altered me both physically and mentally. SKY was a very powerful practice. However, it was not one I felt comfortable doing regularly.

As I delved deeper into how breath affected the body, I learned about a man named Wim Hof, who used breath techniques he'd developed that allowed him to sit in an ice bath for over thirty minutes. Again, sitting in an ice bath was not something I ever wanted to do, but both SKY breathing and Wim Hof showed that how we breathe affects our bodies. These practices showed me how powerfully the breath can affect our well-being.

As I searched to learn more about breath, I stumbled upon a breath workshop at a Poconos center near Scranton, Pennsylvania, and immediately signed up for it.

When I got to the room at the center, about twenty-five of us were there to learn more about ways of using the breath to reduce stress and rewire our nervous systems. Jon, the first of our presenters, stepped onto the dais, a lavalier microphone clipped to his gray sweatshirt, and introduced himself as a psychiatrist with over twenty years of practice. He specialized in helping patients deal with trauma of one sort or another. His hair was short, and he sported a well-groomed beard; both were streaked with gray. He wore navy blue exercise pants and was barefoot.

"You have this stress response system," he said as he wrote the words "stress response" on a whiteboard. "This branch of your nervous system has two parts." He drew two diagonal lines downward, one to the left and one to the right. Under the one on the left, he wrote "action." "There's a part that helps us get rewards. That's the action part; it helps you get those things that make you feel good." As he turned to write on the whiteboard, he added with a smile, "Sex, drugs and rock 'n' roll, those sorts of things." Under the diagonal to the right, he wrote "inhibition." "And then there's the inhibition part—the holding back part—the stop, look, and listen part that keeps you from getting killed. This stress response system is counterbalanced by a recharging side that is part of our social bonding side that helps us tune into other people's feelings."

Jon stood in the middle of the dais; hands cupped one on top of the other at about belt level. "When you're in stress mode, what's your sense of humor like? It's not there, is it? What's your judgment like? Are your movements smooth and coordinated? This mode is pretty good for survival, but it's not so good on an ongoing basis, is it? When you're in stress mode, you're pretty much disconnected from other people, aren't you? It's not about them, is it? When you're in stress mode, it's more about you. It's about you dealing with a difficult situation. It's about your perceived survival."

He continued, standing very erect and composed, "Your breathing can, in a sense, regulate these systems. The way most of us breathe, we're almost constantly in maximal stress mode. Many of us breathe at around twenty or more breaths per minute. Now, when we're recharging, our breath rate slows down naturally so that this recharging can happen.

"And when we can turn on this recharging side of our system, our brains work better, our hearts and lungs work better, the blood vessels relax. Everything works better, and our whole system begins functioning as it should—like when we were young. These facts were noted in ancient Chinese medical texts, and they have since been verified by modern scientific methods without the researchers knowing about those old writings.

"We're going to do some exercises designed to bring our breath rates into the range of five to six breaths per minute."

With that brief introduction, Jon led us through a series of breath exercises designed to slow our breath rate. In those exercises, we visualized the breath moving through our bodies with each inhale and exhale while following his count.

He told us that if we were singers or competitive swimmers, we might already be accustomed to this sort of breathing. He mentioned in passing that many religious chants in the Catholic and Orthodox traditions are sung at the rate of five to six breaths per minute.

After warming us up with simple movements and breathing exercises, he introduced us to a *qigong* series of movements called the Four Golden Wheels. He explained that this ancient Chinese system envisioned a series of "wheels" or swirling energy centers in the body, much like the yogic system's chakras. The exercise, he said, was designed to activate and control these golden or precious energy centers. While some yoga purists may cringe at bringing *qigong* into a yoga practice, I'm all for it if it works.

Through the four-day workshop, we returned to these exercises and practiced them on ourselves and each other until we felt comfortable with them.

Susan was a copresenter with Jon. Probably in her early fifties, she was also a psychiatrist and a partner in his practice. She wore her straight, auburn hair pulled back behind her ears. Around her neck was a colorful scarf that set off her dark pantsuit. She wore no jewelry other than diamond studs in her earlobes.

She told us she would explain some of the science behind Jon's exercises.

"Our ancestors," she said, "tried for thousands of years to understand the brain, particularly how the monkey mind negatively affected our lives. Now, through fMRI studies of the brain, neuroscientists have learned that two important networks within the brain are at play. One of these networks is responsible for self-referencing, understanding the emotions of others, remembering the past, imagining a future, and general mind wandering. This network has been dubbed the default mode network, or DMN. The network comes online whenever our brains are not focused on a specific task."

She moved slowly around the dais, never losing eye contact with us. "When we focus on specific tasks," she said, "the DMN shuts down, allowing another network, the task-positive network, or the TPN, to take over. These two networks act as though a light switch controls them, that is, when one is on, the other is off. So when we focus our attention on a specific task, the TPN takes over, and the DMN shuts down. Our brains are no longer involved in mind wandering or that constant mental chatter. However, just as soon as attention is lost, the DMN comes back online, and mind wandering continues."

She paused in the center of the dais before continuing, "Rigorous studies of meditation and its associated slow breathing have shown a wide range of benefits: it has been shown to lower levels of stress hormones, lower blood pressure, boost the immune system, mitigate depression, anxiety, ADHD, and age-related cognitive decline, reduce the effects of psoriasis and irritable bowel syndrome. Meditation has been demonstrated to control and reduce pain. This may be because the DMN directly stimulates emotional reactivity, often a factor in how we perceive pain.

"Learning how to focus and hold our attention becomes increasingly important as we try to shield our brains from the constant bombardment of advertisements, emails, text messages, and the stream of notifications from our electronic devices. The more we unconsciously allow our awareness to be diverted and misdirected, the less aware we are that it is happening."

Light glistened off one of her earrings as she moved around the dais. "To get an idea of how meditation can do all of these things, we might review the workings of our nervous system," she said. "And this amplifies what Jon said at the beginning of his exercises with you.

"The autonomic nervous system is divided into the sympathetic nervous system (SNS) and the parasympathetic nervous system (PNS). When we are faced with a threatening situation, the SNS prepares us for action, setting us up to fight or flee. To do this, it floods the body with stress hormones, which speed up the heart and increase respiration and muscular tension. The SNS uses a lot of energy, and to be able to do that, it shuts down bodily functions that are not needed to meet the perceived threat, like the digestive and reproductive functions. Then it diverts all of its energy to meeting the threat or fleeing from that perceived danger.

"When the threat is over, what should happen is the PNS should come online automatically to slow down the heart rate and decrease respiration and muscular tension. It begins repairing muscular tissue and cellular

305

damage caused during the SNS activity and restarts digestive and reproductive functions. This is the body's rest and repair function."

Before continuing, she sipped from a glass of water. "That's how it is supposed to work, but the stress hormone level can take several hours to lower naturally. If we are constantly under stress, or if the brain perceives we are under constant threat, like when our breath is fast, these hormones may continue to circulate in the body at high levels, resulting in ongoing muscular tension, high heart and breath rates, and cell damage that doesn't get repaired.

"So where does this leave us? What can we do about it? The answer to that is the breath. We can consciously regulate our breathing or let it work automatically. Our heart rate tends to follow our breath rate. So, by consciously regulating our breath, we can slow or speed up the heart rate, reduce our stress level, and bring relaxation to our muscular system."

A strand of hair had fallen across her face, and she brushed it back behind her ear before continuing. "A key to understanding how to use the breath for these purposes is understanding something called heart rate variability or HRV. When we inhale, our heart rate speeds up slightly, and when we exhale, our heart rate slows down a bit. The difference between the heart rate on the inhale and the exhale is what's called HRV. The greater this difference, the less stressed and the more relaxed we are. By contrast, the lower the difference, the more revved up and the more stressed we are. So a lower HRV is a marker for stress."

Susan paused to let us absorb that fact, then said, "Next, it will help us understand breathing mechanics. We need to breathe like a baby from our diaphragm. When a baby sleeps on its back, its belly rises with each inhale and falls with each exhale. As soon as the baby can sit up, it does so with a straight back, and its belly moves outward with each inhale and back toward the spine with the exhale. Then, somewhere in late childhood, many people begin to think that they don't look cool if their bellies expand when they inhale, so they stop breathing diaphragmatically and begin to rely on their chest muscles to do the work.

"Consequently, we breathe more shallowly and rapidly to get the same amount of air. However, the body interprets this as being under threat because rapid breath signals the SNS that the body is under threat. As a result, stress hormones may be secreted into the bloodstream."

> *Different breath patterns can, as I discovered, produce different mental states. Early in my exploration of yoga, I had learned there were three parts of the body involved with breathing: the shoulders, the chest, and the diaphragm. When the shoulder or chest muscles become the primary muscles for breathing, we breathe in short, shallow breaths and activate the fight or flight reflex.*

> *I once had a woman in class who breathed only from her shoulders and chest, overworking and stressing those muscles. Increased stress on these muscles led to imbalances, which caused irritation and pain throughout her body. Additionally, her short, shallow breathing caused her to experience panic attacks. Unfortunately, in the brief time she came to class, she could not learn to engage her diaphragm.*

> *Three breath patterns are worth learning and using regularly. The first is called balancing breath and can be used to maintain relative calm within the body and mind. The other two are excellent for dealing with acute stress (see Appendix C).*

In other sessions, Susan explained how stress affects the body and the importance of recognizing it in ourselves so we can more effectively deal with it.

She said a person who is not stressed feels safe, comfortable, and relaxed in relationships. Things go smoothly. This person's job is secure and rewarding. The kids are all in good places, and this person is in a loving and stable relationship.

Then there's an edgy person who maybe has a short fuse. This person is revved up, even without realizing it. When sitting, this person may fidget or bounce a leg. Their breath is fast, and they have worries and concerns. Sometimes, they may even acknowledge the feeling of stress or pressure. Distraction therapy is how they deal with their mild stress: drinking, drugs, shopping, and general avoidance. They are defensive because they don't feel emotionally safe. This person may go through the motions but isn't engaged with others except superficially.

Next, she described the truly stressed-out individual. This person may be so stressed that when confronted with a disaster of any sort, they cannot cope without an explosion. Maybe there's a disaster, a flood, a terrorist attack, a shooting at a school or workplace. Perhaps they have an abusive partner or deal with a bully at work or school. This person probably hates to go to work and is constantly on edge and alert. And as a result, this person maintains distance from loved ones.

Then Susan said, "We become so used to stress in our bodies that we aren't even aware it is there. Each major stress event resets our stress points. Constant stress doesn't give the body a chance to repair itself—to rebuild cells that have been damaged because the body is in perpetual stress mode. Over time, constant stress becomes a silent killer."

What do we do with all of this information? We change our habits. We learn to breathe from the diaphragm to control and slow our natural breath, reducing our stress level.

To paraphrase the second line of the Yoga Sutras, "Yoga is the quieting of the mind's self-generated mental gymnastics." In other words, it's trying to teach us how to control the default mode network that Susan described. Yoga is trying to teach us how to deal with stress on a very deep level and Jon's breathing techniques fit nicely into yoga's pranayama, *its breath practices. If we use these techniques properly, we will certainly reap many worthwhile benefits. In short, we have to do it. Don't overthink it; get on with it.*

As I began to work with these breathing techniques and relate them to my meditation, I found that I paid more attention to the technique and not enough attention to the actual practice itself. I learned a valuable lesson: It is essential to set an intention. Setting an intention framed my efforts and directed my focus back to the practice. My unstated intention had been to focus on technique—to create a proper heart and breath pattern using an electronic gizmo I'd bought to measure stress reduction caused by greater HRV through meditation. Then one day, I realized I was not practicing as I'd learned in Rishikesh; I wasn't tiptoeing through the field of sleeping dogs. I was dancing around the edge of the field and ignoring the dogs completely. I was not even heading in the direction of that diamond on the other side of the field. So I packed the heart monitor and other gadgets in a drawer. Now I use my meditation timer and focus as I learned in Rishikesh.

Toward the end of Hermann Hesse's Siddhartha, *a wonderful scene speaks to how we can become sidetracked by our expectations and unframed intentions. Govinda, Siddhartha's childhood friend, comes to a river and asks the old man, Siddhartha, to ferry him across. And Govinda says to his old friend, "You have ferried many monks across the river, are you not also a seeker of the right path?" He adds that he has never stopped seeking. Siddhartha replies that maybe Govinda has been seeking too much, and that's his problem. But Govinda doesn't understand and asks for an explanation.*

Siddhartha says that when we seek, we only see the thing we are seeking, and that focus makes it easy to miss the jewel under our noses. He's saying that being goal oriented sets up expectations that cause us to miss the very thing that we are seeking. He's telling Govinda, and us, to be open to serendipity, that searching, or hunting for something limits the field of view making it easy to miss the jewel we were not expecting to find.

Chapter 43: If Yoga Doesn't Change You

After experiencing that rooftop epiphany in Kerala, I explored Indian symbolism and metaphor and, without realizing it, prepared myself for my first yoga experience. Richard Freeman, an internationally recognized yoga teacher, described yoga as a wish-fulfilling tree. Initially, I thought of it as something other than watching TV in my retirement. I saw it as an exercise program that would keep me strong and flexible as I aged. I got that and much more.

Gradually, yoga nudged me toward paying closer attention to my life and the influences on it. I became more centered and grounded, learning to "control the modifications of the mind-field," in other words, to turn off the chatter of my monkey mind. Through yoga, I became less judgmental, more positive in my outlook, and grateful for the gifts I received.

I am thankful for the power of guru that lit the curiosity and determination to push open the door to yoga. I am grateful for the intricate web of people and events that led to yoga and the full range of its practices. I am appreciative for all of the lessons my Buddhas taught me, for the serendipitous events that led me through a maze of experiences to where I am today, and I reflect on what Joseph Campbell said about knowing we're on the right path when we feel an invisible hand is leading us.

In the late 1920s, Yogananda traveled this country lecturing on the unity of all religions. If I have learned nothing else, it is the truth of that message. Any community of faith could easily teach some of the lessons and values I learned on my journey. The man trying to kill the vyala of desire even as it

311

eats him alive, or Maharathi's painting, Truth Seeking Man Caught in a Whirlpool of Temptation, *could inspire interesting homilies. Maybe someday.*

My relationship with my father was not always positive during our lives together. But through meditation and reflection, I have connected many dots and now see him in a new light. Thich Nhat Hanh said that when he meets someone, he meets that person's entire lineage. We are each a representation of ourselves and our entire history stretching back through time. Each of us is a continuation of our parents, as they were of theirs. Our ancestors, he says, were not always skillful parents because of the difficulties they encountered.

When my father was born, his mother was forty, and his sisters were already married. He was eight when his father left town with a woman in the neighborhood. To support herself and her young son, my grandmother traveled to nearby towns with her son, where she would rent a house for a few months. Then the two of them would go door-to-door as she sold cosmetics and home remedies from a wagon he pulled. She also took book orders. He told me that when the Titanic sank, her book sales soared.

As an older child, he did odd jobs to augment the family income. By age ten, several businesses in town trusted him with the keys to their stores. Arriving at around six o'clock on winter mornings, he lit the coal stoves before the stores opened for business. He and another lad regularly rented a team of horses to deliver newspapers around town. While still a boy, he was a carny at circus and carnival midways, selling tickets to sideshows. Then, when oil was discovered in Southern Illinois, he worked in the nearby oil fields. By his late teens, he was a partner in a photo studio until his

312

partner ran off with the money. So it was no wonder he didn't know how to let a kid be a kid or how to be a parent.

My mother recalled that when she was ten, during the 1915–16 influenza epidemic, her mother nursed her own family as well as her neighbors until she became sick and died. In my mother's anger toward her mother, she had tried to erase her memories. It wasn't until she was in her early sixties that she tried to recover them by talking with her older siblings and painting childhood scenes that recalled better days. So when my parents came into their marriage, they were both, in a sense, broken people.

Before my older sister Mary died, my father had a closer relationship with my older siblings than with Jayne and me. Her death changed everything, as he lost himself in religion and his work. It wasn't unusual for him to spend sixty or eighty hours a week at the stores he managed.

Although he began working full-time after eighth grade, my father continued to educate himself for the rest of his life. Part of our problem may have been my inability to understand and appreciate that he had given me the college education he'd never had for himself. And then I chose to be a wallpaper hanger rather than use my education to make a living.

As my father aged he softened a bit and tried to fix things between us, but I couldn't meet him halfway. This was partly because I didn't recognize his overtures and partly because I didn't know how to soften myself to accept him. Unfortunately, it was many years after his death that I began to understand the role that argument between my parents had played in tainting our relationship. It's too bad we can't conjure up our parents, tell them what we should have told them, and ask the questions we didn't ask when the opportunity was there.

Before Mary's death, my father's company was grooming him to take over their flagship store in Minneapolis. However, when she died, he wanted out of the corporate rat race, but he still had a nine-year contractual commitment to the company. Management's solution was to send him to their worst-performing store in the wilds of South Dakota, hoping he would beg to return to the corporate Promised Land. Instead, he set out to turn around this underperforming store in the company's metaphorical Siberia. After his death, I found detailed records in his files of how he did it. When he left the company, he used this knowledge to turn around other retail stores.

As much as I didn't want to be like my father, I came to realize that I was Frick to his Frack. I kept meticulous work records that allowed me to create an estimating spreadsheet for painting jobs and a computer program to calculate papering jobs.

Despite the difficulties of our relationship, I learned from his example how to run a business and avoid its pitfalls. He taught me the power of advertising and how to ignore advertisers' attempts "to get their hands into my wallet." So I learned to ignore fads and read newspapers without seeing their advertisements.

Randy J. Paterson points out in his book, How to Be Miserable: 40 Strategies You Already Use, *that advertisers create desires in us, but purchasing the objects of our desires only creates a short-lived sense of happiness, maybe lasting a week or so at best. This is one of yoga's central teachings. When we visit an online site, we are bombarded with* notifications telling us that because we were interested in such and such, we might also be interested in this and that. These online world features shorten our attention span in the real world, making yoga meditation even more critical as a counterbalance.

Ultimately, I have accepted that I am very much my father's son and that the acorn didn't fall far from the tree. It got me to where I am today, and for that, I am grateful. Thank you, Dad.

Sam, my former son-in-law, commented years ago that if India didn't change someone, that person wasn't paying attention. The same could also be said about yoga. If yoga doesn't change us, we haven't been paying attention. As in life, yoga tells us, we must be present to win.

Without yoga, I would not have recognized the many Buddhas who taught and guided me. I would not have seen the serendipitous gifts placed in my path to lead me through a maze of experiences. I would not have been aware of Joseph Campbell's invisible guiding hand. I am grateful for all of these and the power of guru, which lit the curiosity and determination that let me push open the door to yoga.

Life is good. Things feel settled. That happy child has taken up permanent residence and will help with whatever lies ahead. And I have at least found the doorway to wisdom.

I hope the lessons recounted here can be a guiding hand for others on their journey.

OM! Shanti. Shanti. Shanti. Peace. Peace. Peace.

Acknowledgments

This book is written in grateful acknowledgments to all of those in my life who made this work possible. That would include just about everyone that I have interacted with in the course of my life, some whose paths I crossed but never knew. I would like to thank all of the Buddhas, whether mentioned as such or not, who came into my life to teach me the lessons I needed to learn. In particular. I would like to thank the members of the writer's group who took me in when I needed their help. I may have bridled at your initial suggestions, but ultimately, I came to see that you were correct in your suggestions.

I am grateful to the web of connections that have brought me to where I am today and will continue to guide me on my path. I am grateful for all of the serendipitous occurrences that have led me to where I am today. I am grateful to my ancestors without whom none of this would have been possible. I am grateful to all who have come into my life both directly and indirectly.

A special thanks goes to all of the Buddhas in my life who steered me to the discovery of yoga's special way of seeing and being. But especially, I would like to thank my very first teacher who introduced me to yoga all those years ago at a workshop I attended. I am sorry I do not remember your name, but you had a tremendous impact on my life. There are many to whom I owe a debt of gratitude for helping no my journey: Iris who helped me fall in love with yoga, Devika who first taught me meditation, Sarah and her three-hundred-hour teacher training course, the Raja Yoga Center where I took my first yoga workshop, Catherine from whom I learned to teach yoga to people with multiple sclerosis, Satya whose Cardiac Yoga training taught me about cardiac issues and teaching yoga to that population, Swami Shantiananda for his thought-provoking teachings on the Yoga Sutras at his retreat center and at his ashram in India, Jon and Susan for their workshop on the power of breath and especially all of my students who have taught me so much over the years.

I have tried to reflect your teachings as accurately as I could. My apologies if I have strayed.

A special thanks to my five technical readers. Your input was invaluable in pulling this work together.

And a very special thank to Bonnie Craig, my copy editor and proofreader, for finding my inconsistencies, and suggesting improvements to the text. Her aid was invaluable in pulling this work together. Any errors in the copy were made by me after she worked her magic.

Thank you all for your inspiration. I endeavor to continue the chain and inspire others as you have me.

Appendices

Appendix A: Yoga Sutras Abridged

Below is the heart, or meat, of the Yoga Sutras for our purposes. Beyond YS 3.6, the Yoga Sutras move into esoteric concepts beyond the scope of this work. To continue study of the Yoga Sutras, the reader is best advised to obtain a complete copy with commentaries.

Samadhi Pada: Concentration—Chapter 1

YS 1.1—After you have looked for understanding of how your head works, you have finally come to yoga for an answer.

YS 1.2—Yoga is the quieting of the mind's self-generated mental gymnastics.

YS 1.3—When we have done this, then the Seer rests in its True Nature.

YS 1.4—When not, well, we identify with those thoughts and live the crazy life of our mental monkey.

YS 1.5—Our thoughts, or *vrittis* can be useful or nonuseful.

YS 1.6—There are five varieties of thought patterns to pay attention to.

YS 1.7—Of these five, there are three ways to gain correct knowledge.

YS 1.8—Incorrect knowledge is illusion based on false information.

YS 1.9—Fantasy is thought pattern with no basis in reality.

YS 1.10—Dreaming is thought based on nonexistent stuff.

YS 1.11—Memory is thought based on reproducing previous impressions.

YS 1.12—Thoughts are mastered by practice and nonattachment.

YS 1.13—Practice means learning and doing mental stabilization exercises.

YS 1.14—A firm foundation is established when practicing with sincerity over an extended time.

YS 1.15—Nonattachment occurs when mental attractions to these nonuseful thoughts, words, and/or deeds are lost.

YS 1.16—When even the subtlest attraction for nonuseful thoughts, words, or deeds is lost, this is Supreme nonattachment.

YS 1.17—Attention develops in four stages.

YS 1.18—In deep absorption there is no object of meditation.

YS 1.19—There are two kinds of aspirants: those naturally advanced and the rest of us.

YS 1.20—The rest of us work to cultivate five core attitudes and goals.

YS 1.21—The more your conviction as you work and practice the better your practice and its results.

YS 1.22—For those with intense practice and conviction, there are three levels of attainment.

YS 1.23—Through meditation on OM we can let go into enlightenment.

YS 1.24—That enlightened state is unaffected by colorings, actions, or results of past acts.

YS 1.25—That is the highest development.

YS 1.26—That is how the most ancient teachers were taught.

YS 1.27—The sound designating this state is OM.

YS 1.28—The sound is remembered with deep feeling for its represented meaning.

YS 1.29—From this comes the realization of Self and the removal of obstacles.

YS 1.30—There are nine distractive hazards that arise and can become disturbances.

YS 1.31—From these nine obstacles arise four consequences.

YS 1.32—Deal with the nine obstacles and their four consequences through "one-pointedness," the focusing with singular attention.

YS 1.33—The mind becomes balanced through practice of the Four Attitudes.

YS 1.34—The mind is calmed by regulating the breath.

YS 1.35—Meditating on the means of sensing calms and stills the mind.

YS 1.36—Special concentration brings stability and tranquility.

YS 1.37—Contemplating a mind free of desires brings stability.

YS 1.38—Meditation on states of unconsciousness brings stability.

YS 1.39—Meditation on one's predisposed object brings stability.

YS 1.40—Once stabilized, the mind can begin examining subtle objects.

YS 1.41—The mind becomes like a transparent crystal.

YS 1.42—Meditation begins to engage a word, its meaning, and the knowledge associated with it.

YS 1.43—With the calming of thought waves, the object shines through.

YS 1.44—This also happens with subtle objects.

YS 1.45—The process extends to unmanifest objects.

YS 1.46—These four kinds of concentrations are only ones having a seed object.

YS 1.47—As we become better, a purity of the inner instrument develops.

YS 1.48—Knowledge gained at this point is essential basic wisdom.

YS 1.49—This knowledge is without words or concepts.

YS 1.50—This creates *samskaras* that impede the formation of less useful *samskaras.*

YS 1.51—When these recede, there is objectless concentration.

Sadhana Pada: Practice—Chapter 2

YS 2.1—Living the practice of *Kriya Yoga*'s triple practice.

YS 2.2—*Kriya Yoga* lessens power of *kleshas.*

YS 2.3—These *kleshas* are five.

YS 2.4—Each lies on a continuum.

YS 2.5—Spiritual ignorance is the cause of all suffering which arises out of these *kleshas.*

YS 2.6—Ego identifies self with thought patterns.

YS 2.7—Desire arises from a sense of a separate self.

YS 2.8—Avoidance is a negative desire.

YS 2.9—Fear is a desire for continuity and avoidance of change.

YS 2.10—With *kleshas* reduced to seed form, only memory remains.

YS 2.11—Meditation reduces *kleshas* to seed form.

YS 2.12—Acting from our mental disturbances deposits their fruits in latent unconscious.

YS 2.13—Actions performed in a mentally disturbed state reinfect our actions.

YS 2.14—Fruits of our actions produce useful or nonuseful results.

YS 2.15—The discerning person sees all as suffering.

YS 2.16—Future suffering can be avoided.

YS 2.17—Suffering is caused by identification of self with objects experienced.

YS 2.18—Objects of experience are of three types.

YS 2.19—Each perception of the seen is different, yet the Seer remains the same.

YS 2.20 That which is Seeing is pure consciousness.

YS 2.21—The relationship between Seer and Seen is same for all objects Seen.

YS 2.22—After Seer has perceived the nature of knowable object Seen, it ceases to exist for the Seer, but not others.

YS 2.23—Alliance between Seer and Seen allows discovery of True Self.

YS 2.24—Spiritual ignorance lets alliance of Seer and Seen appear to exist.

YS 2.25—Once spiritual ignorance is dissolved, the alliance of Seer and Seen dissolves, bringing enlightenment.

YS 2.26—Discriminative knowledge is key to freedom from spiritual ignorance.

YS 2.27—Then certain insights manifest to that person.

YS 2.28—Practice of the eight limbs or steps eliminates impurities, leading to wisdom.

YS 2.29—These are: restraints, observances, poses, breath, sense withdrawal, concentration, meditation, absorption.

YS 2.30—Restraints: nonharming, truthfulness, nonstealing, sexual restraint, nongreed.

YS 2.31—Through practice, these extend to all beings.

YS 2.32—Observances: purity, contentment, hard work, inner exploration, surrender.

YS 2.33—Eliminate negativity through the Four Attitudes.

YS 2.34—Our negativity results in harm to self and others.

YS 2.35—Our nonviolence helps others be so too.

YS 2.36—When truthfulness is established, it flows from all of our acts.

YS 2.37—When nonstealing is established, things come to us.

YS 2.38—With sexual restraint, good comes to us.

YS 2.39—With nongreed comes deep understanding of life.

YS 2.40—With purity comes order.

YS 2.41—With purity comes mental balance.

YS 2.42—With contentment comes happiness.

YS 2.43—When senses are under control, we have full mastery of body and mind.

YS 2.44—Through self-study one gains union of self with Self.

YS 2.45—By surrendering, we come to deepest meditative state.

YS 2.46—The posture for meditation should be steady, stable, and motionless.

YS 2.47—Asana is perfected through relaxed afford.

YS 2.48—Perfected posture lets one transcend the duality of opposites.

YS 2.49—With perfected pose, breathing leads to a natural control of breath.

YS 2.50—Breath is of three types: exhale, inhale, and transition.

YS 2.51—There is a fourth pranayama, deeper and more subtle that the other three.

YS 2.52—Through breathwork mental disturbances are thinned, diminished, and vanish.

YS 2.53—Through breathwork the mind is readied to develop concentration.

YS 2.54—The Fifth Step occurs when sense organs stop engaging with their objects and dissolve.

YS 2.55—Then the senses are completely mastered.

Vibhuti Pada: Progressing—Chapter 3

YS 3.1—Concentration holds attention on an object.

YS 3.2—Holding on one object is meditation.

YS 3.3—When holding on one object, even devoid of its own form, is liberation.

YS 3.4—These last three, when focusing on a single object are called *samyama*.

YS 3.5—Through *samyama*, higher knowledge comes.

YS 3.6—*Samyama* is gradually refined.

For the remaining 50 lines of this and the entirety of the next chapter, *Liberation*, please obtain a complete translation and commentary on the Yoga Sutras.

Appendix B: Meditations

The Four Attitudes

May I be friendly toward the joyful.
May I be compassionate toward the suffering.
May I celebrate the good in others, and
May I be impartial to the faults and failings of others.
Yoga Sutras 1.33

A Loving-Kindness Meditation

May I be filled with loving-kindness.
May I be well.
May I be peaceful and at ease.
May I be happy as I am.
May I cause no pain or suffering.
May I have the patience, courage, understanding, and determination to meet and overcome the inevitable difficulties, problems, failures, and losses in life.

May my friends and loved ones be filled with loving-kindness.
May my friends and loved ones be well.
May my friends and loved ones be peaceful and at ease.
May my friends and loved ones be happy as I am.
May my friends and loved ones cause no pain or suffering.
May my friends and loved ones have the patience, courage, understanding, and determination to meet and overcome the inevitable difficulties, problems, failures, and losses in life.

May all beings be filled with loving-kindness.
May all beings be well.
May all beings be peaceful and at ease.
May all beings be happy as I am.
May all beings feel no pain or suffering caused by others.
May all beings have the patience, courage, understanding, and determination to meet and overcome the inevitable difficulties,

327

problems, failures, and losses in life.

Sixty-One Points of Relaxation
One breath, one point

As you move from point to point around your body, you may visualize these points as skin, bone, joints, or simply as awareness, or perhaps simply as a point of light. However you visualize these points is alright. Try and move from point to point with one inhale and one exhale each. Then move to the next point. If you get lost, you can start over, or simply go back to the last point of your awareness. You can also shorten the process at the lower abdomen and retrace back to the forehead.

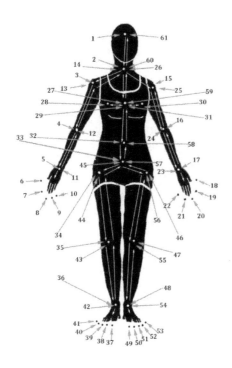

1. Be aware of the forehead. You may experience it as skin or simply as awareness. You may visualize it as a point of light or in some other way.
2. Be aware of your throat. You may experience it as the skin, the joint, or as an awareness. Maybe as a point of light or in some

328

other way.
3. Be aware of your right shoulder.
4. Be aware of your right elbow.
5. Be aware of your right wrist.
6. Be aware of the tip of your right thumb.
7. Be aware of the tip of your right index finger.
8. Be aware of the tip of your right middle finger.
9. Be aware of the tip of your right ring finger.
10. Be aware of the tip of your right little finger.
11. Be aware of your right wrist.
12. Be aware of your right elbow.
13. Your right shoulder.
14. Your throat.
15. Your left shoulder.
16. Your left elbow.
17. Your left wrist.
18. The tip of the left thumb.
19. The tip of the left index finger.
20. The tip of the left middle finger
21. The tip of the left ring finger.
22. The tip of the little finger.
23. The left wrist.
24. The left elbow.
25. The left shoulder
26. The throat.
27. The heart-center.
28. The right chest.
29. The heart-center.
30. The left chest.
31. The heart-center.
32. The navel.
33. The lower abdomen.
34. The right hip.
35. The right knee.
36. The right ankle.
37. The tip of the right big toe.
38. The tip of the right second toe.
39. The tip of the right middle toe.
40. The tip of the right fourth toe.
41. The tip of the right little toe.
42. The right ankle.
43. The right knee.

44. The right hip.
45. The lower abdomen.
46. The left hip.
47. The left knee.
48. The left ankle.
49. The tip of the left big toe.
50. The tip of the left second toe.
51. The tip of the left middle toe.
52. The tip of the fourth toe.
53. The tip of the left little toe.
54. The left ankle.
55. The left knee.
56. The left hip.
57. The lower abdomen.
58. The navel.
59. The heart-center.
60. The throat.
61. The forehead.

Appendix C: Breathwork

What happens to your body and mind when you breathe fast? When you exercise? What happens to your breath and mind when you relax? When you recall a bad memory?

The state of your body, mind, and emotions control how you breathe. Conversely, by consciously controlling your breath, you can control the state of your body, mind, and emotions. Just by deepening and slowing your breath regularly for a few minutes every day, you can begin to lower your heart rate, blood pressure, and stress. Over time and with regular practice, you can make these changes habitual.

Here are some simple exercises to try.

1. **Quick Calming Practices**
    a. Sit upright with a long spine, eyes closed, hands on your lap, palms down, tongue on the roof of the mouth, and teeth slightly apart. Allow a half smile to form on your lips.
    b. Ask yourself without judgment: How am I breathing? Is my breath feeling comfortable or is it feeling restricted?

2. **Heart-Center Practice**
    a. Observe yourself without judgment.
    b. With your eyes still closed, left palm at heart, right hand on top:
        (1) Exhale all of the air out slowly and gently.
        (2) Inhale, expanding in all directions from your heart.
    c. Repeat a few more times slowly—three to five times— lengthening and deepening the breath each time.
    d. Observe yourself without judgment.

3. **Lower Abdomen Practice**
    a. Observe yourself without judgment.
    b. With your eyes still closed, left palm to lower abdomen, right hand on top:
        (1) Exhale all of the air out slowly and gently.

> (2) Inhale, expanding in all directions from your lower abdomen.
> c. Repeat a few more times slowly—three to five times—lengthening and deepening the breath each time.
> d. Observe yourself without judgment.

4. Humming Breath Practice
> a. Observe yourself without judgment.
> b. Inhale, and as you exhale, hum—pay attention to the evenness of the tone:
>> (1) Keep your breath long, slow and steady.
>> (2) Repeat the hum more slowly and strongly three to five times.
> c. Observe yourself without judgment.

Through regular practice for a few minutes a day, you can lower your heart rate, blood pressure, and stress. Over time, a regular practice can be firmly established that will bring big results. An ongoing practice of Balancing Breath for five to ten minutes a day will maintain these gains.

And when encountering stressful situations Square, Breath, or 4-4-6-2 Breath done for five to ten minutes can restore your balance.

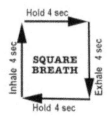

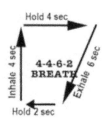

Appendix D: Pronunciation Guide & Terms

Pronunciation Guide

Below is a simplified version of Sanskrit transliteration and the English spelling of those terms. Please note there are no silent letters in Sanskrit. As a general rule, the vowels are pronounced as in Latin or Spanish.

a	as in **fa**ther or **ca**lm
e	as in s**a**ve or w**ai**t
i	as in s**ea**t or c**l**ean
o	as in **co**at or **co**ne
u	as in **coo**t or **boo**t
r	in Sanskrit, **r** is a vowel as **ri** in c**ri**cket
ai	as in **pie** or s**ky**
au	as in **tow**n or **cow**
th	as in **t**op or ho**th**ouse, never as the English **th** sound in **the** or **th**ink
h	after a consonant, **h** gives that consonant an aspirated sound as in up**h**old
jñ	as **gny** or a **g**-sound followed by ca**ny**on
v	following a vowel or beginning a word sounded as **v**
v	following a consonant, it sounds like a **w**

Glossary of Terms

A

Abhinivesha—Fear; one of the *kleshas*; a result of spiritual ignorance, *avidya*

Abhyasa—Practice in the broadest sense; along with *vairagya,* a cornerstone of yoga practice

Ahamkara—Ego, literally the I-maker, the creator of a sense of a separate self

Ahimsa—Nonharming in thought, word, or deed; the first *yama*

Agrajananda—Swami Shanti's teacher

Amritsar—City in northwestern state of Punjab, India

Ananda—The state of bliss; not the emotion of happiness

Anika—A woman's name meaning grace or brilliant

Anjali—Prayer, also a woman's name

Antahkarana—The totality of mind, including buddhi, chitta, ahamkara, and manas

Aparigraha—Nonhoarding; not taking more than one's share; the fifth *yama*

Arjuna —A metaphor for Everyman in the Bhagavad Gita

Arunachala—A mountain west of Puducherry and home of Ramana Maharshi

Asana—Postures or poses; the third of the Eight-Limbs or Eight Petals of Yoga

Aseemanand—A swami accused of bombing a train in 2007, later acquitted

Ashoka—Third Mauryan emperor ruling over much of present-day India (304-232 BCE; converted to Buddhism and promoted righteous living.

Asmita—Ego; one of the *kleshas*; a consequence of spiritual ignorance, *avidya*

Asmita—Literally I-am-ness; the ego creating the sense of a separate self

Ashtanga Yoga—Yoga's eight-fold path; also the Eight Limbs or Eight Petals of Yoga: *yama, niyama, asana, pranayama, pratyahara, dharana, dhyana, samadhi*

Asteya—Not taking anything not freely given; nonstealing; the third *yama*

Atman—Life principle, roughly analogous to the soul

Atha—Now in the sense of after a period of preparation; the first word of the Yoga Sutras

Aurobindo—Indian philosopher, yogi, poet and nationalist (1872–1950)

Auroville—International community founded by a follower of Sri Aurobindo

Avidya—Spiritual ignorance; one of the *kleshas*

Ayyappan—Hindu deity of truth and righteousness; a modern temple in the city of Tiruchirappalli, Tamil Nadu, India

Ayodhya—City in state of Uttar Pradesh and birthplace of Ram

B

Baba Ram Dass—American spiritual teacher and author of *Be Here Now*

Babri Masjid—Mosque in Ayodhya destroyed by mob in December 1992

Basant Lok—Upscale shopping center in Delhi

Bharatanatyam—A classical Indian dance form originating in the state of Tamil Nadu

Brahmacharya—Appropriate sexual behavior; the fourth *yama*

Bharatiya Janata—Hindu nationalist political party

Brahman—The ultimate reality underlying all of the manifest and unmanifest reality

Buddhi—The executive functioning part of the mind

C

Chamundi—A local name for Shiva's consort Parvati, the Destroyer of Ignorance

Charpoy—A low bed constructed of a wood frame and rope straps also used as a couch

Chennai—City on Bay of Bengal, Tamil Nadu, India, formerly Madras

Chitta—The part of the mind representing emotional and unconscious responses

D

Darshan—Literally, a glimpse or viewing that imparts merit to the viewer

DMN—The brain's default mode network responsible for rumination and mind wandering

Dhaba—A roadside rest stop, usually with a restaurant

Dharma—The Truth of things and our relationship to that Truth

Dharana—Concentration; the sixth of the Eight Petals of Yoga

Dhoti—A long loincloth traditionally worn by Hindu men in south Asia

Dhyana—Meditation; the seventh of the Eight Petals of Yoga

Dvesha—Aversions; one of the *kleshas*; a consequence of spiritual ignorance; *avidya*

Dukkha—Pain, suffering, unhappiness; opposite of *sukha*

F

Four Attitudes—Four positive attitudes counterbalancing negativity; YS 1.33

G

Ghat—Flight of steps to a body of water; a mountain pass

Gopuram—An entrance tower to a Hindu temple

Gujarat—Western state in India on Arabian Sea and the Pakistani border

Guru—A power or force that brings understanding

H

Harappa—Indus Valley civilization that thrived approximately 2500–1700 BCE

Haveli—A traditional merchant's mansion in Rajasthan, India

Hawa Mahal—Building in Jaipur, formerly housing for court women

HRV—Heart rate variability; the variation of heart rate on inhale and exhale

I

Indra's Web—A metaphor for describing the interconnectedness of all creation

Indriyas—The senses; specifically, the senses of knowing and of action

Ishvara Pranidhana—That which is greater than ourselves; fifth *niyama*; also third element of *Kriya Yoga*

J

Jhansi—Historic city in the Indian state of Uttar Pradesh

Jhula—A bridge

K

Kaivalya—The idea of total and absolute detachment; title of the fourth chapter of the Yoga Sutras

Kerala—State in southwest India on the Malabar Coast

Khajuraho—Town in Chhatarpur district of the state of Madhya Pradesh with eighty-four temples displaying erotic sculptures

Karma—Action, including thoughts, words, and deeds

Kathakali—A dance style originating in the Indian state of Kerala

Karmashaya—The storehouse of *samskaras*; the unconscious

Kleshas—The five hindrances to spiritual growth: *avidya, asmita, raga, dvesha, abhinivesha*

Klishta—Distressed, afflicted, tormented

Klishta Vritti—Colored or clouded memory traces

Krishna—Avatar of Vishnu, Arjuna's charioteer in the Bhagavad Gita

Kriya Yoga—A method of purifying actions through *tapas, svadhyaya,* and *ishvara pranidhana*

Kriyamana—Future consequences of actions

Kshipta—A disturbed mental state

Kumbakonam—City near Thanjavur, Tamil Nadu, India

Kumarakom—Town in the southwestern State of Kerala

L

Lalit—Man's name

Lakshmi—Goddess and consort of Vishnu; also a woman's name

M

Madras—City in state of Tamil Nadu, India, now called Chennai

Madurai—City in state of Tamil Nadu, India and home of Meenakshi temple

Mahabharata—Indian epic narrating events and aftermath of Kurukshetra War; also a metaphor for man's spiritual struggle

Malabar Coast—The coastal region of the southwestern Indian subcontinent

Manas—The lower animal mind; the reactive mind

Mandawa—Town in Rajasthan containing former homes of wealthy merchants

Mandukya—An Upanishad describing three states of consciousness

Matrimandir—The meditation center at Auroville near Puducherry

Meenakshi—A large temple in Madurai dedicated to a form of Shakti and Shiva

MBSR—Mindfulness Based Stress Reduction; a mindfulness program to reduce stress

Mindfulness—Being attentive on purpose, in the present moment without judgment

Mudha—A dull state of mind

Mudra—A symbolic gesture of the hands or body

Mylapore—Suburb immediately south of the Chennai

N
Niyama—The second of the Eight Petals of Yoga; observances to create inner peace

O
OM—Symbol of Consciousness; composed of sounds A-U-M and silence

P
Paramhansa—Title of honor of an enlightened person

Patanjali—Codifier of the Yoga Sutras probably around 500 BCE

PNS—Parasympathetic nervous system responsible for rest and recovery

Prajna—The sleep state; represented by the "M" in the OM mantra

Pranayama—The fourth of the Eight Petals of Yoga; practices of breath awareness

Prarabhda—Consequences of our past actions playing out in the present

Pratyahara—The fifth of the Eight Petals of Yoga; the control of our reactions to sensory inputs

Puducherry—The former French colony of Pondicherry located on the southeastern coast of India

Purana Qila—Old Fort in Delhi

R

Raga—Desires; one of the *kleshas*, a consequence of spiritual ignorance or *avidya*

Ramana Maharshi—Indian saint who lived at ashram in Tiruvannamalai, Tamil Nadu, India (1879–1950)

Ramayana—-Indian epic narrating the life of Ram, prince of Ayodhya

Ranganatha Swamy—Temple in Tiruchirappalli, Tamil Nadu, India

Ravana—Demon king who kidnapped Prince Rama's wife, Sita in the Ramayana

Rishikesh—City in northern state of Uttarakhand on the Ganges River

S

Sadhana—Practice, particularly the practice of yoga; second chapter of the Yoga Sutras, progressing

Sadhaka—A spiritually adept individual

Samadhi—Total absorption; title of the first chapter of the Yoga Sutras, concentration; also the eighth of the Eight Petals of Yoga

Samskara—Negative impressions caused by our actions and stored in the unconscious (*karmashaya*)

Samyama—The triple practice of *dharana*, *dhyana*, and *samadhi*

Sanchitta—Accumulation of past good and bad acts stored in the unconscious

Santosha—Contentment; the third *niyama*

Satya—Truth that does no harm; the third *yama*

Saucha—Purity; the second *niyama*

Shravanabela Gola—Jain temple in the vicinity of Mysore

Sikhara—The mountain-like structure of a Hindu temple housing the temple deity

SKY—Sudarshan Kriya Yoga; a very intense *pranayama*

SNS—Sympathetic nervous system responsible for the fight or flight response

So-Ham—Simple mantra meditation relating to the breath pattern of inhaling and exhaling

Sudarshan—Literally meaning good or auspicious vision or seeing

Sukha—Happiness, pleasure, ease, joy; opposite of *dukkha*

Svadhyaya—Self-study; fourth *niyama*; also the second element of *Kriya Yoga*

T

Taijasa—The Dream State as represented by the sound "U" in the OM mantra

Tapas—Determination; the third *niyama*; also first element of *Kriya Yoga*

Thanjavur—City in Tamil Nadu, India

TPN—The Task Positive Network of the brain responsible for focused awareness

Tiruchirappalli—City, whose nickname is sometimes shortened to Trichy, in southern Tamal Nadu, India

Tiruvannamalai—City in state of Tamil Nadu, India

Tripura—Literally the three cities or states of consciousness referenced by the A-U-M mantra, anthropomorphized into a goddess.

Trichy—Short for Tiruchirappalli, a city in southern Tamal Nadu, India

Turiya—The Fourth State of Pure Consciousness as represented by the silence at the end of OM

U

Upendra Maharathi—Artist who painted *Truth Seeking Man Caught in a Whirlpool of Temptation*

V

Vairagya—Nonattachment; a cornerstone of yoga practice along with *abhyasa*

Vaishvanara—The Waking State as represented by the "A" sound in the OM mantra

Vibhuti—The idea of accomplishments; third chapter of the Yoga Sutras; Progression of Practice

Vikshipta—A distracted mind

Vivekananda—An influential philosopher and social reformer who addressed the Parliament of Religions in Chicago in 1893

Vritti—Fluctuations of the mind; rumination, mind wandering, monkey mind, internal chatter

Vina—Musical instrument on subcontinent; evolved into lute, zither, and arched harp

Vyala—A mythical creature representing desire's attempt to eat us alive

Y

Yama—The first of the Eight Petals of Yoga; five behavioral restraints fostering harmony with others

Yoga—To yoke or join together from the Sanskrit word *yuj*

Yoga Sutras—The collection of 195 aphorisms on the theory and practice of yoga codified by Patanjali

Appendix E: Further Reading

Abhedananda, Swami, *The Gospel of Ramakrishna*, Kindle

Anderson, Sandra, 2000, *Yoga Mastering the Basics,* Honesdale, PA: The Himalayan Institute

Austin, James, 1999, *Zen and the Brain,* Boston: First MIT Press

Bhaskarananda, Swami, 2009, *Journey from Many to One: Essentials of Advaita Vedanta*, Seattle, WA: Viveka Press, Kindle

Bouanchaud, Bernard, 1997, *The Essence of Yoga,* Portland, OR: Rudra Press

Brown, Richard P. & Gerbarg, Patricia L., 2012, *The Healing Power of Breath,* Boston: Shambhala

Brown, Richard P. & Gerbarg, Patricia L., "BreathBodyMind," Accessed December 5, 2023, https://www.breath-body-mind.com

Buck, William, 1975, *Mahabharata*, Berkeley, CA: University of California Press

Buck, William, 1978, *Ramayana*, Berkeley, CA: University of California Press

Chödrön, Pema, 1994, *Start Where You Are*, Boston: Shambhala Publications

Clarke, Karen O'Donnell, "Yoga Heals Us," Accessed December 5, 2023, https://www.breath-body-mind.com

Coulter, David, 2001, *Anatomy of Hatha Yoga,* Honesdale, PA: Body and Breath

Cunningham, M. Mala, "Positive Health Solutions," Accessed December 5, 2023, https://www.cardiacyoga.com

Dalrymple, William, 1993, *City of Jinns,* New Delhi: Penguin Books

Dalrymple, William, 2009, *Nine Lives,* London: Bloomsbury Publishing Plc

Dass, Baba Ram, 1971, *Be Here Now*, Kingsport, TN: Kingsport Press

Davenport, Barrie & Scott, Steve, 2017, *10-Minute Mindfulness*, Mahwah, NJ: Oldtown Publishing LLC, Kindle

Davidson, Richard J., with Begley Sharon, 2012, *The Emotional Life of Your Brain*, 2012, New York: Penguin Group

Dayananda, Swami, 2009, *Introduction to Vedanta*, New Delhi, India: Vision Books Pvt, Ltd

Desikachar, T. K. V., 1998, *Health, Healing & Beyond*, Aperture Foundation

Desikachar, T. K. V., 1995, *The Heart of Yoga*, Rochester, VT: Inner Traditions International

Easwaran, Eknath, 2009, *The Upanishads*, Nilgiri Press

Easwaran, Eknath, 2008, *The Bhagavad Gita for Daily Living, Vol I, II, & III*, Nilgiri Press

Farhi, Donna, 2004, *Bringing Yoga to Life*, New York: Harper Collins

Farhi, Donna, 2000, *Yoga, Mind, Body and Spirit*, New York: Henry Holt & Company

Farhi, Donna, 1996, *The Breathing Book*, New York: Henry Holt & Company

Feuerstein, Georg, 2001, *Yoga Tradition, Its History, Literature Philosophy and Practice*, Prescott, AZ: Hohm Press

Frawley, David, 2000, *Vedantic Meditation*, Berkely, CA: North Atlantic Books

Frawley, David, 2006, *Yoga and the Sacred Fire*, Delhi: Motilal Banarsidass

Frawley, David, 2002, *From the River of Heaven*, Twin Lakes, WI: Lotus Press

Gates, Rolf, 2002, *Meditations from the Mat*, New York: Anchor Books

Goldstein, Joseph & Kornfield, Jack, 1987, *Seeking the Heart of Wisdom*, Boston: Shambhala

Gormley, JJ., "Surya Chandra Healing Yoga School," Accessed December 5, 2023, https://www.schys.yoga

Hanh, Thich Nhat, 1976, *The Miracle of Mindfulness*, Boston, MA: Beacon Press

Hanson, Rick, with Richard Mendius, MD, 2009, *Buddha's Brain*, Oakland, CA: New Harbinger Publications, Kindle

Hesse, Herman, 2023, *Siddhartha*, New Delhi, India: Double 9 Books, Kindle

Holmes, Hannah, 2011, *Quirk: Brain Science*, New York: Random House, Kindle

Iyengar, B. K. S., 1979, *Light on Yoga*, New York: Schocken Books

Iyengar, B. K. S., 2003, *Light on Pranayama*, New York: Crossroad Publishing Company Iyengar, B. K. S., 2005, *Light on Life*, Emmaus, PA: Rodale Press

Jnaneshvara Bharati, Swami, "Yoga Sutras of Patanjali," Accessed October 30, 2023, https://www.swamij.com/yoga-sutras.htm

Kabat-Zinn, Jon, 1990, *Full Catastrophe Living*, New York: Dell Publishing

Kabat-Zinn, Jon, 1994, *Wherever You Go, There You Are*, New York: Hyperion

Kingsland, James, 2016, *Siddhartha's Brain,* New York: HarperCollins Publishers

Kornfield, Jack, 2001, *After the Ecstasy, the Laundry*, New York: Bantam Books

Lassiter, Judith, 2000, *Living Your Yoga: Finding Spiritual in Everyday Life,* Berkeley, CA: Rodmell Press

Maharaj, Nisargadatta, 2012, *I Am That,* Durham, NC: The Acorn Press

Maharshi, Ramana, 1998, *The Spiritual Teachings of Ramana Maharshi*, Boston, MA: Shambhala Publications

Mahathera, Gunaratana, 1991, *Mindfulness in Plain English*, Taipei, Taiwan: Buddha Educational Foundation

Merullo, Roland, 2007, *Breakfast with Buddha*, New York: Workman Publishing, Kindle

Nester, James, 2020, *Breath*, New York: Riverhead Books, Kindle

Paterson, Randy J., 2016, *How to Be Miserable: 40 Strategies You Already Use*, Oakland, CA: New Harbinger Publications, LLC, Kindle

Pirsig, Robert, 1984, *Zen and the Art of Motorcycle Maintenance,* New York: William Morrow and Company

Rama, Swami, 1985, *Perennial Psychology of the Bhagavad Gita*, Honesdale, PA: Himalayan Institute Press

Sapolsky, Robert M., 1998, *Why Zebras Don't Get Ulcers*, New York: W. H. Freeman and Company

Satchidananda, Swami, 2004, *The Yoga of Patanjali*, Buckingham, VA: Integral Yoga Publications

Satyananda Saraswati, Swami, 2013, Asana *Pranayama Mudra Bandha*, Yoga Publications Trust, Kindle

Singh, Khushwant, 2003, *Gods and Godmen of India*, New Delhi, India: HarperCollins Publishers, India, Kindle

Steindl-Rast, David, 1984, *Gratefulness, the Heart of Prayer*, Ramsey, NJ: Paulist Press

Vivekananda, Swami, 1972, *Ramakrishna and His Message*, Calcutta, India: Advaita Ashrama, Mayavati, Almore, Himalayas

Watts, Allan, 1989, *The Book*, New York: Random House

Weintraub, Amy, 2004, *Yoga for Depression*, New York: Broadway Books

Zimmer, Heinrich, 1989, *Philosophies of India*, Princeton, NJ: Princeton University Press

About the Author

Photo:
ECUHealth/Thomas Grimes

The author in Dog-on-a-Wall and Head-to-Knee poses

Don was a latecomer to yoga. He consciously avoided it for the first fifty-seven years of his life. Then, by accident, he was introduced to yoga, and from that point on, he was fully committed. At sixty-three he taught his first yoga class, and five years later, he completed a three-hundred-hour teacher training course. He is now qualified through the Yoga Alliance as an Experienced Registered Yoga Teacher (E-RYT®) and a Yoga Alliance Continuing Education Provider (YACEP®). Soon after his seventy-second birthday, he spent three months in India, with three weeks spent at an ashram studying the Yoga Sutras. In addition to teaching regular Hatha Yoga classes, Don has taught yoga to people with multiple sclerosis and cancer, led meditation workshops, and is the second author on a paper detailing the effects of yoga on a small population of cardiac patients. In addition to his commitment to yoga, Don is also an avid cyclist, aiming to ride sixty to ninety miles a week.

During the COVID pandemic (2022) Don created a YouTube channel in which he shared some of his classes, meditations, photo journeys, and thoughts.

These can be accessed via the keyword YogiDonaldo.
(https://www.youtube.com/@yogidonaldoenglish9427/videos)